C000084836

Italian Painters V2: The Galleries Of Munich And Dresden

Giovanni Morelli

In the interest of creating a more extensive selection of rare historical book reprints, we have chosen to reproduce this title even though it may possibly have occasional imperfections such as missing and blurred pages, missing text, poor pictures, markings, dark backgrounds and other reproduction issues beyond our control. Because this work is culturally important, we have made it available as a part of our commitment to protecting, preserving and promoting the world's literature. Thank you for your understanding.

ITALIAN PAINTERS

CRITICAL STUDIES OF THEIR WORKS

By GIOVANNI MORELLI

(IVAN LERMOLIEFF)

THE GALLERIES OF MUNICH AND DRESDEN

TRANSLATED FROM THE GERMAN BY

CONSTANCE JOCELYN FFOULKES

WITH ILLUSTRATIONS

Vol. 2

LONDON
JOHN MURRAY, ALBEMARLE STREET
1893

PREFACE.

THIS volume deals with the Italian pictures in the galleries of Munich and Dresden. It is in the main a reproduction of my former book—'Italian Masters in German Galleries'—which has long been out of print. I have, however, added to and I trust improved it in certain parts. Beyond an account at some length of the drawings of the Venetian Domenico Campagnola, which are commonly ascribed to his great contemporary and prototype Titian, and a few pages devoted to Giovanni Cariani, a little-known painter of Bergamo, the reader must not expect to find much new matter in this volume. I have, however, touched upon a point which appears to me not without importance in the history of Italian art, and to which I would direct special attention—the question of the authorship of a great number of pictures in public and private collections as to which I am convinced, after many years of careful study, that, although they pass for works by Italian masters, they are in reality for the most part imitations by Northern and principally by Flemish painters.

By commenting more fully than has hitherto been done upon the large number of Italian pictures, whether with right or wrong attributions, which are to be found in other European collections besides those especially noticed, I trust that I may have assisted beginners in art-criticism, and have afforded them more copious materials for their own studies.

I take this opportunity of briefly noticing some adverse criticisms directed against me. Among other things, it has been said that my writings lacked that grave and learned tone which is alone calculated to impress the reader, and which distinguishes a serious student of art from a superficial dilettante. This is very possible; but in this world many persons say the most foolish things with an air of the greatest solemnity, while others treat of very important subjects in a light and playful manner. I must confess that nothing appears to me more ludicrous than that self-complacent assurance and pretentious gravity which, according to Socrates, moved even the gods to laughter. It has also been said that my books are badly written. This I willingly admit, for I certainly do not lay claim to any special gifts of style or rhetoric. It has always been my aim to think clearly and correctly rather than to write brilliantly.

Again, my writings have been stigmatised as being without form, and as lacking that systematic treatment essential to a book of any pretensions. It was not, however, my intention to produce a book to be admired, but rather one that might be read with profit before the pictures themselves. This object I have, I think, attained.

In addition to all my other shortcomings, I have been found fault with for having only touched upon subjects which were deserving of fuller treatment. Had I been more exhaustive, however, I should have deprived my readers of the pleasure of thinking and studying for themselves, which I always consider a fault in tact on the part of a writer.

If it be true, as some of my friends are kind enough to say, that I have had the good fortune to correct several glaring misstatements in the history of Italian art, it is entirely owing to the fact that I hold no official position, and am, therefore, free to devote myself to my studies and to express my views without reserve. I have thus one immense advantage over my opponents at Berlin and Paris, though in learning and intellectual attainments they are doubtless my superiors. A director of a gallery or a professor is apt to think it due to his high office that he should lay down the law to others, and to feel himself debarred from admitting that he has anything more to learn or that he may have committed mistakes. I, on the contrary, am still able to learn even in my old age, and I trust to be able to do so as long as I live.

I must not omit to notice a few words of censure courteously expressed by an English art-critic in reviewing the first volume of these 'Studies.' This gentleman, Mr. Claude Phillips, considers that my

writings are of too controversial a character, and
would gain by being modified in this respect. From
an English point of view he is undoubtedly right.
The polemical attitude, which only produces ill-
feeling, is rootedly distasteful to me. I was forced,
however, to defend myself against the repeated and
virulent attacks of my opponents, not only on my
own account, but also for the sake of those who
agreed with me in my views. I should have pre-
ferred to do so in one of the leading German art
reviews. But this was out of the question, as all
opinions running counter to those of certain accepted
authorities have been for some years past excluded
from these periodicals. At Berlin, the 'centre of the
scientific study of art,' the critics have found it de-
sirable to form an alliance, offensive and defensive.
Like the Triple Alliance, which was formed in that
city for the preservation of the peace of the universe,
this league was to ensure to its members a peaceful
and unmolested existence and to uphold its own
prestige in matters of art. Under these circumstances
I have felt bound to say something further in my own
defence, though I am aware that this is hardly the
place to enter upon a controversy.

Some of the most persistent among my numerous
opponents at Berlin condemned my interpretation
of the history of Italian art as unscientific. They
more especially disparaged the experimental method
which I recommended. None of them, however,
were able to show that my opinions were unsound,
nor were they capable of proving, by arguments to

the contrary, that the conclusions to which my
researches had led me were erroneous. To deny
the opinions of others, and yet be incapable of pro-
ducing any well-founded reasons for doing so, is
simply childish. That I have committed mistakes,
notwithstanding a close study of over thirty years, I
am ready to admit. The more serious of them, how-
ever, would scarcely, I think, have been discovered
by my opponents had I not pointed them out myself
and rectified them in this edition. There are doubt-
less many still remaining ; I must leave it to future
art-historians to expose them.

In judging of works of art there are two kinds
of errors into which we are liable to fall. As
theologians distinguish, and rightly, between venial
and deadly sins, so in the various attributions of
pictures the same distinction may, I think, be drawn.
The method of study which I have recommended
must not, however, be held responsible for the mis-
takes which I made ten years ago. On the contrary,
in nearly every instance where I have been misled
in forming a judgment upon a picture, I had either
misapplied the method or had not made use of it
at all. Of course, however, I do not pretend to
say that it is infallible, for in no branch of science
is there any infallible method.

One of my younger opponents, who considers
my experimental method far too material, observes
that ' every art-critic will have his own method.' Be
it so, answer I, and let us judge of the value of these
different methods according to their several results.

The same writer proceeds to inform me that the
critical study of art cannot yet claim to be called a
science, but is only a means to a higher end, and he
considers it his duty to exhort the German student
'above all to be true to the precepts of his fore-
fathers.'

Now let me ask any unprejudiced reader, who
may have glanced at my unpretending writings,
whether on one single page of my 'Critical Studies'
I have ever claimed for them the rank of a scientific
treatise? To have done so would have been simply
ludicrous on my part. As it happens, however, I
took every opportunity of impressing upon my reader
that the experimental method was only to be regarded
as an aid in determining the authors of works of
art—an aid, that is to say, to connoisseurship—and
that in time it might come to serve as a more solid
basis for that science of art-criticism which we all
alike desire to see established. As the Italian proverb
says, however, 'Non v' ha peggior sordo di chi non
vuol sentire' ('There are none so deaf as those who
won't hear').

On the other hand, I must acknowledge that I
fully deserved the rebuke which two distinguished
directors saw fit to administer to me on another
point. I had actually imagined that in a picture by
Gerrit Lunders, in the Borghese gallery, I could
detect the influence of Dusart, who was several years
his junior. In addition, I had spoken of the elegant
formality of Van Dyck's portraits, I had character-
ised Backhuysen as somewhat monotonous and un-

interesting, and I had written 'Brower' instead of 'Brouwer.'

My acquaintance with the Dutch schools of painting is so slight that it was extremely unwise of me to venture an opinion at all, and this time I am really much indebted to my German censors for their criticism. It will serve as a warning to me never again to speak on subjects of which I have little or no knowledge. And, in conclusion, I would only ask leave to close these remarks by the suggestion that my opponents should themselves lay to heart the words of admonition which two of the most eminent German critics have addressed with such ready zeal to me.

IVAN LERMOLIEFF.

GORLAW : *December* 1890.

CONTENTS.

————◆◇◆———

LIST OF ILLUSTRATIONS.

———•◦•———

FULL-PAGE ILLUSTRATIONS.

Erratum.

Page 43, note 1, *for* ' (No. 295) ' *read* ' (No. 194A).'

THE MUNICH GALLERY.

INTRODUCTORY.

'One day telleth another.'

I AM aware that my friend, the late Mr. Mündler, published a criticism on the pictures contained in the Munich gallery, but I refrained from reading it, not wishing to be influenced in my own judgment by one for whose ripe knowledge and penetrating insight I have the greatest respect.

His ' Essai d'une analyse critique de la Notice des tableaux italiens du Musée National du Louvre ' (1859) was at the time, in many particulars, a model of art-criticism, and I feel sure that even Messrs. Crowe and Cavalcaselle, the most prominent critics of the present day, would acknowledge that they have derived many hints for their own researches and attributions from this little volume.

Mr. Mündler's nature was that of a true artist—simple, unaffected, endowed with a strong sense of the beautiful, and capable of great enthusiasm. This latter quality, indeed, sometimes led him astray, but in his day he was almost unrivalled in the appreciation and intimate knowledge of Italian Painting. Why, then, did he, with his fine perception and his passion for art, occasionally commit such palpable mistakes ? It was, I think, because he pursued no method in his studies, but was wont to be guided solely by the general impression produced upon him by a picture, relying too implicitly on his instinct and his truly prodigious memory. Yet even the most highly gifted and accomplished connoisseur will never attain to certainty of judgment without a definite system of study, and this, I believe, must be that so-called ' experimental method ' which, from the time of Leonardo da Vinci, of Galileo, and of Bacon, to that of Volta and Darwin, has led to the most splendid discoveries. In the history of Art it can, of course, only be regarded as a means to assist in identifying the author of a picture.[1]

The barbarous 'restoration' to which pictures of the best period have, for the most part, been subjected, renders it often all but impossible to recognise the hand of the master in his work, inasmuch as what we have before our eyes, instead of the true features of the original, is either a black mask with which the restorer has concealed them, or an utterly flayed and disfigured countenance which he has given us instead.[2] Under such circumstances it would be impossible to distinguish between an original and a copy were it not for the forms peculiar to each master in his treatment of the human frame; hence definite results can only be attained by a careful examination of these.[3]

[1] It has been asserted in Germany that I profess to recognise a painter solely by the form of the hand, the finger-nails, the ear, or the toes in his work. Whether this statement is due to malice or to ignorance I cannot say; it is scarcely necessary to observe that it is incorrect. What I maintain is, that the forms in general, and more especially those of the hand and ear, aid us in distinguishing the works of a master from those of his imitators, and control the judgment which subjective impressions might lead us to pronounce.

[2] In the last century the pictures were merely repainted; in more recent times they have been first rubbed down, which, especially as regards Venetian pictures of the beginning of the sixteenth century, is far worse.

[3] The matter or contents of a picture are inseparable from the form, but in the study of art our judgment must be guided by the form rather than by the subjective impression of the whole. Those who deny the importance of studying ' form ' only prove that they shrink from studying art scientifically. (See vol. i. of these studies, the Borghese and Doria galleries, pp. 73-6.)

I refer, of course, only to true artists, who are distinguished
by a characteristic and independent mode of conception
and expression; imitators, whether in art or science, are
mere ciphers who do not come under consideration here;
tedious themselves, their sole attraction is for tedious
people, and that only on account of such technical skill as
they may possess.

As my own studies have convinced me that this experi-
mental method, applied to the identification of works of art,
may be of use to students, I shall endeavour in the follow-
ing pages to enter more fully upon the subject and to
illustrate my meaning by examples as occasion offers. But,
as I have elsewhere observed, it is not as easy as might
be supposed to recognise the forms characteristic of each
painter, and in order to learn to see correctly the eye must
be trained by long and constant practice. Time and trouble
are requisite in every branch of study, and no one can
master a foreign language, or even his own, without due
application; a truth which might with advantage be laid
to heart by many young critics who think themselves
qualified, after a six months' sojourn in Italy, to reject
offhand the conclusions to which others have come after
years of patient research.

I will begin with the Venetian school, because it is better
represented in the Munich gallery, in point of numbers,
than any of the numerous other schools of Italy, perhaps
because of the constant intercommunication which for
centuries existed between Bavaria and the City of the
Lagoons. By the Venetian school, however, I do not mean
that of Venice alone. Properly speaking, this should be so,
but in these days it is usual to include in this category all
the schools of painting in the territory once belonging to
the Republic in North Italy, which felt the influence of
the capital in a greater or less degree without losing their

distinctive and local characteristics. This individuality
of each school—the direct outcome of diversity of race,
natural scenery, soil, climate, &c., more strongly developed
in some districts, less strongly in others—cannot, of course,
be adequately studied and understood in picture galleries,
the contents of which are for the most part eclectic in
character. It must be studied in the district where it ori-
ginated, in the history of which it forms so integral a part.

In no country has art been so essentially the language,
or rather the dialect, of the people as in Italy. Unchecked
in its growth, it flourished like a living organism in its native
soil, while, from various causes which cannot be touched
upon here, the literature of the Italians never assumed a
popular form and expression. This relation between speech
and representation—that is to say, between the spoken
language of a race and the visible language of art, between
two modes of expression differing in form though prompted
by the same spirit—is due, not to chance and external con-
ditions, but to innate causes.[1]

In Venetia, where this indigenous art-language, so to
speak, was never perverted and denationalised, as in other
parts of Italy, by the foreign domination of the Spaniard,
its evolution may be traced from its rise in the thirteenth
century to its final extinction in the time of Tiepolo,
Canaletto, and Longhi; for Canova, David, Carstens,
and Cornelius certainly did not exterminate the art of the
perruque period, as is usually supposed, and as has been
represented by Kaulbach on the walls of the New Pina-

---

[1] In the declining period of art
in Italy, shortly after the death of
Raphael, the painter lost all indivi-
duality; hence the forms, which are
the expression of character, cease to
be distinctive. We have, therefore,
nothing left to guide us in recognising
his work but the general impression
and certain external and accidental
signs. These mannerisms, which
are like · flourishes in calligraphy,
are, however, very untrustworthy
guides, and of small value for iden-
tifying pictures.

cothek at Munich. Art had died a natural death long before these distinguished persons began to lay the foundations of the 'New Art' so called.

It is only in Italy itself—in remote village churches, and on the walls and façades of dwelling-houses—that this popular art-dialect can be studied. In the province of Bergamo, for instance, in the fertile valleys of the Serio and the Brembo, we meet with pictures of the school of the Boselli, the Gavazzi, and the Scipioni of Averara, and with frescoes of the first half of the fifteenth century, in which we can trace the characteristics still remarked in the appearance, the gestures, and even in the idioms, of the people in the streets—those of a rough, energetic mountain-race uniting caution, but not always refinement or charm, with their natural strength and vigour. The same fundamental character is seen in a modified degree in the works of other Bergamasque artists, who left their homes at an early age in order to pursue their studies at Venice— Palma Vecchio, Previtali, Cariani, the two Santa Croce, and others.

These remarks apply in a general sense to all the Italian schools. But among those races of the peninsula who showed less aptitude for the fine arts, we shall find that the development is not always continuous and unbroken, especially in the epochs of transition from the 'heroic' or Giottesque to the 'scientific' or realistic period, when the study of linear perspective and the faithful imitation of nature were the principal aims of the artist.[1]

[1] In his second commentary, Lorenzo Ghiberti observes: 'Ho sempre seguito l' arti con grande studio e disciplina, conciò sia cosa che io abbia sempre coi primi precetti cercato d' investigare in che modo la natura proceda in essa [arte] et in che modo io mi possa approssimare ad essa, come le specie venghino all' occhio e in che modo la teorica dell' arte statuaria e della pittura si dovesse condurre;' that is, 'I have ever with diligence and method pursued the study of art. From the time of my earliest training I have sought to discover

The school which shows the most complete development, and in this and other respects takes precedence of all others, is the Florentine. The Veronese, as Dr. Richter in a forthcoming work will prove to the conviction of all students, may perhaps rank second. The attempts of the Venetians in the fourteenth and the early part of the fifteenth centuries were weak and faltering, as Messrs. Crowe and Cavalcaselle have justly observed, until Gentile da Fabriano and Pisanello—and not the much-overrated Johannes Alemannus, as some German writers affirm—gave a new impulse to painting. In architecture and sculpture, on the other hand, much admirable and characteristic work had already been achieved—to mention only a few names—by Filippo Calendario, the delle Massegne, and Maestro Bartolommeo.[1] This important fact must not be overlooked, for, in order to do justice to a school, and to understand the history and development of art, the student must not limit his attention to one form of artistic expression, viz. the graphic alone.

Towards the close of the fifteenth century, when painting attained its full development under the Vivarini and the Bellini, we find this art thrusting that of sculpture into the second place and taking it in tow, not only in Venice but throughout North Italy, though the two sometimes curiously reflect one another. Thus, in the works of the Lombardi,

how nature develops herself in art, and how it may best be approached; how the forms present themselves to the eye, and on what principles the arts of painting and sculpture should be practised.' (See *Vasari*, ed. Le Monnier, i. xxx.)

[1] The sculptures on the Ducal Palace, of the middle of the fourteenth century, those in the churches of San Marco, the Frari, and San Giovanni e Paolo, should be examined as a proof of this, as also the rare medals by the Venetian medallists Lorenzo, Marco, and Alessandro Sesto (1393–1417), the forerunners of Pisanello. The latter, during his sojourn in Venice (1421–1423), must certainly have seen and studied the works of these artists.

and even in those of Alessandro Leopardi, we recognise at times the Vivarini, or, again, Giovanni Bellini; the figures of the sculptor Antonio Riccio of Verona have the impress of the Veronese school of painting,[1] whence proceeded Riccio's fellow-countryman, the painter Liberale; while a high-relief over the door of a house (No. 2857) in the Campo S. Tomà, at Venice, might be a picture in stone by Mansueti or Carpaccio. The statues in many of the churches at Verona should also be studied from this point of view. Again, we recognise the spirit of Dosso in many a sculpture by Alfonso Lombardi,[2] and that of Paul Veronese in Alessandro Vittoria's statues.

In the Milanese district, however, sculpture not only maintained its ground, but even continued to influence painting[3] to some extent, a result to which the numerous

[1] As, for example, the statues of Adam and Eve in the Court of the Ducal Palace at Venice.

[2] See, for instance, the busts on the façade of the Palazzo Bolognini at Bologna.

[3] In modelling heads, Andrea Solario surpassed all his contemporaries, as may be seen in his " Ecce Homo " in the Poldi-Pezzoli collection at Milan. His excellence in this respect was probably due to the teaching of his brother Cristoforo the sculptor, surnamed ' il Gobbo ' (the Hunchback). The close connection between the two is seen in a head in bas-relief by Cristoforo in the Trivulzio collection at Milan, which bears a strong resemblance to Andrea's portraits. Again, the influence of the sculptor Amadeo is strikingly apparent in a picture by Bartolommeo Suardi, known as Bramantino, in the Ambrosiana, the "Nativity," No. 278. Messrs. Crowe and Cavalcaselle (ii. 82) deny that it is by this painter; but it appears to me to be undoubtedly a genuine and an early work by him, and it has been accepted as such in the Ambrosiana. The landscape background is very characteristic of Bramantino, so, too, are the forms of the hand and the ear and the quaint drapery on the head of the Madonna. A headdress of this description is not met with in pictures by any of his fellow-pupils under Foppa, as Borgognone, Bevilacqua, Buttinone, or Civerchio, though it is seen in an early work by Andrea Solario in the Brera (No. 105 bis), in one by Luini in the Church of the Passione at Milan, and in nearly all the early works of Gaudenzio Ferrari, as also in a series of frescoes in the Brera (Nos. 41, 43, 51, 53, 69 and 73), formerly in the Church of S. Maria della Pace at Milan. These latter, ascribed in the Brera to Luini, should, I think, be attributed to a pupil or imitator of Bramantino (†).

sculptures in the Certosa at Pavia and on the Cathedral
at Milan may have contributed.

I would especially recommend a careful study of the
drawings by the old masters in addition to that of the three
contemporary forms of art already touched upon. For,
while pictures have been so damaged by time, and so mal-
treated by the restorer, that it is well-nigh impossible to
recognise in them the hand and the spirit of the master,
original drawings, not having been tampered with in the
same degree, reveal the personality of the painter with all
his merits and defects. To the student, the drawings are
indispensable, as they enable him to acquire a more intimate
knowledge of each master and to impress more sharply
upon his mind those marks of identity, whether material
or intellectual, which distinguish different painters and
different schools; for instance, peculiarities in the disposi-
tion of the drapery, or in the treatment of light and shade,
all of which are more apparent in drawings than in pic-
tures; or again the preference shown by a given master for
drawing with black or red chalk or with the pen.

For purposes of serious and comparative study photo-
graphy is an invaluable aid, and I should therefore advise
all who intend to devote their attention to original drawings
to procure reproductions of those which I have mentioned
in these pages as peculiarly characteristic. This, of course,
presupposes some familiarity with the works of the great
masters both in painting and sculpture, for drawings
merely bewilder novices, as has been abundantly proved,
especially in recent years. To a practised eye, however,
their study is one of the purest of enjoyments.

Ten years have elapsed since these criticisms on the
Munich gallery were first published. Dr. Marggraff, the
author of the catalogue of that day, has since died, and
Dr. von Reber, the present director—a distinguished art-

historian—has issued a new catalogue with the co-operation
of the most eminent writers on art in Germany and Holland.
Now art-critics, who personally may have the greatest regard
for each other, are often unable to agree in their appreciation
of works of art, for a German sees things differently from a
Frenchman, a Russian, or an Italian. ' Non è bello quel
che è bello, ma è bello quel che piace,' [1] says an Italian
proverb. I would remind my readers of this fact, lest they
should suppose that, because I cannot always agree with
the directors of galleries in their estimate and attribution
of Italian pictures, I must of necessity be systematically
opposed to them. During the last ten years I have ad-
hered more strictly than ever to the counsel of Pangloss,
' cultivons notre propre jardin,' and I trust that I have
thus been enabled to repair certain shortcomings in my own
studies.

In once more reviewing the pictures in the Munich
gallery I return to the task with fresh ideas and renewed
vigour. No doubt I shall find that I committed some mis-
takes ten years ago, but I hope, on the whole, to be able to
confirm many, or indeed most, of the judgments which I
passed at that time.

THE VENETIANS.

In the first edition of these 'Critical Studies' this
chapter opened with the following words, which I think it
desirable to repeat :—

' Turning to Dr. Marggraff's new catalogue (of 1879), to
see whether the early masters are worthily represented
in this gallery, our attention is at once arrested by
the names of two great artists—Giovanni Bellini and

---

[1] 'The beautiful is not that which is beautiful, but that which pleases.'

Andrea Mantegna, the principal representatives respectively of the Venetian and Paduan schools in the fifteenth century. Assuming that all writers on art must be familiar with the style of two painters of such marked individuality, are we therefore to accept the statements of the catalogue without reserve? Scarcely, I think; for the compiler himself observes, in his preface, that man's judgment is not infallible. The mind, moreover, is as much addicted to habit as the body, and clings to traditional delusions more pertinaciously than to the truth.[1]

'I should, therefore, recommend all young students, who honestly desire to learn in a gallery, to examine the pictures impartially, unbiassed by the opinions of others. No doubt they will commit many mistakes, as it is in the nature of man to err; but eventually, after repeated failure, they will attain to independence of judgment, for, as Nelson said, it is only at sea that a man can learn to be a sailor.

'The most eminent critics and connoisseurs of recent times—Rumohr, Waagen, Mündler, and Crowe and Cavalcaselle—studied in this way; hence their views as to the attribution of pictures do not always agree either with each other or with those of Dr. Marggraff. I am often unable to accept their opinions as to pictures in this collection, but I hope to be pardoned for not doing so, provided that in every case I state my reasons for differing from them. These are based upon indisputable and practical facts, accessible to every observer, and are not merely subjective and æsthetic, dependent upon individual taste and impressions, as is usually the case in critical writings on art.'

To my satisfaction I see that justice has now been done

---

[1] Leonardo da Vinci observed: 'Il massimo inganno degli uomini è nelle loro opinioni' ('Men are chiefly deceived by their own preconceived opinions').

in the new catalogue to Giovanni Bellini and Mantegna, and that the names of both have disappeared from its pages. After being subjected to a critical examination, the so-called Giovanni Bellini [1] has, I am told, been banished to Schleissheim. The sentence was well-merited, though somewhat harsh when we consider how many of the works attributed to his fellow-countrymen in this gallery—including that assigned to his brother, Gentile Bellini (No. 1030)—are deserving of a similar fate.

Dr. Marggraff's "Mantegna" (No. 1023), though not sent to Schleissheim, has now been transferred to the Ferrarese school. The authorities were right in not adopting the name I had suggested for this inferior little picture, for it is of no consequence whether it was produced in the workshop of the Veronese Benaglio, or in that of some Paduan painter. One thing, however, is certain—that it has no claim to the great name of Mantegna, while, to connect it even interrogatively with that of the characteristic "Stefano da Ferrara" of the Brera, that is, with Ercole de' Roberti,[2] is heresy. His name should certainly be omitted from future editions of the catalogue of the Munich gallery.

We now come to Marco Basaiti, whose works are rarely met with out of Italy. The Munich Pinacothek, more fortunate in this respect than the Louvre or the public galleries of Madrid and Dresden, claims to possess two pictures by him. One (No. 1031) represents the Madonna and Child. The Virgin lays her hand on the head of the donor; on her right is St. Jerome, on her left St. Sebastian; in the background is a landscape watered by a river. This

---

[1] No. 1196 of Dr. Marggraff's catalogue.

[2] The fine altar-piece in the Brera, once erroneously attributed to an otherwise unknown painter, Stefano da Ferrara, is now acknowledged to be the work of Ercole de' Roberti.

picture was formerly assigned to the 'school of Giovanni
Bellini,' but it is now rightly ascribed to Basaiti, to whom
Messrs. Crowe and Cavalcaselle also attribute it. Though
genuine, it is much injured and repainted. The other
picture (No. 1032, Cabinet XVIII.), which, at my suggestion,
has been accepted as an original, represents the "Pietà,"
the dead Christ resting on the knees of the Madonna,
bewailed by Joseph of Arimathea and the Holy Women.
Messrs. Crowe and Cavalcaselle [1] were much reminded in
this work of 'so poor a character' of Nicolaus (?) de'
Barbaris. Dr. Marggraff, with more caution, threw doubts
upon its authenticity, and I, too, must now admit that this
unattractive production cannot possibly be either an early
or a late work by Basaiti, but that it is merely a copy after
that master, executed probably by one of the many inferior
Flemish artists who flocked to Italy in the first half of the
sixteenth century, to the detriment of their own manner of
painting.

The hand of a feeble northern artist is apparent in
every part of this picture: in the types, which are mere
caricatures—for instance, the man in the turban who
shows all his teeth [2]—in the wooden treatment of the
hair—more especially that of the Magdalen—in the folds
of the mantle of the doleful St. John, and in the dry,
miniature-like treatment of all the details—the stones, the
book, &c. The un-Italian character of this picture may

---

[1] i. 266, note 3.

[2] The early Flemish and German
painters, even Dürer and his pupils,
were wont to represent strong emo-
tion by depicting their figures with
open mouths, so that the teeth and
even the tongue are visible. See,
for example, many works in this
gallery by northern painters of the
fifteenth and sixteenth centuries; in
the Uffizi, Nos. 704, 713, 724, 768, 777,
779, and 1143; in the Doria gallery
at Rome, No. 26, and others. This
tendency is rarely observable in
Italian pictures, with the exception,
perhaps, of those by Antonio Pollai-
uolo, Jacopo de' Barbari, Liberale da
Verona, Andrea Solario, Defendente
Ferrari, and of a few others.

MADONNA WITH SAINTS. BY BASAITI.

(In the Berlin Gallery.)

To face p. 13.

perhaps explain why Messrs. Crowe and Cavalcaselle were reminded in it of Jacopo de' Barbari.

Basaiti's early works, such as No. 24 in the Museo Civico at Venice,[1] and No. 40 in the Berlin gallery, recall the school of Alvise Vivarini;[2] whereas those of his later period—for example, the figures in the altar-piece in the Church of the Frari at Venice, which was left unfinished by Vivarini, and completed by Basaiti in 1503—point to a connection with Boccaccino, notably in the types of the angels and in the hard zigzag folds of the drapery.[3] Basaiti's works of the years 1515 and 1516 appear to me to be in his best *quattrocento* manner. The following belong to this epoch :—

The "Ecce Homo" in the gallery at Bergamo (of 1517) ; the "Christ" in the Ambrosiana (Sala Pecis), signed MARCVS BASITI ; an excellent little picture representing the "Calling of the Sons of Zebedee," in the public gallery at Vienna; a "St. Catherine" (No. 103) in the Esterhazy gallery at Pesth, and a "St. Sebastian" in the Doria gallery at Rome.

Later, Basaiti's manner of painting becomes broader, and his colours are more thickly laid on, owing probably to his study of the works of Giovanni Bellini and Cima. We may consequently, I think, assume that from the years 1515 to 1521 he must have been in his prime, and could not therefore have been born much earlier than 1470. His latest works are those in the Berlin gallery.

Basaiti is said to have been the son of Greek parents who had settled in Venice—a tradition which his name

---

[1] Correr collection, Room IX.

[2] The little picture in Berlin recalls the Madonna with angel musicians by Alvise Vivarini in the Church of the Redentore at Venice. The form of the thumb[is characteristic in all the pictures by Basaiti above mentioned.

[3] "A Madonna with Saints," a work belonging to this middle period of Basaiti's career, is in the collection of Signor Frizzoni-Salis at Bergamo.

confirms. As an artist, however, he is wholly Venetian.
Lanzi and other writers—on what grounds I am unable to
say—consider that Basaiti was a native of the Friuli. Had
this been the case, Vasari would certainly have heard it
from Grassi, who supplied him with information about
Friulian artists, and it would have been mentioned by
Count Maniago in his careful ' Storia delle belle arti
Friulane.' I may add that beginners in art-criticism,
when in doubt to whom to ascribe some Venetian picture—
whether to Cima or to Catena—have invariably taken
refuge in the name of this little known master. I have,
therefore, thought it desirable to give reproductions here
of three of his works. I have never met with a single
drawing bearing the name of Basaiti, nor one which had
any claim to be even doubtfully attributed to him.

Of the two pictures ascribed to Giorgione in Dr.
Marggraff's catalogue, one has now been rightly given to
Titian (No. 1110, Room IX.), the other (No. 1107) is
attributed to Palma Vecchio. The first of these two in-
teresting pictures represents an allegorical female figure
known as " Vanity." Before being placed in the Munich
gallery, this picture, if I mistake not, was rightly named,
and was only attributed to Giorgione at a later period.'

' It has been reserved for critics
of the nineteenth century to draw
attention to the absurd names be-
stowed upon pictures in the seven-
teenth century and the beginning of
the eighteenth. The following may
suffice, though I could name many
more examples of celebrated pictures
which have only recently received
their rightful names :—

1. The fine portrait of the Comte
de Morette in the Dresden gallery.
During the seventeenth century it
was always regarded as the work of
Hans Holbein, and as such we find
it described in the *Microcosmo della
Pittura* (p. 266) by Francesco Scan-
nelli in 1677. In the eighteenth
century it was renamed Leonardo
da Vinci, the portrait being then
pronounced to be that of Lodovico
il Moro. The confusion probably
arose from the name Morett, which
may have been found on the back
of the panel. Morett was taken to
mean ' Moro '; hence Leonardo da
Vinci, the greatest painter at the
Court of Lodovico Sforza ' il Moro,'
would naturally have been chosen
to portray his patron. To Baron

MALE PORTRAIT. BY BASAITI.
(In the Morelli Collection, Bergamo.)

To face p. 14.

MADONNA AND CHILD WITH SAINTS.   BY BASAITI

(In the Gallery at Padua.)

To face p. 14.

Messrs. Crowe and Cavalcaselle are in doubt whether to give it to that master or not; in any case they consider it to be ' in the spirit of Pordenone ' (ii. 150) ; subsequently (ii. 287) they ascribe it to the latter. Originally, therefore, they regarded it as the work of Giorgione, executed in the spirit of Pordenone; later as that of Pordenone executed in the spirit of Giorgione. I shall return to this picture, and will therefore say no more about it here,

Rumohr is due the merit of having restored this fine portrait to its true author—Holbein.

2. The small "Crucifixion " with SS. Jerome and Christopher in the Borghese gallery at Rome. In the second half of the last century Vermiglioli described it as the work of Pintoricchio, and it is incomprehensible why, on being placed in the Borghese gallery in the beginning of this century, it should have been named Carlo Crivelli. The present writer had the satisfaction of restoring it to Pintoricchio in 1874.

3. The so-called "Bella di Tiziano," once in the Sciarra-Colonna gallery at Rome. In the seventeenth century the picture was in the celebrated collection of the Archduke Leopold William at Brussels, under the name of Palma Vecchio, and, as such, a small copy was made of it on copper by David Teniers the younger. This copy I saw, in 1868, at Blenheim. It had inscribed on the back, 'd'après Palma Vecchio.' The name of Titian was bestowed upon the original when it came to Rome, but all connoisseurs agree that this beautiful work is unmistakably by Palma Vecchio.

4. The " Sleeping Venus," by Giorgione, in the Dresden gallery. In the middle of the seventeenth century it passed as a work by that master; later it was attributed to Titian, for, even in Venice, Giorgione was held of no account in the eighteenth century. As a Titian, therefore, it came to Dresden in 1721. There, incredible as it may appear, it was pronounced to be a copy, probably by Sassoferrato. This attribution was adhered to until 1879, when the author recognised the spirit and characteristics of Giorgione in this exquisite painting.

5. The "Finding of Moses," in the Brera. At the time of Ridolfi— that is, in the middle of the seventeenth century—it was always regarded in Venice as the work of Bonifazio ; towards the close of the last century the name of Giorgione was substituted. Recent criticism has restored to Bonifazio Veronese this fine and brilliantly coloured work.

6. The large altar-piece by Foppa, in the Brera. In the sixteenth century it was in the Church of S. Maria delle Grazie at Bergamo, and the ' Anonimo ' mentions it as the work of Vincenzo Foppa. When, at the end of the last century, it came to Milan, the name was changed to that of Zenale, without any apparent reason. The picture has now been restored to its rightful owner, at the suggestion of the writer.

beyond congratulating the director upon having restored it to Titian.

The other picture (No. 1107) came to the gallery as the work of Giorgione, and is cited as such by Vasari's Florentine commentators.[1] The late Mr. Mündler was the first to recognise in this painting the one mentioned by Vasari as Palma's portrait of himself. He was followed by Messrs. Crowe and Cavalcaselle, and quite recently by Professor Locatelli of Bergamo,[2] and by the director of the Munich gallery. Vasari describes it as Palma's portrait of himself, and though he does not appear to have seen the picture, he mentions it, on the authority of his informant, as 'the best of all the master's works.' The broad drawing and modelling of the head undoubtedly point to Palma more than to any other Venetian, yet in the pose of the head, which seems calculated for effect, in the almost defiant expression of the features, I was unable, when I first saw the portrait, to discern the spirit, and still less the features, of this simple and unassuming painter, and a second visit to Munich only confirmed this impression. A man who, like Palma, selected as executors of his will a wine-seller and a fruiterer, would never have borne himself so haughtily as this young man.

I think it not improbable that a few decades after the death of Palma this picture, like many others by his imitator Cariani, was ascribed to the master himself. The portrait has been deprived of its original surface through over-cleaning, otherwise there would have been no difficulty in distinguishing between the master and the pupil—

[1] See *Vasari*, vii. 86, note 2 (ed. Milanesi, iv. 99). 'The portrait of a Fugger is now (1846), we may confidently affirm, in the Munich gallery. It is a half-length figure of a man with long hair, a foxskin over his shoulder, and gloves in his left hand. The catalogue describes it as the portrait of Giorgione, by himself.'

[2] See *Notisie intorno a Giacomo Palma il Vecchio ed alle sue pitture*, Bergamo, 1890.

MALE PORTRAIT. BY CARIANI.
(In the Munich Gallery.)

To face p. 16.

Palma's flesh-tints being always clear, while those of
Cariani are of a violet-reddish tone. The head, as already
observed, is wholly unlike Palma in its defiant, almost
insolent expression; so, too, is the form of the ear, and the
glaze of a red tone which is too strongly marked on the bridge
of the nose; all these considerations incline me to regard
this lifelike portrait as an admirable work of Palma's pupil,
assistant, and imitator, Giovanni Cariani,[1] a native of the
Val di Brembo, near Bergamo. A very old tradition, con-
firmed in 1648 by Ridolfi,[2] the Venetian painter and
writer on art, spoke in favour of the authorship of Gior-
gione, and recently both Vasari's Florentine commentators
and Dr. Marggraff have unanimously ascribed it to that
gifted artist. On the other hand, three critics of recent date,
among them Mr. Mündler, whose opinion carries great
weight, rejected this attribution, and concurred with Vasari
in giving the portrait to Palma Vecchio. I regret to say
that no critic except myself seems to have thought of
Giovanni Cariani in connection with it. The authorities
at Munich have prudently chosen a middle course, and
have unhesitatingly ascribed it to Palma. But as by so
doing they have, as it were, challenged me to give my
reasons for differing from them, I feel bound to devote
rather more space to this striking portrait than they, or
indeed I myself, should otherwise have wished. Should
my view prove incorrect (which in this case is not unlikely),
this digression may at least encourage some fellow-worker
to make a closer study of this painter, who, though by no
means without importance, is as yet scarcely known.

I will begin by mentioning some of the characteristics

---

[1] Several good portraits by him
are in the gallery at Bergamo,
among them one, formerly ascribed
to Giorgione, of a man with a hooked
nose, wearing a broad-brimmed hat.

[2] See Carlo Ridolfi, *Delle mera-
viglie dell' arte, ovvero delle vite
degli illustri pittori Veneti e dello
Stato*, vols. i. and ii. (Venezia,
1648).

whereby Palma's works may be distinguished from those of his more immediate pupils and imitators, Cariani and Bonifazio Veronese.[1] Palma's ear is large and rounded in form, and terminates in a pointed and well-defined lobe; Cariani's is also rounded, but has no distinct lobe; Bonifazio's ear, on the contrary, is always long. Palma's scale of colour is deeper than that of Lotto or Bonifazio; his hands are more bony than those of Cariani and of Bonifazio, coarser and less spiritualised than those of Lotto. In Cariani's early works, however, we meet with a form of hand which nearly approaches Palma.

Palma's great talents, as all connoisseurs are aware, lay in representing idealised female heads. These beautiful Venetian types are the very essence of his art, a source of delight and satisfaction to himself, and the immediate cause, in all probability, of his European reputation. On the other hand, I know of only two male portraits by this

---

[1] Palma is not only confounded with Cariani and Bonifazio Veronese, but often with Titian. Thus an exquisite early work by the latter in the Bridgewater gallery, "St. Joseph receiving the Infant Saviour from the Madonna" (No. 29), is attributed to Palma. Messrs. Crowe and Cavalcaselle (ii. 487) observe of it: 'This spirited little picture is too feeble for Palma, and is painted in a style (!) reminiscent of Bernardino Licinio or Polidoro Lanzani.' On the other hand, many pictures by Palma are ascribed to Titian. For instance, the so-called "Bella di Tiziano" in the Sciarra-Colonna gallery, the "Woman taken in Adultery" in the gallery of the Capitol, and a "Holy Family, with SS. John the Baptist and Catherine" at Hampton Court (No. 115). The latter picture, though much damaged, is genuine, which Messrs. Crowe and Cavalcaselle (ii. 486) will not allow. They observe, however, that, of all the pictures at Hampton Court under Palma's name, this 'most recalls the master's manner.' The portrait in the English National Gallery (No. 636), erroneously said to represent Ariosto, was also at one time thought to be by Titian; but Sir Frederick Burton recognised in it the hand of Palma. Messrs. Crowe and Cavalcaselle, in their *Life of Titian* (i. 200), would attribute this portrait to Dosso or even to Pellegrino da San Daniele, on the grounds that the latter was often at Ferrara, where Ariosto lived. From this it would appear that they look upon it as the authentic portrait of the poet, a proof, I think, that these writers are as little acquainted with Ariosto's characteristic features as they are with Palma Vecchio's equally characteristic manner of painting.

master, and both, unlike the deliberately idealised head
at Munich, are faithful imitations of nature. One, much
injured by recent restoration, is in the Querini-Stampalia
collection at Venice, and represents a young patrician rest-
ing his hands upon a window-ledge; a grey niche forms
the background.[1] The other is in the English National
Gallery (No. 636), and formerly passed for the portrait of
Ariosto by Titian, but, as already observed, has been re-
stored to Palma by Sir Frederick Burton. By Cariani, on
the other hand, I could name over a dozen male portraits,
the treatment of which is at times ideal and decorative, at
others the reverse. But I am far from asserting that, on
these grounds alone, this portrait cannot be by Palma,
but must of necessity be by his imitator, Cariani, and
this time I am not prepared to consider my attribution as
final.

Even in these days the name of Giovanni Cariani, the
fellow-countryman, contemporary, and pupil of Palma, is
scarcely known to students of art. By the middle of the
sixteenth century he appears to have been wholly for-
gotten in the Venetian territory, and Vasari makes no men-
tion of him. His works, like those of many other secondary
artists, were ascribed to his more renowned contemporaries
only a few years after his death, and, as his manner of
painting underwent several changes, it is not surprising
that his pictures should have been attributed to Giorgione,
Sebastiano del Piombo, or Lorenzo Lotto, and most fre-
quently to Palma Vecchio.

We will now examine what appear to me the more
mature among Cariani's early works, which for centuries
have borne the name of Giorgione.

The earliest I know, mentioned as a work by Cariani in

[1] The portrait very probably represents one of the Querini family, who
were Palma's patrons.

the 'Anonimo,'[1] is "Christ bearing the Cross," formerly
in the Palazzo Brembati, and now in the Public Gallery at
Bergamo.[2] It is on panel, though, as a rule, Cariani
employed canvas. The technic recalls Andrea Previtali's
early works (of 1502 to 1506), and points to the school of
Giovanni Bellini. I venture, therefore, to place it between
the years 1506 and 1508. The drawing is hard and un-
skilful, the treatment of the beard minute and timid, and
the hands, though carefully executed, are wanting in life.

I should place some years later those works in which
the imitation of Giorgione—the most admired painter in
Venice from the middle of the first decade of the sixteenth
century—is apparent. Eventually, all these pictures were
ascribed to Giorgione himself by students of art and picture-
dealers. The following belong to this period :—

1. The portrait of a man in a large black hat, with a
hooked nose and a keen, uncanny expression. It hangs in
the public gallery at Bergamo (Carrara collection, No. 135).[3]

2. The portrait of a woman with long fair hair—coarse,
and not very attractive, but with an expression of life and
energy (No. 85 of the same collection).

3. The bust portrait of a young monk in a white habit,
ascribed to Sebastiano del Piombo (No. 153 of the same
gallery, Lochis collection).

4. The full-faced portrait of a black-robed scholar, with
a view of the sea in the background. This portrait, which
came from Venice to Bergamo under the name of Giorgione,
is now in the Morelli collection.[4]

---

[1] See *Notisia d'opere di disegno*,
p. 188. Edited by Dr. G. Frizzoni.

[2] Lochis collection, No. 172.

[3] Ridolfi, in the *Life of Cariani*,
observes : ' Signor Jacopo Pighetti (a
native of Bergamo living at Venice)
possesses the portrait of a man in a
broad-brimmed hat ("berettone"),
which is always regarded as the
portrait of Cariani by himself.' This
latter assertion is scarcely likely to
be correct.

[4] Now in the public gallery at
Bergamo.

PICTURE BY CARIANI.

(In the Gallery at Vienna.)

To face p. 21.

5. A picture in the public gallery at Vienna (No. 217), which is described as follows in Dr. von Engerth's catalogue : " A youth crowned with vine leaves, attacked by an assassin, turns his head over his left shoulder and grasps his sword." Ridolfi and Boschini both mention this picture as the work of Giorgione.[1]

To this Giorgionesque period of the master (1512–1514) I should be disposed to ascribe the renowned portrait in the Munich gallery. Of all Cariani's works of this date it is undoubtedly the most successful and attractive. It has been highly extolled as the work of Giorgione himself by all later biographers of that master. That this portrait should have been regarded, even by Venetian art-historians, as identical with the one mentioned by Vasari [2] as that of a Fugger, proves how superficial was the knowledge of both Giorgione and Cariani as far back as the middle of the seventeenth century. Vasari says : ' È nel nostro libro una testa colorita a olio, ritratta da un Tedesco di casa Fuccheri, che allora éra dei maggiori mercanti nel Fondaco dei Tedeschi, la quale è cosa mirabile.' [3] A century later, it was described by Ridolfi as the work of Giorgione : " Il ritratto d' un Tedesco di casa Fuccheri con peliccia di volpe in dosso in atto di girarsi." [4]

It is evident that this picture was no other than the one now at Munich, which, at that date, was in the possession of a Fleming named Van Veer, who lived at Venice. In the present day Vasari's Florentine commen-

---

[1] Messrs. Crowe and Cavalcaselle (ii. 152, 547) and other art-critics, rightly recognised the Giorgionesque manner of Cariani in this celebrated picture, of which we give a reproduction here.

[2] vii. 86 (ed. Milanesi, iv. 99).

[3] ' There is in our book (of original drawings by the great masters) a head, painted in oil, a portrait of a German of the house of Fugger, who was then one of the greatest merchants in the Fondaco dei Tedeschi, which is an admirable work.'

[4] " The portrait of a German of the house of Fugger, with a foxskin round his shoulders, in the act of turning his head."

tators have added to the confusion by affirming that
Giorgione's portrait of a Fugger, described by Ridolfi, 'is
now in the Munich gallery, and is there regarded as the
master's portrait of himself.' [1] But, before proceeding
further, let me ask all unprejudiced observers one question.
Has this defiant and bold-looking youth the appearance of
a German, and, moreover, of a German merchant of the
aristocratic standing of the wealthy Fuggers? Is it not
far more probable that it is the idealised portrait of a
young Venetian of the people, full of life and vigour?
The painter flung a foxskin, or, as Vasari has it, a camel's
skin, round the shoulders of his model, and gave him a pair
of gloves to hold, his object being to produce one of those
mysterious pictures after the manner of Giorgione. Cer-
tainly, in this happily inspired portrait, Cariani succeeded
in approaching nearer to the spirit and feeling of his great
prototype than the more unimaginative Palma Vecchio was
ever able to do. I am acquainted with about forty works
by Cariani, but this portrait, assuming it to be really by
him, attracted me more powerfully than any others I know.

We now come to the master's second period, from
about 1514–1516, when he entered into closer relations
with his fellow-countryman Palma, and perhaps assisted
him. In Palma's workshop he not improbably became
more intimately acquainted with another of the master's
pupils, Bonifazio Veronese. This seems to me to be con-
firmed by the similarity noticeable, especially in the rosy
flesh-tints, between Bonifazio's early pictures and those
of Cariani's middle period. No one at all acquainted with
the works of these two imitators of Palma will, I think,
question that they approached each other closely in this
respect. I will now enumerate a few characteristic works
of Cariani's Palmesque period :—

[1] vii. 86 (ed. Milanesi, iv. 99, note 2).

MADONNA AND SAINTS. BY CARIANI.

(Belonging to Signor Federigo Frizzoni Salis at Bergamo.)

To face p. 23.

1. The Triptych with SS. Stephen, Catherine and James, which he painted for the Church of Locatello, in the Val d'Imagna near Bergamo. The two first-named saints —full-length figures standing in a landscape—are in the gallery at Bergamo (Lochis collection, Nos. 192 and 196). The St. Catherine more especially recalls Bonifazio. The St. James was formerly in the possession of Count Petrobelli at Bergamo.

2. A splendid picture belonging to Signor Federigo Frizzoni-Salis at Bergamo—the "Madonna and Child" between SS. Francis and Jerome.[1] The rosy flesh-tints of the Madonna, like those of the St. Catherine before mentioned, so closely resemble those of Bonifazio, that the inexperienced would doubtless be led to attribute pictures such as this one by Cariani to the former painter. The Madonna in Signor Frizzoni's picture should be compared with the Virgin in an early work by Bonifazio in the Ambrosiana, and I think that every unprejudiced critic will then be disposed to share my opinion. A comparison between the works of the Bergamasque and those of the Veronese painter is also interesting from an ethnological point of view. Both were pupils of Palma. Cariani, who came of a mountain race, is always earnest and energetic to rudeness in his works, but without grace. Bonifazio, on the other hand, who was a son of the plains and belonged to

[1] Some forty years ago this admirable picture by Cariani was bought by the late Sir Charles Eastlake from the picture-dealer and painter Schiavone, at Venice. A large sum was given for it, for both Mr. Mündler and the late director of the National Gallery—two of the most eminent connoisseurs of Italian painting in their day—considered it to be by Palma. After having been brought to London, the picture was carefully cleaned, and, to the general surprise, a *cartellino*, inscribed 'I. CARIANVS,' came to light, which had been painted over with intent to deceive. The picture was subsequently exchanged for one by Cosimo Tura (now No. 772 in the English National Gallery). Thus we see that even experienced critics may occasionally mistake the pupil Cariani for his master Palma.

the Venetian stock, is always graceful and attractive; his figures are slender, refined, and easy in their movements, though they lack the look of vigour, energy, and decision—qualities which we always find exemplified in Cariani's somewhat coarse and robust saints.

Among the works of Cariani's middle period I should include the following: The "Nativity" in the parish church at Zogno, in the Brembo Valley; a "Holy Family" in a landscape, in the Morelli collection;[1] and a "Madonna" between SS. John the Baptist and Catherine, in the Vienna Academy. To Cariani's Palmesque period must also have belonged an altar-piece, which he painted in 1514 for the church at Lonno, in the Serio Valley.[2] About 1516 or 1517, as Messrs. Crowe and Cavalcaselle have observed, Cariani's technic underwent another change. He laid on his colours in a thin and liquid manner, grounding his pictures in tempera of a grey tone, and finishing them with thin glazes of oil. This method is apparent in the following works:—

1. The portrait of a physician, who was a professor in the University of Padua (No. 184 in the gallery at Bergamo). This fine and well-preserved portrait is inscribed: 'Io. Bened. Caravag* [of Caravaggio, in the Bergamasque district] Philos. et Medicus ac Studii Patavini Lector et

[1] Now at Bergamo.

[2] This picture represented the Madonna with the Infant Saviour blessing the kneeling donor and his wife, between SS. Anthony and Catherine. It was signed 'I. CARIANI. P. 1514.' (See *Vite de' Pittori, Scultori e Architetti Bergamaschi, scritte dal Conte Cav. Francesco Maria Tassi*, i. 37.) In 1553 it was removed to make room for a much larger one, representing St. Anthony between SS. Peter, Paul, Stephen, Jerome, Bernard, and Catherine, and with the Madonna and Child in the upper part. It is inscribed, '*Julius Licinius Venetus florente suæ ætatis anno 26 pingebat*,' and may still be seen in its original place in the church. This Friulian artist, Julius Licinius, must, to judge by this picture, have been a very inferior painter, though, according to Maniago (*Storia delle arti Friulane*, p. 91), he was employed to decorate with frescoes several houses at Augsburg, and fulfilled his task so satisfactorily that the chief magistrate of that place bestowed upon him the right of honorary citizenship.

Rector IOANNES CARIANVS.' The conception is so simple, true, and lifelike, the colouring so fresh and luminous, that it may challenge comparison with the best portraits.

2. The portrait of a young man in black, turning to the right, with a keen unpleasant expression. The signature is I. C. (No. 165 in the gallery at Bergamo, Lochis collection).

3. The little picture in the Ambrosiana—the "Procession to Calvary"—probably belongs to this period. Cariani evidently made use of northern engravings for it; and it was even formerly attributed to Lucas van Leyden. The late Mr. Mündler was the first to restore it to its true author.

4. In 1519 Cariani painted the group of the Albani family, a signed and dated picture, now belonging to Count Roncalli at Bergamo. The Albani were Cariani's patrons, and he painted portraits of several members of the family; that of Francesco (?) now belongs to Mr. Salting, in London, while that of a very unattractive old woman, in profile, is in the Museo Civico at Milan (Tanzi collection).

A Madonna with the donor, signed and dated 1520, is in the possession of Signor J. Baglioni at Bergamo, and of the same date are the "Resurrection" belonging to Count Marazzi at Crema,[1] and the portrait of the Doge Andrea Gritti in the Palazzo Morloni-Beroa at Bergamo, there ascribed to Titian.

Cariani must at this time have settled at Bergamo, for his mode of expression and representation once more underwent a change. The Venetian element gradually disappeared from his works, his Bergamasque nature reasserted itself, and henceforward he expressed himself, so to speak, in the dialect of his native province. This change of manner may be observed in the much-

[1] This picture is signed as follows : ' IOANNES. CARIANVS. P.M.D.XX.'

repainted altar-piece of St. Helena and other saints in the
gallery at Bergamo, and in that executed by the master
for the Church of S. Gottardo at Bergamo, which in 1803
was removed to the Brera. The latter picture represents
the Madonna and Child enthroned between SS. Augustine,
Catherine, Apollonia, Joseph, Philip, Grata, and Adelaide,
and numerous angels in many-coloured robes. There is
much that is awkward and boorish in the conception,
drawing, and colouring of this picture; the saints, however,
are powerful and earnest in expression. According to
Count Tassi, the landscape-painter Zuccarelli pronounced
this picture to be the finest at Bergamo—a city which
contains some of the most glorious works of Lotto and
Moretto!

Tassi (*op. cit.*) mentions that Cariani executed numerous
frescoes at Bergamo on the façades of private houses and on
public buildings; but scarcely a trace of them now remains.
They have been ruthlessly destroyed by the ravages of time.

The same writer ascribes to Cariani the lunette fresco
over the side door of S. Maria Maggiore at Bergamo, and is
followed by Messrs. Crowe and Cavalcaselle. I consider it
to be an undoubted work of Andrea Previtali (†). As to the
frescoes in the Castle of Malpaga, near Bergamo, Cariani
certainly had no part in them, as Messrs. Crowe and
Cavalcaselle would have us believe.[1] They were executed
by Romanino and his assistants.

We gather the following facts about Cariani from a
document formerly in the possession of Don Cavagnis, of
Fuipiano, of which I have a copy. It states that on
September 5, 1508, Zuan de Zuan de Busi was at Fuipiano,
and promised a donation of three ducats to the parish
church. He had probably been recalled from Venice by
the illness of his father, who must have died soon after-

[1] ii. 556.

wards, for under date November 5, 1508, we find the painter called 'Mr. Zuan quondam Mr. Zuan ditto Cariani,' &c. In 1529 Cariani is mentioned as one of the heads of the guild of SS. Philip and James present in Fuipiano, and under date 1541 we read that the sum of 97l., Denari 20, is to be paid to 'Mr. Zuan fù Mr. Zuani ditto Cariani,' for the altar-piece with St. Roch, which he sent to Fuipiano by the hand of Geronimo de Donado. This is the last record we have of the master.

We may conclude that Giovanni Busi, called from his father Cariani, was born at Fuipiano, a village in the Brembo Valley, between 1480 and 1485. Like his Bergamasque fellow-countrymen—Palma Vecchio, Francesco and Girolamo da Santa Croce, Galizzi, and others—he probably was sent to Venice, while yet a boy, to learn his art. There he must have spent the greater part of his youth, and only settled at Bergamo about 1520.

His works are numerous in the neighbourhood of his home. I am acquainted with two-and-twenty in the Bergamasque district, and with eight at Milan; but out of Italy he is rarely met with. Three or four of his pictures are at Vienna; one, formerly in the Schönborn collection at Pomersfelden, belongs to the Grand Duke of Oldenburg, and a portrait is in the Berlin gallery. In England, I only know of two works by him—one in the collection of Mr. Salting, and a "Madonna and Saints" of no great merit which has recently been acquired by the National Gallery (No. 1203). The "Lucretia" in the Holford collection, which Messrs. Crowe and Cavalcaselle attribute to Cariani, is by Lotto, and the double portrait in the Louvre (No. 1156) is certainly not by Cariani.

Palma Vecchio is undoubtedly the most accomplished, complete, and well-balanced of all the Bergamasque artists, but I think I shall not be far wrong if I characterise

Cariani as the most vigorous and full of vitality among them.

To return to Palma Vecchio. A much-damaged picture by him hangs in Room IX. (No. 1108). It represents the Madonna and the Child, who gives a rosary to St. Roch. On the right is the Magdalen. It is a work in Palma's third or so-called 'blonde' manner (1520–1526). The form of the ear both in the Madonna and the Child is very characteristic, having a wide and rounded auricle and a well-defined lobe.

The new catalogue, like the former one, states that Palma first studied under Giovanni Bellini, and afterwards perfected himself under Giorgione and Titian. This, I may add, is the generally accepted opinion ; but Messrs. Crowe and Cavalcaselle, the most recent historians of Italian painting, are very decidedly opposed to it. They assign to him, as a pioneer, almost the highest place in the Venetian school of the first half of the sixteenth century. 'From the borders of Piedmont,' they observe, ' to the Gulf of Triest . . . . in the plains watered by the Adige and the Po there is not a city of any pretensions that did not feel the influence of Palmesque art.' Moreover, they believe that Pellegrino da San Daniele, Pordenone, Morto da Feltre, and many other celebrated painters of that date, derived their style in part from Palma. They therefore assume that he must have been born before 1480, that he was contemporary with Pellegrino and Giorgione, and older by a few years than Titian, Pordenone, and Sebastiano del Piombo. All these considerations lead them to conclude that 'Palma shared with Giorgione and Titian the honour of modernising and regenerating Venetian art' (ii. 456, 457). The question is one of some importance in the history of Venetian painting, and I shall, therefore, devote a little space to it in order to state my views on the subject.

Palma's earliest biographers, Vasari and Ridolfi, represented the master as being younger than Titian and Giorgione; and the Venetian who furnished Vasari with information about Palma and Lotto stated that the former died at the age of forty-eight. This was evidently the account of the matter current among painters at Venice, and why should we doubt it ? Do we possess any conclusive evidence to the contrary ? By no means. Dates of this description were usually supplied to Vasari by impartial and unprejudiced persons, and, as we shall see in the life of Antonello da Messina, are generally pretty correct. It is only when drawing upon his imagination and adding to the narrative, in order, as he supposed, to render it more interesting, that the biographer often went grossly astray. Some years ago a document was discovered containing Palma's will and the year of his death—1528.[1] If, there-

[1] Extract from the *Raccolta Veneta, Dispensa* ii., March 1866: 'Testamentum magistri Jacobi Palma pictoris de confinio Sancti Bassi.'

'Die XXVIII IULIJ MDXXVIII.'

'Die 28 mensis Julij 1528 Indictione prima Rivoalti. Cum vite sue terminum etc. Quapropter ego Jacobus Palma pictor qm. ser Antonij de confinio Sancti Bassi, sanus Dei gratia mente et intellectu, licet corpore pergravatus, timens hujus seculi pericula, ad me vocare feci presbyterum Aloysium Natalem plebanum etc.... ut hoc meum scriberet testamentum. . . . In primis namque animam meam Altissimo commendans, instituo et esse volo meos fidei commissarios et hujus mei testamenti exequtores ser Marcum de bajeto, mercatorem vini, ser Joannem frutarolum [fruit-vendor] in confinio Sancti Angeli, et ser Fantinum de Girardo tinctorem [all three probably Bergamasques settled at Venice], qui omnes concorditer exequantur etc. . . .

'Item volo quod per meos commissarios dispensetur ducatos viginti quinque inter meos affines et consaguineos magis indigentes, tam in presenti civitate Venetiarum, quam in territorio bergomensi pro anima mea. . . .

'Item volo quod mittatur Assisium ad orandum pro anima mea cum elemosyna consueta. Item dimitto Margaritæ nepti meæ, filiæ quondam ser Bartholomei olim fratris mei, ducatos ducentos pro suo maritare seu monachare. Et ipsa descedente ante suum maritare vel monachare, ipsi ducati ducenti deveniant in meam commissariam' . . . . The remainder of his fortune : 'Dimitto et relinquo Antonio, Joanni et Marietae, fratribus, nepotibus meis,

fore, Vasari's information—that he died at the age of forty-
eight—be correct, he must have been born in 1480, though
whether at Serinalta or at Venice it may be difficult to
decide. Vasari calls him 'Palma Viniziano,' from which
we might infer that, like his grand-nephew Palma Giovine,
he was a native of Venice. Later writers, however, con-
sider that he was born at Serinalta, the home of his
parents.[1]

It is of little importance where he was born; as a
painter he is a Venetian, as an artist a Venetianised Berga-
masque; for, notwithstanding his training in the City of
the Lagoons, he never entirely lost his hardy mountain
nature. Compared with the figures of Giorgione, Lotto,
and Bonifazio Veronese, who were all children of the
plains, those of Palma appear of a more grave and vigorous,
though at the same time a ruder stamp.

I know of no work by Palma bearing either signature
or date, while we have signed pictures by Lotto as early as

filijs prefati quondam ser Bartholo-
mei olim fratris mei, equaliter et
equis portionibus inter eos ' etc.

From his will we therefore gather
that Palma was never married and
had no legitimate children. Among
the unfinished pictures found in his
workshop after his death—about
forty in number, some of them
mere sketches—we find mentioned
a "Retrato de messer Francesco
Querini." This is probably the
much-repainted male portrait in the
Querini-Stampalia collection at
Venice. The Querinis were Palma's
patrons. Another half-finished por-
trait found in the master's work-
shop is described as follows in the
inventory of his property. 'Quadro
di una donna retrata con forni-
menti de nogera, le qual depenture,
e scorzade e descolade con maneghe

de razo zalo de circa b¹ I.' This
might be identical with the exquisite
female portrait in the Querini col-
lection. From the opening sentences
of his will, we may infer that Palma
had been ailing for some years,
perhaps since 1525. He probably
suffered from consumption. His
large altar-piece—the "Adoration
of the Magi," now in the Brera, No.
172—was in great part executed by
a pupil or assistant, owing to the
master's failing health.

[1] Signor Elia Fornoni, of Ber-
gamo has proved from documents
that Palma Vecchio was born at
Serinalta, and he considers that he
belonged to the Nigretti family. At
Serinalta a house in the Contrada
Nigretti is still called 'la cà (casa)
del pittùr ' (pittore) (the house of the
painter).

1500, 1505, and 1506. One of Palma's earliest works is, I think, the very interesting little picture representing "Tobias and the Angel" in the Stuttgart gallery. As works of a few years later, I would name the "Lucretia" in the Borghese gallery, the "Adam and Eve" at Brunswick, and the "Woman taken in Adultery" in the gallery of the Capitol. Dr. Bode, on the other hand, regards a Madonna in the Berlin gallery (No. 31) [1] as one of the first works of Palma's early period. The panel bears a *cartellino* with IACOBVS PALMA, and as this appears to be of early date, the Berlin director infers that the signature must be above suspicion. Had Dr. Bode, who is so intimate with the technical methods of the Italian masters, examined this picture with a critical eye, instead of only observing the label, he would have seen that it could not be the work of a beginner, but that it revealed a practised hand. The picture appears to me to be by some uninteresting and remarkably commonplace imitator of Francesco da Santa Croce.[2] As to the label with its very old signature and the crossed palm branches above, I believe it

---

[1] 'Une Vierge avec l'Enfant, qui porte en grosses lettres la signature, "Jacobus Palma," paraît au premier coup d'œil trop faible pour ce maître. Son coloris est fruste et clair, son dessin gauche. Mais le tableau porte incontestablement la marque d'un peintre de Bergame, successeur de Bellini, et comme la signature est sans aucune doute (!) contemporaine du tableau, nous pouvons y voir avec vraisemblance une œuvre de la première jeunesse de Palma, ce peintre étant originaire de Bergame.'—*Gazette des Beaux-Arts*, décembre 1889, p. 613.

[2] Francesco di Simone, of Santa Croce, a village in the Brembo Valley, is one of those Bergamasque artists who left their homes at an early age to study painting in Venice. An "Annunciation," signed FRANCISCVS DE SANTA CRVCIS (*sic*) FECIT 1504, was a few years ago removed from Spino, a village in the Brembo Valley, to the public gallery at Bergamo. It shows a very juvenile hand, and proves that the painter was an imitator of Giovanni Bellini. In a picture of 1507 in the Church of S. Pietro Martire at Murano, Francesco added D.I.B. after his signature, that is, Discipulus Joannis Bellini.

to be one of the many forgeries which were perpetrated centuries ago (†).[1]

And now I must ask, which are the works of Palma's contemporaries in North Italy—at Vercelli, Milan, Pavia, Lodi, or even at Bergamo, Brescia, and Verona—wherein Messrs. Crowe and Cavaleaselle have detected his influence? They must, I think, have confounded him with Giorgione. The only painters directly connected with Palma were his immediate pupils, Cariani and Bonifazio Veronese, and his uninteresting follower, the Bergamasque Galizzi.[2]

It was long before Palma attained to any reputation beyond the limits of Venice, and except the altar-pieces for Serinalta, Dossena, and Peghera—all villages in his native valley—he received commissions for others only from Fontanelle near Oderzo, from Zerman near Treviso, and from Vicenza. These pictures are evidently the work of a finished artist, and must have been produced between 1515 and 1525. Lotto, on the other hand, was actively employed at Treviso as early as from 1503 to 1506. In the latter year he obtained a commission from the Dominicans of Recanati, and in 1509 he even received the flattering invitation to decorate some of the apartments in the Vatican. All this, I think, makes it very doubtful whether Palma was older than Lotto and Titian. As regards Messrs. Crowe and Cavalcaselle's statement that Pordenone, Pellegrino, and Morto da Feltre derived their style from Palma, are we to accept it as a recognised fact? Morto da Feltre we may dismiss at once, as I know too little of him. Pordenone in his early works—such as the beautiful altar-

[1] See on this point my *Critical Studies in the Borghese and Doria Galleries*, p. 296.

[2] There are several signed works by this very feeble painter in the public gallery at Bergamo and in the Casa Agliardi in the same city. His best work is probably a Triptych in the collection of Dr. Gustavo Frizzoni. It represents the Madonna and Child between SS. John the Baptist and Alexander.

piece at Sussignana and the frescoes in the Castle of S. Salvadore—was undoubtedly influenced by Giorgione, and especially by Titian in his Giorgionesque period. The frescoes by the latter at Padua, of the years 1510–1511, seem to have been carefully studied by Pordenone, but of Palma's influence I can find absolutely no trace in his works. Pellegrino da San Daniele, whose best work, according to Count Maniago, is the altar-piece of 1528 at Cividale, certainly appears as an imitator, though not as a direct pupil, of Palma in that picture. As I can only regard this Friulian artist as a very inferior painter, which is quite contrary to the view taken by the most recent writers on art, I feel bound to state my reasons for differing from them.

Vasari was never in the Friuli himself, and Pellegrino's works were therefore wholly unknown to him. For information about them he relied blindly on Giovan Battista Grassi, a painter of Udine, and Pellegrino's fellow-countryman. Grassi, like many other writers of his day, was induced by local vanity and partiality to unduly exalt Pellegrino, who was an artist of small capacity. He represented him to Vasari as a pupil of Bellini, and added that the master was so astounded at his scholar's extraordinary progress that he called him ' Pellegrino,' that is, the rare, the remarkable, the unparalleled. It is strange, however, that neither the ' Anonimo ' in the sixteenth century, nor Ridolfi in the succeeding one, should mention this painter. Grassi's story, as related by Vasari, was first brought into notice again by Lanzi, who was followed by Count Maniago. In recent times the fame of Pellegrino was increased by Harzen and Passavant, who attributed to him the fine engravings signed ' P. P.'

From my own studies and from notices of him in documents, for which I am indebted to Dr. Joppi of Udine, the principal events of this painter's life must, I think, have been somewhat as follows: Pellegrino's father, Battista, was a Dalmatian settled as a painter at Udine as early as 1468. In 1470 he was living at San Daniele, near Udine, where he was commissioned to decorate a church with paintings. In 1487, his son Martino (afterwards known as Pellegrino) acted as a witness at Udine, from which we may infer that he was born between 1460 and 1470. He is called 'Maestro Martino' in a contract of 1491, by which he undertook to execute frescoes in the Church of Villanova, near San Daniele, none of which have been preserved. In another contract of April 5, 1494, relating to a picture at Osopo, which is still in existence there, he is named 'Maestro Martino dicto Pellegrino di Udine.' The Italian word 'pellegrino' means both stranger and pilgrim, but in poetry anything remarkably rare and beautiful. The picture at Osopo would certainly not lead us to suppose that the word in its latter sense could ever have been applied to Martino da Udine, and I think that it will be generally admitted that this painter was merely called Pellegrino because at Udine he was regarded as a stranger, in the same way that Jacopo de' Barbari was called 'Walch'—the foreigner—at Nuremberg. The picture at Osopo must have been executed some years after the contract was concluded, for the composition vividly recalls Bartolommeo Montagna's altar-piece of 1499, now in the Brera. It is therefore very probable that Pellegrino made use of Montagna's drawing for his own picture, for it is out of the question that so great an artist as Montagna should have borrowed the design of one of his best works from so inferior a painter as Pellegrino. The contrast, moreover, in the picture at Osopo, between the fine composition and the feeble execution, is very striking. In the years 1497 and 1498 Pellegrino executed frescoes in the Church of S. Antonio at San Daniele, and about the same time he married in that place. In these frescoes

as well as in the picture at Osopo he appears as a feeble
and archaic painter. His master was probably no other
than his father, Battista. His altar-piece with St. Joseph
in the cathedral at Udine, of 1501, is so entirely repainted
that I can form no opinion with respect to it. In 1504 he
was at Ferrara, working for the Duke Alfonso d'Este. In
1505 and 1506 he was partly at Udine, partly at Ferrara—
where he was employed in the Palazzo Schifanoja by
Sigismondo d'Este—and partly at San Daniele. In this
year he is first called 'Pellegrino di San Daniele.' In 1506
he was again employed at Ferrara by Duke Alfonso, but
returned after a few months to Udine, where he remained
throughout the year 1507. From 1508 to 1512 he visited
Ferrara regularly every autumn. In 1513 he painted two
allegorical figures in chiaroscuro in the Loggia of the
Palazzo Pubblico at Udine, some portions of which still
exist. In 1516 he undertook to furnish a carved and
painted statue of St. Margaret to San Daniele. In 1519–
1520 he painted the shutters of the organ in the cathedral
at Udine ; and in these works, notably in the ample folds
of the drapery, we first perceive the influence which
Giovanni Antonio da Pordenone must have exercised over
him.

From 1519 to 1521 Pellegrino continued to paint in the
choir of the Church of S. Antonio at San Daniele. The
frescoes he executed there are his best works, and prove, I
think, that he was an imitator not only of Pordenone, but
of Romanino. On his journeys to and from Ferrara,
Pellegrino must often have been at Padua, and in that city
he would have seen and studied Romanino's admirable
picture of 1513, then in the Church of S. Giustina. His
colouring recalls that master ; the ample folds of his
drapery remind us of Pordenone ; while in some of his
heads he approaches Titian and Palma. The works of the

two latter painters he had probably seen at Oderzo, at
Zerman, and in the ' Scuola del Santo,' at Padua. In 1526
he went to Venice—apparently for the first time—in order
to ' buy colours ' for the large picture which he had under-
taken to paint for the church at Cividale. In Venice he
undoubtedly saw many works by Palma, whose splendid
" St. Barbara " must already have attained celebrity; and
he certainly took him for his model, as the altar-piece at
Cividale clearly proves.

A male portrait by Pellegrino in the public gallery at
Vienna (No. 219), which Herr von Engerth's catalogue de-
scribes as that ' of a young hero,' may belong to the master's
Palmesque period (†). It is there ascribed to Palma him-
self, while Messrs. Crowe and Cavalcaselle are disposed to
attribute it either to Pordenone or to Bernardino Licinio.[1]

In 1530 and 1531 Pellegrino was engaged in a trade in
wood; but, notwithstanding, we find that in 1546 and 1547
he again accepted commissions for pictures. In December
1547 he died, aged over eighty.

Pellegrino's large "Annunciation," in the Venice
Academy, bears the following signature :—

' Pelegrinus faciebat, 1519.'

P . . . P

In the eyes of Herr Harzen, these two letters were
profoundly significant. ' Eureka ! ' he exclaimed in his
delight on discovering them, and forthwith ascribed to
Pellegrino the celebrated engraving signed with two p's,
without stopping to inquire whether the drawing and the
feeling in this picture coincided with those in the engraving.
All other writers on art, including even Passavant, followed
blindly in his steps. But I think that anyone who compares

[1] In the seventeenth century this
portrait was considered to represent
Gaston de Foix, who fell at the
battle of Ravenna in 1512.

this beautiful engraving—the " Triumph of Selene " [1]—
with Pellegrino's pictures, will agree with me that it has
no connection with that painter, but shows the hand of an
excellent Ferrarese master. That an artist of so little origi-
nality as Pellegrino should have been highly thought of in his
own home need surprise none acquainted with the works of
other Friulian painters. Everything in this world is com-
parative, and those who have leisure and inclination to de-
vote a short time to this interesting district will see that
Pellegrino's works contrast most favourably with those of
painters like Leonardo da San Daniele, Domenico da Tol-
mezzo, Miani (at Cividale), Andrea Bellunello, Gianfrancesco
da Tolmezzo (at Barbeano), Giovanni and Girolamo Martini,
Luca Monverde, Seccante, Calderari, Girolamo Grassi, and
others. The Friulians, unlike their neighbours of the March
of Treviso, were not endowed with much artistic talent;
shrewd, industrious, and active, they were, like all mountain
races, homely and prosaic by nature. Giovanni Antonio da
Pordenone, it is true, was partly of Friulian parentage,
that is, on his mother's side; but his father was a Brescian
of Corticelle del Lodesano, near Cremona, and his artistic
training was mainly derived from a study of the works of
Giorgione and Titian, and was certainly not due to the
teaching of Giovanni Francesco da Tolmezzo, a tire-
some and insignificant painter, whom Messrs. Crowe and
Cavalcaselle, on what grounds I cannot imagine, most
erroneously regard as his master. Fortunately for these
writers, the fresco which they cite in support of their
view is in the remote village of Barbeano, and I shall not
recommend any student to go so far out of his way in order

[1] It is incomprehensible that
M. Laborde, in his excellent work on
engravings, actually does not men-
tion this example. A writer treating
of the heavens would surely not
omit all mention of the moon! In
my opinion, the forms in this en-
graving point to an artist who nearly
approached Ercole Roberti (†).

to instruct himself on this point. Another Friulian by
birth, a gifted and spirited painter who died young, was
Sebastiano Florigerio. He married the daughter of Pelle-
grino da San Daniele. His father, Giacomo da Bologna,
lived at Conegliano. I am only acquainted with three or
four works by this master,[1] among them the altar-piece in
the Church of S. Giorgio at Udine, which displays much
talent. I have treated Pellegrino somewhat diffusely, but
I felt bound to support my own views about this painter
as far as possible, as they differ so widely from those of
Messrs. Crowe and Cavalcaselle. The character of local
Friulian art is dry and prosaic. All that is best in it is
derived from without ; hence it is impossible that these
artists should have exercised the slightest influence on the
development of Venetian painting. We will now return to
Palma Vecchio.

Vasari does not mention who was Palma's master.
Ridolfi conjectures that he came to Venice when young,
and there learnt much from Titian, so much indeed ' that he
acquired a certain sweetness of colouring which approached
that of Titian's early works ' (' ch' egli apprese certa
dolcezza di colorire che si avvicina alle opere prime dello
stesso Tiziano '). How is it that the researches of writers
so competent as Messrs. Crowe and Cavalcaselle should
have led them to form an opinion of Palma so diametrically
opposed to that of Vasari and Ridolfi ? They are unable
to produce a single document in support of their theory,
which is based, it appears to me, upon a delusion. My
readers should know that in the Duc d'Aumale's collection
there is a Madonna by Palma bearing his signature, and
a date, which some affirm to be M D. This is the only
instance with which I am acquainted of a signed and

[1] In the Venice Academy there
is a picture by this artist represent-
ing the Madonna and Child between
SS. Sebastian and Roch.

dated picture by the master. The workmanship is in no respect that of a *quattrocento* painter, and belongs to a period at least ten years later than that attributed to it. It is, moreover, entirely disfigured by repainting. The ear of the Infant Saviour is not of Palma's characteristic form, having been altered by the restorer, as also the left hand of the Madonna; the sky has been painted over, and both the beard and the nimbus of St. Jerome are modern. On examining the *cartellino* the question at once suggests itself whether the name and date are genuine, or are they a later addition? Taking into consideration all these points, I cannot but decide in favour of the latter view.[1] The solution of this problem is not

[1] Messrs. Crowe and Cavalcaselle (ii. 110), misled by their conviction that Palma influenced Titian, whilst the reverse was really the case, trace his influence in Titian's beautiful early work in the Madrid gallery, which is there ascribed to Giorgione. It represents the Madonna and Child, to whom St. Bridget offers some flowers, whilst her husband, St. Ulfus, clad in armour, stands behind her. Titian probably painted the picture between 1512 and 1514, at a time, therefore, when Palma was forming his style entirely upon the works of this master. The type of the Madonna at Madrid vividly recalls that of the woman accused by her husband in Titian's once splendid fresco at Padua, which has been irreparably injured by repainting. Messrs. Crowe and Cavalcaselle would also trace the influence of Palma in the Madonna with St. Anthony in the Uffizi (No. 633), in the "Amor sacro e Amor profano" of the Borghese gallery, and in the Antwerp picture of the Bishop of Palo—a member of the Pesaro family—presented to St. Peter. The "Amor sacro e Amor profano" (which they suggest should be renamed "Amor sazio e Amor ingenuo," i. 63) must, according to them, have been painted in 1500, the Antwerp picture in 1503. I must confess that I am unable to share their opinion. The Borghese picture is undoubtedly an early work, and thoroughly Giorgionesque, but the treatment is so free and broad that I should place it eight or ten years later—that is, about 1509. The Antwerp picture must have been executed for the Pesaro family later than 1503, though certainly earlier than the Borghese picture (the inscription is, I should say, an addition of the seventeenth century). I should therefore class it among the following early works of Titian: The Infant Saviour between two saints, in the Church of S. Marcuola at Venice; "Tobias and the Angel," in that of S. Marziale; and the Madonna of the Cherries in the public gallery at Vienna. The artistic development of Titian and

without importance in the history of Art, for, should
the *cartellino* prove genuine, then Messrs. Crowe and
Cavalcaselle will be right in their conclusions, and the
development of Venetian painting in the first twenty years
of the sixteenth century must have been much as they
represent it.   If, on the other hand, it can be proved
that the inscription was added after the death of Palma by
some picture-dealer (which I am quite convinced was the
case), then their theory breaks down, and Palma's place
among his renowned contemporaries will be a much lower
one than that hitherto assigned to him by them.   It would,
therefore, be most desirable if the present possessor would,
in the interests of art, allow the picture to be carefully
cleaned.

I am not acquainted with any drawings by Palma.
That of the " Holy Family " mentioned by Sir J. C.
Robinson in his catalogue of the Malcolm collection
(No. 363) is, I consider, by Palma Giovine ; the Italian
signature—Giacomo—also proves this (†).

Let us now examine the other pictures in the Munich
gallery ascribed to Palma Vecchio.   Some critics continue
to attribute to him the large figure of " St. Jerome writing "
(Room VIII., No. 1088), while the new catalogue assigns
it to a Brescian painter.   Messrs. Crowe and Cavalcaselle
do not believe it to be by an Italian master.   I am now

Palma, who both came of mountain
races, was not so rapid as Messrs.
Crowe and Cavalcaselle would have
us believe.   Had Titian produced
such admirable works as those just
mentioned as early as 1500 and
1503, he would certainly have been
employed in the service of the Re-
public at that date, and Dürer
would have mentioned him in 1506.
But it was not until 1510 and 1511
that he gave proof of his remarkable

powers in his frescoes in the Scuola
del Santo at Padua, which are still
wholly Giorgionesque in style.   Im-
mediately after their completion he
received commissions from the city
of Vicenza.   Even at that date he
never signs himself ' maestro,' but
simply, ' Io tician di Cador depintore
1511, 2 decembrio.'   (See Gozzati's
work on the Church of the Santo at
Padua.)

also of this opinion, and look upon it as an enlarged copy of a figure by Moretto or by his pupil and imitator, Giovan Battista Moroni. In the same room we find a "Madonna with Saints" (No. 1086), which was formerly catalogued as Palma Vecchio. Ten years ago I unfortunately ascribed this feeble production to Girolamo da Santa Croce, misled by various peculiarities, among others the parrot so frequently introduced by this painter into his pictures. There is nothing for it now but to acknowledge that I made a mistake, which is the more to be regretted as the director of the gallery has adopted my over-hasty suggestion. The picture, I think, must be allowed to remain among the large class of anonymous works by unknown and unimportant imitators of the Bellini and of Alvise Vivarini.

The number of Palma's pictures which have come down to us is comparatively limited, a further proof that his life was not a long one. Messrs. Crowe and Cavalcaselle enumerate about fifty-three or fifty-four as authentic. I think the following should be omitted from their list :—

1. A Madonna and Child with St. John the Baptist and other Saints, formerly belonging to Signor Andreossi at Milan, and now in the English National Gallery. It is an undoubted work of Bonifazio Veronese (†), though at the Bergamo Exhibition it was catalogued as 'Palma.' This fine work of brilliant colour is regarded by Dr. Bode (Cic. ii. 782) as a copy of what he considers Bonifazio's original in the Venice Academy (Room XVI. No. 28), which there bears the name of Andrea Schiavone or Meldola. Few connoisseurs of the Venetian school will, I think, agree with him.

2. The "Schiava di Tiziano" in the Barberini gallery, a feeble copy by a much later painter.

3. A "Holy Family" in the Stuttgart gallery, by Bonifazio the younger.

4. No. 17, in the same gallery, is not by Palma.

Several works, on the other hand, of which Messrs. Crowe and Cavalcaselle would deprive Palma, are, I consider, genuine, among them the " St. John the Baptist " in the public gallery at Vienna (No. 223), which, though much repainted, shows all the characteristics of the master, and has now been ascribed to him at my suggestion (†). Messrs. Crowe and Cavalcaselle (ii. 488) describe this picture as ' A feeble and injured panel in a style commingling that of Palma with that of Pordenone.'

There are other works, and some of them may be reckoned among Palma's masterpieces, which receive no mention from these writers. Such are: (1) the " Lucretia " of the Borghese gallery (No. 106) ; (2) the " Woman taken in Adultery " in the Capitol (No. 180) ; (3 and 4) the altar-pieces at Peghera and Dossena—two villages in the Brembo Valley ; (5) a " Madonna " in the gallery at Rovigo (No. 39), which, though much injured, is, I think, genuine, whereas the portrait mentioned by Messrs. Crowe and Cavalcaselle (No. 123) appears to me to be merely an old copy after Palma ; and so, too, is the female portrait in the gallery at Modena, which is there ascribed to Giorgione ; (6) " Tobias and the Angel " in the Stuttgart gallery ; (7 and 8) two damaged portraits in the Querini-Stampalia collection at Venice ; (9) " Jacob and Rachel " in the Dresden gallery ; (10) a " Madonna with Saints " in the Brignole-Sale collection at Genoa.

There are, therefore, I think, about sixty-four known works by Palma, of which thirty, including some of his finest and most important, are still in Italy ; the remainder are dispersed abroad. I must, however, observe that those mentioned by Messrs. Crowe and Cavalcaselle in private collections in England I have not been able to examine. Even for a painter who died at forty-eight this number is very limited, consisting as it does mostly of comparatively small cabinet pictures. Even if Palma painted very slowly and with extreme care, he might have produced at least three or four such in the course of the year.

On the other hand, Lotto's works are far more numerous. In the province of Bergamo alone we find more than twenty, exclusive of his frescoes at S. Michele, Trescorre, and other places in the neighbourhood, and among them seven large altar-pieces. At Milan there are seven of his pictures; at Brescia one; in the March of Treviso two; at Venice three altar-pieces and several portraits; at Florence two—one in the Uffizi and one in a private collection; twelve in the March of Ancona; about eight in Rome; one at Naples; and one, a fine portrait, at Modena, in a private collection. Italy alone, therefore, possesses from fifty-nine to sixty of his works, and in other countries he is also well represented.[1] In Messrs. Crowe and Cavalcaselle's list of Lotto's works we find only thirty-two mentioned in Italy, and twenty-six in other countries.

Lotto and Palma Vecchio may have been acquainted in their early youth in the workshop of Giovanni Bellini, but from 1500 to about 1510 they appear to have had little connection with each other. Lotto was then often absent from Venice, and his signed works of that date have not the least affinity with those of Palma. From 1510 to 1515, however, more intimate artistic relations seem to have sprung up between the two. To this period I should ascribe those pictures of Palma's showing a rich Giorgionesque

[1] A work of Lotto's Bergamasque period, of 1523, is in the Museo del Prado at Madrid; in the Louvre we find three pictures by him; three in the English National Gallery; two at Hampton Court; one in the Bridgewater gallery; one in the Holford collection; and one in that of Professor Conway in London. Several are in the Berlin gallery, two at Vienna, one at Munich, one at Dresden (No. 295), and one in the Hermitage at St. Petersburg, of 1522.

colouring together with the sharp strongly-marked lights
which are characteristic of Lotto ; such, for instance, as the
" Adoration of the Shepherds " in the Louvre (No. 1399), a
female portrait in the public gallery at Vienna, and another
beautiful portrait of a young woman in the Berlin gallery
(No. 197ᴬ). It appears to me that at that time Lotto and
Palma must have studied together the works of Giorgione
and sought to imitate them, and that Palma was then in-
fluenced to a certain extent by Lotto, rather than Lotto by
Palma. Palma's finest and most perfect work is, perhaps, the
large altar-piece in the Church of S. Sebastiano at Vicenza,
the figure of St. George in it recalling the glorious figure
of St. Liberale in Giorgione's celebrated altar-piece at
Castelfranco. One of his last works was the large " Ador-
ation of the Magi," now in the Brera (No. 172); it was
begun by the master for the Church of S. Elena in Isola,
near Venice, and finished by one of his pupils, probably
Cariani.[1] It may be compared with a picture by Cariani
hanging near. Messrs. Crowe and Cavalcaselle see in it
the influence of both Cima and Carpaccio (ii. 468). Among
all the painters of the Venetian school after the time of the
Bellini, Palma Vecchio is, I think, the most powerful and
accomplished, as his pupil, Bonifazio Veronese, who is often
confounded with him, is the gayest and most brilliant.

We will now proceed to Lorenzo Lotto, the friend and
colleague of Palma Vecchio. I am inclined to think that
he was born in 1476, and not in 1480, as is usually assumed.

[1] The contract for this picture
has been published in the *Archivio
Veneto* (tom. I. parte 1, p. 167). It was
ordered by Orsa, the wife of Simone
Malipiero. "Jacopo Palma qdm.
Ser Antonij" received 100 ducats
for it in 1525. In the following year
Palma appears to have fallen ill.
The forms of the hand and ear in
the Madonna, the Infant Saviour, St.
Joseph, and St. Helena are charac-
teristic of Palma, while the colouring,
the landscape, the type of the angels,
and the form of the hand and ear
of the kneeling king on the right,
all point, I think, to Palma's pupil
Cariani, who probably completed
the picture.

His picture of " St. Jerome " in the Louvre (No. 1350), dated 1500,[1] already shows considerable skill and experience. In 1555, moreover, Lotto appears to have been a very old man, for, according to a MS. document referring to this painter in the library of the Correr Museum at Venice, he had then 'almost lost his voice.' In that year the Holy House of Loreto paid to ' Messer Lorenzo Lotto, oblato di Santa Casa,' a monthly allowance of one florin or 44 bolognini for food and clothing, because Lotto had dedicated himself and all his possessions to the Madonna of Loreto.[2]

Lotto seems to have died at a great age, between 1555 and 1556; even in the year 1542 he appears to have believed that his end was not far off, for in the archives of S. Giovanni e Paolo at Venice (*Libro Consigli*, 3, *Carta* 96) we find the following entry : ' Item ms. Lorenzo Loto dat scire relinquit conventui de credito suo pro palla Sc̄ti Antonini[3] omne creditum suum ultra ducat : nonaginta, hoc videlicet pacto quod conventus teneatur in morte sua

---

[1] I have examined this date in a good light and in company with several intelligent art-critics — Vicomte de Tauzia, the late director of the Louvre, Count Clément Ris, and Dr. Gustavo Frizzoni of Bergamo — and we all agreed that it was genuine and had not been tampered with, as Messrs. Crowe and Cavalcaselle affirm. As these writers hold that in studying art four eyes are better than two, they will, I doubt not, acknowledge that the testimony of eight eyes must therefore be more worthy of credence than that of four. These two pictures, then, the Palma in the Duc d'Aumale's collection and the Lotto in the Louvre, are the subject of dispute between myself and Messrs.

Crowe and Cavalcaselle; for, while they pronounce the *cartellino* in Palma's picture to be genuine, and the date in Lotto's to have been altered, I feel convinced that the latter, though renovated, is authentic, whereas I can only look upon the *cartellino* in Palma's picture as spurious, and the painting itself as of a much later period of Palma's career than 1500.

[2] This document was kindly brought to my notice by Commendatore Niccolò Barozzi, in a manuscript in the library of the Correr Museum at Venice.

[3] This fine altar-piece has now been temporarily removed from the Church of S. Giovanni e Paolo to the Academy.

gratis sepelire eum in aliquo sepulcro et dare sibi habitum ordinis.'

Lotto was not born at Bergamo but at Venice,[1] where he entered the school of Giovanni Bellini. Here Palma, his junior by a few years, was probably his fellow-pupil. Both painters were by nature simple, unaffected, and religious, and very likely felt mutually attracted.

The following early works by Lotto are very Bellinesque in character :—

(a) A small panel representing "Danae." She is depicted fully draped, reclining in a forest glade, resting her head upon her right hand, and looking upwards, while she receives the golden rain showered upon her by Cupid. A female faun casts glances from behind a tree on the left at a satyr, who is stretched on the ground to the right. Nothing could be more decorous and ingenuous than the manner in which the young painter has here represented the fable of Danae. The drawing is hard and awkward, but the colour already shows much refinement and delicacy. It is now in London, in the possession of Professor Conway, who had the good fortune to acquire it a short time ago at Milan.

(b) The little picture representing "Lot and his Daughters," in the Museo Civico at Milan (No. 106), may

---

[1] See Bampo, *Spigolature dall' archivio notarile di Treviso.* With regard to Lotto, Vasari was better informed than later writers, who, on the very untrustworthy authority of Lomazzo, wished to correct the biographer's statements. Vasari tells us that Lotto was a Venetian and a pupil of Giovanni Bellini, and that later he sought to imitate the manner of Giorgione. In contracts existing at Bergamo, Lotto calls himself 'Lotus Venetus,' and in one he adds : *Nunc habitator Bergomi.* In a document of 1509, now in the Corsini Library at Rome, he, however, signs himself 'Lotus de Trivisio.' The extract is as follows :—
'9 Martii 1509. Magister laurentius Lottus de Trivisio confessus recepisse,' ' for paintings to be executed in rooms in the upper storey of the Vatican, 100 ducats.' At that time Raphael had been more than six months in Rome. Did Lotto ever execute these paintings?

be a few years later in date than the preceding (†) ; it shows a considerable advance in the drawing.

(c) The " St. Jerome " in the Louvre of the year 1500. This is the earliest signed and dated work by Lotto with which I am acquainted.

(d) The allegorical picture of 1505, which is fully described by Federici (*Memorie Trevigiane*, ii. 78). It was until lately in the possession of Signor Gritti, the artist, at Bergamo.[1]

(e) The picture in the Naples Museum.

(f) The altar-piece in S. Cristina, near Treviso (of about 1505 or 1506 ?) ; a spirited work, unfortunately much damaged by restoration.[2]

(g) The " Madonna " in the Bridgewater gallery.

(h) The altar-piece in the parish church at Asolo of 1506.[3]

[1] An inscription on the back of this much damaged little picture runs as follows :—

' Bernardus Rubeus [Rossi] . Berceti . comes, Pont . Tarvis [he was bishop of Treviso], aetat . ann XXXVI . mens . X . D . [dies]. V . Laurentius . Lotus . P . Cal . Jul . M.D.V.'

[2] Like all this master's early works, the altar-piece in S. Cristina is signed in Latin: ' LAVREN . LOTVS . P .' The form of the hands and the folds of the drapery are Bellinesque in character ; the expression of the Madonna is earnest, that of St. Christina pure and devout ; St. Liberale is Giorgionesque in type. Lotto is very restrained in this picture, and we find nothing of that nervous restlessness, often verging on mannerism, which is apparent in his later works, and which at first is apt to prejudice the spectator against him.

[3] This picture, like the one in the Munich gallery, is signed ' LAVREN LOTVS,' with the addition of ' JVNIOR M.D.VI.'—that is, completed in the month of June. Som writers have misunderstood this inscription, and have deduced from it that there were two painters of the name, an elder and a younger. But the picture at Asolo disproves such an assumption. It must have been finished in the beginning of June, for on the 20th of that month we find Lotto at Recanati, where he signed a contract in which he agreed to paint a " Last Supper " for the Dominicans of that town. ' 20 Junii 1506. Laurentius Lotus Pictor Venetus promittit fratri Augustino hispano Priori Sancti Dominici pingere Cœnam, latam novem pedes et dimidium, altitudinis proportionatæ, sumptuosam et splendidam, et deauratum secundum designum, pro florenis 100 et expensis pro se et famulo ' (Archives at Recanati, Protocol of Ser Piergiorgio Antonio). In the summer of 1509 Lotto returned to Recanati from Rome.

(*i*) The picture in the Borghese gallery of 1508.

(*k*) The picture at Recanati of 1509.

In his works at Jesi, however, of only a few years later
—1511 and 1512—the great influence which his fellow-
countryman Giorgione exercised over him is apparent ;
both painters were inhabitants of the March of Treviso.
Messrs. Crowe and Cavalcaselle, I regret to observe, enter-
tain a quite different conception of Lorenzo Lotto from that
which my own studies have led me to form. They regard
him as a native of Bergamo, though Lotto's temperament is
essentially different from that of the Bergamasques ; they
further consider that he was a disciple of the ' Bellin-
.esques ' (?) ; that he passed his youth with Previtali, and
later inclined to the manner of Palma and Giorgione,
though he never succeeded in freeing himself from his
Lombard tendencies (? !). Tassi, in his ' Vite dei Pittori
Bergamaschi ' (i. 115) certainly described him as a pupil
of Previtali. It was Lomazzo who first stated that he
was a scholar, in some degree, of Leonardo da Vinci, solely,
it appears, because Milan and Bergamo are not very far
apart. He was followed by other writers, including Lanzi,
who all looked upon Lotto as a Bergamasque. In his later
period Lotto, according to Messrs. Crowe and Cavalcaselle,
approached Titian, though he continued to be also strongly
influenced by Previtali. To make the measure of analogies
and influences complete, they further conclude that Lotto
—whose brain, in consequence of these many influences,
must, it might be supposed, be in a state of utter confusion
—visited Bologna in the first decade of the sixteenth
century, and there made a diligent study of the frescoes
by Francia, Costa, Tamarozzo, Chiodarolo, and Aspertini,
in the chapel of S. Cecilia,[1] as they ' find a reflex of this

---

[1] These beautiful frescoes were completed in 1506.

visit in one of his pictures.' [1] Finally, they discover in his works a miscellaneous compound of the styles of Cima, Bellini, Carpaccio, Montagna, Previtali,. and Santa Croce, and, as they hold that he visited Palma's workshop, they infer that the latter must have furnished the sketch for Lotto's picture of 1508 in the Borghese gallery. I can but congratulate these writers upon the profound learning which they display in this exhaustive analysis; at the same time I must confess that it does not appear to me to be quite in accordance with facts, at least as I understand them.

Lotto's naïve and charming early work in the Borghese gallery, which must have been painted in Rome or in the March of Ancona for some convent, appears to me a singularly characteristic example of his own individual manner and mode of expression, and bears no trace of the influence of Palma. The drawing of the Madonna's hand, the arrangement of the hair of the Infant Saviour, with the manner in which the lights are treated and the folds of the drapery, all recall the style of Bellini. The S. Onofrio, as the late Professor Thausing justly observed, has some connection with Dürer, and more especially recalls one of the heads in the "Christ among the Doctors" painted by that master at Venice in 1506, and now in the Barberini gallery. This ' coincidence ' is, however, easily explained, as both painters in all probability made use of the same Venetian beggar as a model. Vasari says : ' Fù compagno ed amico del Palma Lorenzo Lotto ; ' that is, Lotto was Palma's friend and fellow-pupil, not his ' journeyman,' as Messrs. Crowe and Cavalcaselle have rendered ' compagno ' in order to support their theory that Lotto was the pupil or imitator of Palma. Some works, however, of Palma's middle period—1512–1520—so vividly recall Lotto, especially in the treatment of the lights, that the late

[1] See *History of Painting in North Italy*, ii. 503.

Mr. Mündler even pronounced Palma's picture in the Louvre,
No. 1399, to be by Lotto.[1] Taking him all in all, Palma
is a more accomplished and pleasing painter than Lotto,
who in his works frequently overleaps himself and loses
balance ; but in power of imagination, artistic conception,
and poetic fire Lotto ranks far higher than Palma.

The portraits of Alessandro Martinengo and his wife
Barbara, in Lotto's altar-piece of 1517 in San Bartolommeo
at Bergamo, are almost unsurpassed in the whole range of
Italian painting for poetic charm of conception and repre-
sentation. Lanzi observes rightly : ' Se Palma è meno
animato del Lotto e meno sublime, è forse più bello, co-
munemente parlando, nelle teste delle donne e dei putti.'
Lotto was certainly never influenced by Previtali, a dry,
uninteresting painter, though excellent as regards his
technic ; but the reverse may very well have been the case,
as we shall see presently. As to the supposed connection
between Lotto and Leonardo da Vinci, it seems to me pure
fiction.[2]

On the other hand, Lotto was Correggiesque some time
before Correggio himself had attained to fame. The two
were kindred spirits who worked at the same period.
Both sought, as Leonardo before them had done, to give
expression to the inward beauty of the soul, a tendency
which marks the final step taken by Art when it has
reached the zenith of its greatness. This strain was evi-
dently due to the natural development of the artistic
faculty itself.[3]

[1] See *Beiträge su Burckhardt's Cicerone*, p. 57.

[2] The 'Lorenzo' who, at the age of seventeen, entered Leonardo's work-shop in Florence in 1505 was probably the sculptor Lorenzetto. Lorenzo Lotto was at that time at Treviso ; and when, in 1515, he settled at Ber- gamo, Leonardo went to France.

[3] How is it that portraits by Lotto are so often ascribed to Correggio ? In a portrait painted from life there can be no question of the painter being swayed by extraneous influ- ences, for the conception can only proceed from himself.

Lotto was working at Bergamo from 1515 to 1524.[1] He was in the March of Ancona and at Rome from 1506 to 1510, and again from 1554 to 1556. In the intervals he appears to have resided in Venice, in the monastery of S. Giovanni e Paolo. Unlike Correggio, Lotto confined himself almost entirely to the representation of religious subjects. I am only acquainted with two mythological pictures by him : the so-called " Triumph of Chastity " in the Rospigliosi gallery at Rome, and the " Danae " belonging to Professor Conway. His portraits are worthy to rank with the finest works of his contemporaries ; the best are in Rome ; in the Brera and the Museo Civico (No. 83) at Milan ; in the English National Gallery ; at Hampton Court ; in the Holford collection ; and in the gallery at Madrid. A very attractive portrait by him is in the public gallery at Vienna (No. 443) (†), where it formerly bore the

---

[1] Lotto first came to Bergamo in 1513, and here he signed the contract to paint a large picture for the Church of the Dominicans with the portraits of the donors, Alessandro and Barbara Martinengo. He then returned to Venice to the monastery of S. Giovanni e Paolo, where he commenced the preparation of his design for this picture. It was painted on panel—four feet high by two wide—and signed : 'Lav. Lot. in Io. Pav. Pinxit' (that is, in the monastery of S. Giovanni e Paolo. Some years ago I saw this sketch at Bergamo ; later it was sold, and is now in France. The altar-piece is the largest which Lotto ever painted. He began it in 1515, and it was completed in the following year. In it Lotto shows himself more Correggiesque than even Correggio himself in his Madonna of St. Francis in the Dresden gallery (No. 150), which was painted in 1514. This Correggi-esque feeling is particularly noticeable in the action of St. Alexander, of St. John the Baptist, and of the angels playing at the foot of the throne. The three beautiful panels, forming the predella to this picture, are in the sacristy of the Church of San Bartolommeo ; the picture itself hangs behind the high altar. In the early part of 1515, before Lotto went to Bergamo, he was probably at Padua, and here must have painted the fine portrait of Agostino della Turre, a professor in that university. It is now in the English National Gallery, and bears the following inscription : ' Dño Nicolao de la Turre nobili Bergomensi amico Sing°, 1515, Bgmi.' Lotto probably took the picture with him to Bergamo, and delivered it to Niccolò della Turre. He must then have added the other portrait—probably that of Niccolò himself—for this second figure is very awkwardly placed in the picture.

name of Titian, to whom the late Dr. Waagen also attributed it; recently it has been ascribed to Correggio.[1] It represents a young Venetian noble of a refined type, with a pale complexion, light brown hair and beard, and blue eyes. The hands are white and delicate, with greenish shadows— a characteristic of this master.   In his left hand is a bird's claw in gold.   The head, as in all Lotto's portraits, is full of subtlety, intellect and distinction.   According to Herr von Engerth's catalogue, it represents the naturalist Ulysses Aldrovandi.   This is impossible, however, as Aldrovandi, who was born in 1522, was scarcely twelve years old when Correggio died.   A good portrait of him by one of the Caracci is in the gallery at Bergamo, but it bears not the slightest resemblance to the supposed likeness at Vienna. This is not the only portrait by Lotto ascribed to Correggio, and the same confusion occurs at Hampton Court.   Lotto's best portraits, like those of Leonardo, Andrea del Sarto, and Correggio, are signalised by that instinctive refinement, the natural expression of inward sensibility, which characterises the best period of Italian art in the last stage of its development; whereas the elegance displayed in the portraits of the Tuscan Bronzino and of the North Italian Parmegianino is not spontaneous, but artificial and external, standing in no relation to the inward personality of the subject represented.   This new tendency marks the first period of decline in art.   With Lotto and Correggio this elegance of sentiment, as already observed, occasionally degenerates into restlessness and affectation.   The temperament of the two artists had much in common; both were by nature reserved and given to solitude and retirement, Lotto's life being principally passed in the seclusion of a monastery in the society of Dominican monks.   Neither he nor Correggio ever courted the favour of the great and

---

[1] This portrait is now rightly attributed to Lotto.

prosperous of this world, and their works show less realism than any others of the time in which they lived and of the schools to which they belonged.

Titian, who may have been Lotto's contemporary in age, appears to have thought very highly of him, as is proved by the following passage from a letter of Pietro Aretino to Lotto bearing date April 1548 : ‘ Titian, who writes to me from Augsburg, sends you his affectionate greetings, and adds that his pleasure in hearing his own works praised by the Emperor would be doubled if he could show them to you and discuss them with you.’ Lotto's charming early work in the Munich gallery (Room VIII., No. 1083) represents the “ Marriage of St. Catherine,” and is signed ‘ LAVREN . LOTVS F.’ The form of hand recalls Bellini, and the movement of the Child and of St. Joseph is very characteristic of the master. It is probably of the same period as the pictures at Treviso and Asolo (1505–1507). In his later period, from 1520 to 1530, he usually signs himself in Italian : ‘Lorenzo’ or ‘Laurentio,’ ‘Loto’ or ‘Lotto.’ This picture is painted after the method of Dürer, Van der Goes, Bellini, and of other painters north and south of the Alps —that is to say, after the method of the Van Eycks.[1] The sky has been almost entirely repainted.

There is, I think, a second work by Lotto in this gallery —the very attractive and interesting little picture of a faun in Cabinet XIX. (No. 1094). It probably represents Pan ; he is seated upon a stone playing on his pipes ; beside him lies a cithara ; in the background a roe-deer is grazing in a meadow. It is strange that it should have come to Munich under the name of Correggio ; critics, however, paid small

[1] This method consisted in laying in the picture in *grisaille* with tempera, and finishing with thin glazes of oil colours. The linseed or walnut oil, having been purified by repeated filterings, was mixed with varnishes. Pictures painted in this method never darken, but preserve their transparency of colour, as this little work of Lotto's proves.

attention to it, and evidently considered it unworthy of study, as it showed little affinity with Correggio's style—that is, with his more popular and better known manner. The importance of this picture did not, however, escape Mr. Mündler's critical eye. He ascribed it, I believe, to Palma Vecchio, and it certainly strikes us at once as a Venetian work. The method of the painting is that of Bellini, Lotto, and other Bellinesque painters, as is plainly visible in those parts from which the glazes have disappeared. The fiery redness of the horizon and the emerald green of the meadow recall both Palma and Lotto. But the form of the hands, the light blue drapery about the shoulders of the god, the knot of ribbon confining this drapery in front, the treatment of the subject, and the fresh and spirited conception point, I think, to Lotto rather than to Palma. This precious little picture has unfortunately suffered severely from repainting and over-cleaning.

Thus I thought and wrote about this picture some ten years ago, for, instead of studying the forms, I allowed myself here, as in a few other instances, to be led astray by the colouring. This appeared to me so thoroughly Venetian, that, like Mr. Mündler, I mistook this early work of Correggio for the work of a Venetian master, and ascribed it to Lotto, while he considered it to be by Palma. A few years later, however, I found out my mistake, for, on obtaining a photograph of it, I was able to study the forms without being misled by the deceptive colouring. The long folds of the blue drapery, the strongly developed shinbone, the arch expression of the god, wholly unlike Lotto's manner of treatment, all convinced me that this was an early work by Correggio of the period when he studied Giorgione, and more especially Lorenzo Lotto. The name of Correggio, moreover, would scarcely have been bestowed upon it had it not always borne this attribution. We may look upon this instance as one of the few in which tradition may be relied upon, for, considering the opinions entertained about Correggio as far back as the middle of the sixteenth century, it is not likely that a picture of so distinctly Venetian a character would have then been attributed to the painter of the "Notte." For the history of Correggio's early training it is of the highest importance. The directors of this gallery showed great discretion in adhering to the traditional name in spite of the opinions expressed by Mr. Mündler and myself. This little picture affords another proof that the painters of the best period were accustomed to try their hands on works of small dimensions.[1] It must have been painted about 1511–1512, the same time as the picture in the Uffizi (No. 1002).

We will now proceed to Lotto's fellow-countryman, Giorgio Barbarelli, called Giorgione. The portrait ascribed to this master by Dr. Marggraff (Room IX.) is not, as we have seen, by him, but probably by Cariani or, as some would have it, by Palma Vecchio. We will, therefore, examine the second picture attributed to him in the old catalogue. It hangs in Room IX. (No. 1110), and, as

---

[1] The following are all of small dimensions :—Correggio : the "Marriage of St. Catherine," in the Frizzoni collection at Milan ; the "Madonna," in the Malaspina collection at Pavia, there ascribed to Francia ; the "Madonna," under the name of Titian, in the Uffizi ; the "Faun," in the Munich gallery.

Raphael : The "Dream of a Knight," in the English National Gallery ; the "St. Michael" and the "St. George," both in the Louvre ; the "Three Graces," in the Duc d'Aumale's collection ; the "Madonna and Child with SS. Francis and Jerome," in the Berlin gallery.

Lotto : the "Danae," belonging to Professor Conway ; "Lot and his Daughters," in the Museo Civico at Milan ; the "St. Jerome," in the Louvre ; the "Allegory," lately in the collection of Signor Gritti at Bergamo.

Giovanni Bellini : The "Crucifixion," in the Correr Museum ; the "Ecce Homo," in the English National Gallery ; the "Madonna and Child," belonging to Dr. Frizzoni, at Milan.

Giorgione : The "Judgment of Solomon" and the "Ordeal by Fire," both in the Uffizi.

already mentioned, was once ascribed to Titian. Later, the
name of Giorgione was substituted, while Messrs. Crowe
and Cavalcaselle are of opinion that it is by Giovan Antonio
da Pordenone. The present authorities of the gallery
agree with me in restoring it to Titian. The type of this
beautiful woman is very similar to that in other pictures of
this master's Giorgionesque period—for instance, in No.
1590 in the Louvre, which is known as "Alfonso d'Este
and Laura dei Dianti." The violet tone of the flesh-tints,
which is still discernible in the Munich picture, is charac-
teristic of Titian (as, for instance, in the "Flora" of the
Uffizi), so, too, are the brownish-yellow headdress worn by
this figure and the form of her hand. The fold in the drapery,
forming an acute angle $\wedge$, is also a distinguishing mark
which recurs in many of Titian's pictures; for example, in
the "Daughter of Herodias," the "Amor Sacro e Amor Pro-
fano," the "Flora," and the picture in the Louvre, No. 1590.
All these positive proofs, leaving the negative ones alto-
gether out of the question, have convinced me that this
Sibyl cannot be either by Giorgione or Pordenone, but is
an undoubted early work of Titian, whose lofty spirit still
breathes freshly from the painting, wreck of its former self
though it be.

We will now examine Titian's other works in this gallery.
Some of them are of great value. According to the old
catalogue this master was born about 1477, and was first
a pupil of Gentile and then of Giovanni Bellini, and later
was influenced by the precocious genius of his friend and
contemporary Giorgione. These notices appear to me
correct, except that I should be inclined to agree with Dolce
and to omit Giovanni Bellini. I have no admiration for
Titian's personal character, yet it is hard to believe that he
could have intrigued, as he did in 1513, in order to supersede
Bellini and obtain his stipend in the 'Senseria' of the

Fondaco de' Tedeschi, had he ever been that master's pupil.

Whether Titian learnt the rudiments of his art from Antonio Rosso, Sebastiano Zuccato, Gentile or Giovanni Bellini, is not a question of great historical moment. But one point is indisputable, that in Titian's early period (from 1504–1512) the influence of Giorgione is so striking, that the works of these two masters have not unfrequently been confounded.[1] In 1505 Titian was still Giorgione's assistant, and, according to the 'Anonimo,' on the death of his friend and master in 1511 he finished several of his pictures. Giorgione's influence is felt not only in the early works of Titian, but in the paintings of nearly all his Venetian contemporaries—in those of Lotto, Boccaccino, Palma Vecchio, Giovan Antonio da Pordenone, Bonifazio Veronese, Cariani, Dosso, Romanino, and of many others, not to mention his pupil Sebastiano del Piombo.

Messrs. Crowe and Cavalcaselle acknowledge the influence of Giorgione over Titian, and even draw special attention to it in the early work by the latter in the sacristy of S. Maria della Salute at Venice [2]—St. Mark between four

[1] This occurs, for example, in the following pictures: "Christ bearing the Cross," in S. Rocco at Venice; the "Concert," in the Pitti (No. 185); the "Daughter of Herodias," in the Doria gallery; the "Madonna between SS. Ulfus and Bridget," in the Madrid gallery (No. 236). Messrs. Crowe and Cavalcaselle (Life of Titian, i. 54, 55) contend that Titian's charming "Madonna" (No. 276) in the public gallery at Vienna was painted in the fifteenth century, and they are reminded in it of the Bellini, Carpaccio, and even of Palma Vecchio (!); the landscape background they mention as particularly fine. This landscape, however, should have proved to them, I think, that the picture was at least six or eight years later in date. This broadly-treated landscape is in striking contrast to the backgrounds of Giovanni Bellini, Cima, Basaiti, and even of Previtali.

[2] The following pictures appear to me to be earlier than that in the sacristy of the 'Salute': "Christ bearing the Cross," in S. Rocco the "Infant Saviour between SS. Andrew and Catherine," in S. Marcuola; "Tobias and the Angel," in S. Marziale; the "Baptism of Christ," in the gallery of the Capitol; and

saints. But, in addition to the influence of Giorgione, they also see in this picture that of Fra Bartolommeo della Porta, especially in the drapery and in the attitudes of St. Sebastian and St. Roch. Such astute criticism can only be adequately appreciated and understood when we recollect that in 1508 Fra Bartolommeo spent some weeks with the Dominicans of S. Pietro Martire at Murano, and even began to paint an altar-piece for them.[1]

According to the catalogue of the Munich gallery, there are about a dozen pictures by Titian in the collection, and we will now proceed to examine them. In Room IX. there is a fine and genuine work by the master, representing "Christ crowned with thorns" (No. 1114). Though painted by Titian when he was ninety, it shows a firmness of touch and a power of which few painters would have been capable at so advanced an age. The master has confined himself in this picture to four colours—black, white, red, and orange—the only ones, it is said, employed by the earliest Greek painters. This system of colouring adopted by Titian was sometimes followed by Rubens, Van Dyck, and the elder Franz Hals, the most brilliant examples being two celebrated portraits by the latter painter in the Haarlem gallery.[2] The "Christ crowned with thorns" is said to have come to Germany from the Netherlands, and in the retouches to which it has been subjected Messrs. Crowe and Cavalcaselle[3] affirm that they can detect the hand of Rubens, or perhaps Van Dyck, as in the man in profile on the right who menaces the Saviour. The hand, with its long tapering fingers and academic character, was certainly not the work of Titian, and was

the "Bishop of Pesaro," in the Antwerp Museum. I consider them to be earlier than the "Amor Sacro e Amor Profano," in the Borghese gallery.

[1] See Padre Marchese, *Memorie dei più insigni Pittori, Scultori e Architetti Domenicani*, ii. 59-64.

[2] Nos. 60 and 61.

[3] ii. 401, note.

probably painted by a Fleming, but whether by Van Dyck or some other artist of the Netherlands it is impossible to say.

Another excellent work is the portrait of a man in black, erroneously called that of Pietro Aretino (No. 1111). In the new catalogue the personage represented is said to be identical with the "Knight of Malta," whose portrait by Giorgione is in the Uffizi; but this appears to me very doubtful. In Giorgione's portrait the nose is sharp and aquiline, the eyes are smaller and their glance keener than in that by Titian, the beard is thicker, and the expression far more resolute.

In the same room we find a "Madonna adoring the Infant Saviour," who lies on her knee (No. 1117). She is seated in a landscape between SS. Francis, Jerome, and Anthony; the latter touches the foot of the Child. The picture has suffered severely from restoration; if I am not mistaken, it was originally a good work of the school, and Titian himself may even have executed some portion of it. His imitators frequently reproduced this composition with modifications.[1]

In the same room we find the full-length portrait of the Admiral Luigi Grimani, which is certainly neither by Titian nor by Tiberio Tinelli, nor is it in the manner of Pietro Vecchia, as Messrs. Crowe and Cavalcaselle pronounce. As this kind of groping is distasteful to me, I prefer to say at

[1] Messrs. Crowe and Cavalcaselle (*Life of Titian*, ii. 452) ascribe this picture to Francesco Vecellio, and the director of the gallery has adopted their view. My knowledge of that painter is too limited for me to venture on an opinion; but if the picture ascribed to him in the Venice Academy (Room VII., No. 58) be really his work, he cannot, I think, be the author of the example in Munich. My impression, as I said before, is that we have in it a good work of the school, the drawing having perhaps been by the master himself. The 'Anonimo' mentions that many pictures in Titian's workshop were executed by a 'Stefano del Tiziano' and by a certain 'Girolamo.' The picture may have been painted by one of these artists.

once that I do not know the painter. In the new catalogue it is assigned to the school of Tintoretto, which may very likely be right, as that school comprised a large number of painters.

No. 1115 is a finely conceived portrait, but neither the drawing nor the technic of the painting show the hand of Titian, and I must confess that they afford me no clue as to its authorship. The picture has suffered severely and the glazes have almost disappeared, but it is still a striking and impressive work.[1]

No. 1121 represents a man in black. In front of him, on a table, are some pearls and other trinkets; behind him stands a woman. It is an interesting though damaged work, which Messrs. Crowe and Cavalcaselle have rightly assigned to Paris Bordone.

No. 1112 is a fine and genuine portrait of Charles V. The landscape in the background is painted with marvellous lightness of touch. In tone, it vividly reminds us of several landscapes by Rubens, as, for example, those numbered 794 and 797 in this gallery. Rubens appears to have taken Titian for his model in landscape-painting on his return from Madrid, where he had been sent on a diplomatic mission. He must there have had ample opportunity for studying the numerous pictures painted by Titian for Charles V. and Philip II. In the portrait at Munich the Emperor looks ill and depressed. It must, I think, have been painted a few months earlier than the wonderful equestrian portrait of Charles V. at Madrid, which, in my estimation, is in every respect one of the finest portraits in the world. The inscription on the Munich portrait—

[1] Messrs. Crowe and Cavalcaselle (ii. 453) think it may be by Tintoretto, but both the conception and representation appear to me to be far too simple for this master, and the handling of the brush differs from that of Tintoretto; but, as already observed, I can venture upon no opinion as to its author.

'Titianvs F., 1548'—is genuine, though it has been re-touched.

No. 1116, Venus with a Bacchante, a Satyr, Cupid, and other figures. This picture is hard in the outlines, and the treatment of the hair lacks freedom. The catalogue ascribes it to Titian, in which I cannot concur; it appears to me to be not even a school picture, but merely a copy.

The "Madonna and Child" in a landscape, with the little St. John and the donor (No. 1109), is described by Messrs. Crowe and Cavalcaselle [1] as a 'masterpiece,' dating from between 1520 and 1525. 'The treatment,' they observe, 'in the style of that period being perfect, and the profile of the donor very fine.' The liquid Titianesque colouring is certainly splendid, and the portrait of the donor excellent, but the modelling is far too weak for the master, the body of the Child is defective in drawing, the ear is not of that rounded form so characteristic in Titian's works of this period; the forms of the trees are too petty, the painting of the lamb too spiritless, while the Madonna appears to have but one arm. If the director of the gallery would compare this feeble picture with the "Vierge au lapin" in the Louvre (No. 1578)—a beautiful signed work by Titian—he would, I feel sure, agree with me that the picture in Munich, notwithstanding its fine colour, is only a copy by some painter of the school (†).

No. 1113 represents the Madonna in a landscape with a sunset sky. The signature, 'Titianus Fecit,' is spurious. It appears to me to be a work of the school, finished by the master himself, the landscape being, I think, entirely by his own hand. It is of his later period, and has been much injured by restoration.

No. 1120, the portrait of a man in black, dated 1523.

[1] ii. 424.

Messrs. Crowe and Cavalcaselle [1] suggest that Paris Bordone may be the author of this much injured work, and the attribution is plausible, though I am unable to accept it, as I can see no trace of Paris Bordone's manner, either in the technic or in the form of the hand. The drawing is extremely hard. It might possibly be an old copy of an original by Titian, but I must refrain from assigning to it the name of any particular painter. On the other hand, I have no hesitation in ascribing the small picture of "Apollo and the Muses," [2] 'with its succulent richness of colouring,' to Andrea Schiavone. It is a charming little work, probably intended for the decoration of a spinet; the influence of Parmegianino, as well as that of Titian, is apparent in it.

No. 1133—"Jupiter and Antiope," a fragment—is certainly neither by Titian nor by Giovanni Contarini, as Messrs. Crowe and Cavalcaselle conjecture, and still less by Paul Veronese, as the new catalogue suggests. Such pictures are as nameless waifs in the history of art.

After passing in review all these pseudo-Titians, it is satisfactory to find two undoubtedly genuine works by Moroni, the eminent Bergamasque portrait-painter. Both are in Room IX. ; one, No. 1124, is a good though somewhat over-cleaned work, painted between 1560 and 1570. It represents a woman in a fur-trimmed dress, and has all Moroni's characteristics. The new catalogue concurs with me in ascribing it to this master (†). The other—the portrait of an ecclesiastic, No. 1123—was once rightly attributed to Moroni, but Dr. Marggraff, at the suggestion of Mr. Mündler, gave it to Moretto. The present director, to my surprise, accepted this attribution, and other modern critics also concur in this very erroneous view. It is, however, one of the finest and most characteristic of Moroni's

---

[1] ii. 453.　　　　[2] Cabinet XVIII., No. 1089.

portraits. Those who are not very intimately acquainted with the manner of this painter might perhaps confound him with Moretto—whose pupil he was—especially when he copies that master's pictures, as, for instance, in the reading St. Jerome in the gallery at Bergamo, and an early picture in the Brera, No. 256. But in portraits painted from life Moroni differs materially from Moretto in the form and feeling of the hands. With the latter the fingers are tapering and somewhat academic, lacking the truth to individual nature which Moroni knew well how to give when he chose. Moretto's flesh-tints are for the most part light and silvery in tone, while Moroni's incline to earthiness and more nearly approach to reality. In the Munich portrait, the form and colouring of the hands are so characteristic of Moroni, that they ought to leave no connoisseur in doubt as to its authorship. I may add that, when Moroni painted portraits from life, he always drew the ear in proper proportion, whereas in his figures not taken from living models it is almost invariably too small.

Giovanni Battista Moroni was born at Bondo, near Albino, in the province of Bergamo, most likely about 1525. In his earliest works the flesh-tints are of a brick-red tone, and as this is a characteristic which occurs in some of Moretto's works after 1540, it is probable that Moroni became his pupil about that date.

Moretto was a Brescian by birth, but his ancestors—the Bonvicini [1]—only settled there in 1438, and the family came originally from Ardesio, which, like Albino, is a village in the Serio Valley. The earliest dated work by Moroni that I know of is of 1553, though he may, of course, have painted others before this time. It is in the Berlin

[1] 'Ambrogio and Moretto quondam Guglielmino of Ardesio, called Bonvicini.' (See *Disionario degli* *Artisti Bresciani di Stefano Fenaroli.*)

gallery. Another of his early period, in which he ap-
proaches Moretto more nearly than in any other, is in the
parish church of Gorlago [1] (†). Several others of this date
are in the city of Bergamo and its vicinity; for example, a
head of Christ in profile in the public gallery. In the
Poldi-Pezzoli Museum at Milan there is an angel by him
belonging to the same period.

Moroni succeeded in representing the surface and out-
ward aspect of the human countenance on canvas with
extraordinary truth and fidelity, and in this respect is
unsurpassed. His portraits must have been speaking
likenesses, reproducing his sitters to the life, and to the
general public this is always the principal attraction.
Though an excellent painter, he was not a poet in the true
sense of the word. He saw his subject from the point of
view of the average man, and his portraits are all more or
less prosaic. Occasionally, however, he attains to a remark-
able degree of excellence, and succeeds in penetrating
through the outward envelope to the soul of his sitter.
Such portraits are almost worthy to rank with those of
Titian.

Moretto consistently shows himself an artist of a
higher type than Moroni. In conception and drawing he
is more noble and refined than his homely pupil, but those
subtle differences which distinguish the two artists are
not visible to every eye, nor are they always sufficient to
enable students to tell a good work by Moroni from a feebler
one by Moretto. In such cases certainty of judgment can

---

[1] This picture is ascribed to
Ceresa. It hangs on the wall to the
left of the door, and represents
Christ in a glory of angels holding
the cross; below kneel St. John the
Baptist and a warrior saint. The
angels and the warrior are taken
from Moretto; the head of Christ
recalls Romanino even more than
Moretto; the drawing is very care-
ful, though somewhat timid. It
was probably painted at Brescia
in the workshop of his master
Moretto.

only be attained by a thorough and intimate knowledge of the form of hand and ear peculiar to each master.

It is only in this century that Moroni has attained the European reputation as a portrait-painter which he deserves. During his lifetime he was doubtless highly thought of in the province of Bergamo, but beyond the limits of the Venetian Republic he was scarcely known. Up to the beginning of this century his works were nearly all in that province, and the few which had passed out of Italy at an earlier period were assigned to other masters. Thus two male portraits in the public gallery at Vienna, formerly in the collection of Archduke Leopold William at Brussels, are still ascribed respectively to Titian and Johannes von Calcar, that attributed to Titian being said to represent the anatomist Vesalius.[1] The life-sized portrait of Cardinal Cristoforo Madruzzi in the Casa Salvadori at Trent [2] also appears to me to be by Moroni (†), and not by Titian, as Messrs. Crowe and Cavalcaselle and Dr. Bode [3] consider.

Among Moroni's finest pictures are three in the English National Gallery; [4] the " Scholar " in the Uffizi; and several

[1] In the catalogue of 1892 both are for the first time attributed to Moroni.

[2] Two other full-length male portraits in this collection are ascribed respectively to Titian and Moroni. I consider both to be by the latter. One represents a man in black, with a pair of gloves in his right hand and a dog beside him; the other is the portrait of a man in brown with a fur-trimmed tunic.

[3] Cicerone, ii. 768.

[4] Even a practised eye will occasionally confound portraits by Moroni and Moretto. Thus Mr. Mündler, in his Beiträge zu Jacob Burckhardt's Cicerone, p. 67, ascribed the three life-sized portraits in the Casa Fenaroli at Brescia to Moretto, to whom they were attributed in that collection. The author had the good fortune to recognise in two of them the spirit and the hand of Moroni, and to restore them to that painter (†), under whose name they were subsequently sold to the English National Gallery, through Signor Baslini, a picture-dealer of Milan. One represents an Italian nobleman with a wounded foot, wearing a black cap; the other a lady in a brocaded dress, seated in a chair. The third, a splendid portrait, now also in the National Gallery, represents a young nobleman in a red cap; it is dated 1526, and is one of Moretto's most elegant and refined works of this class. A

at Bergamo—in private collections and in the public gallery. The portrait in the Louvre, of an ecclesiastic seated in an easy chair, belongs to his last period, and is not a good example of the great portrait-painter. Many altar-pieces by him are preserved in the province of Bergamo,[1] which, though possessing much technical merit, are for the most part dull and dry in conception.

Moroni died in 1578, while engaged upon a picture of the "Last Judgment" for the parish church of Gorlago, two hours from Bergamo. Among his imitators the following may be mentioned: Giampaolo Lolmo, who died in 1595; Francesco Zucco; Carlo Ceresa and Giovan Battista Moneta—all natives of Bergamo. Portraits by the last-named painter are extremely rare.

We find portraits by Moroni in nearly every important gallery in Germany; the one at Munich (No. 1123), and that of a Dominican lay-brother, in the Staedel Institute at Frankfort, being, I think, the finest among them. His drawings are very rare, and I have never seen but one. It represented St. Roch kneeling, and was washed with water-colour. Many years ago it was in the collection of Signor Carlo Prayer at Milan, and it is said to be now at Berlin.

In Room IX. hangs a curious portrait (No. 1125), representing a young man holding a rose. It is signed 'Franciscus Turbidus,' and dated 1516. Francesco Torbido, called 'il Moro,'[2] was certainly not born so late as 1500, as

few years later he may have painted the other portrait in the same collection, No. 299, representing Count Sciarra Martinengo. I know few other portraits which appeal to us os powerfully as this admirable work.

[1] Moroni's works may be found in the churches at Bergamo, and in the villages of la Ranica, Fiorano and Desenzano Madonna della Ripa) in the Serio Valley; and in the parish churches of Cenate, Fino, Almenno, Roncola, Romano, and others.

[2] The profile portrait of Torbido in red chalk is in the Christ Church collection at Oxford (Grosvenor Gallery Publication, No. 37). Torbido in this portrait has the features of a Moor, hence probably his nickname of 'il Moro.'

the new catalogue informs us, nor yet so early perhaps as 1486, as Dr. Cesare Bernasconi, in his ' Studij della Scuola pittorica Veronese,' conjectures, but more probably in the last decade of the fifteenth century. The catalogue further informs us that Torbido was still living in 1581, though where it derived this information it is impossible to say. He was alive in 1545, but the year of his death is not known. Vasari records that he worked under Giorgione, which is both possible and probable, but his real master was his fellow-countryman Liberale, as the biographer also tells us. Vasari's informant as to Veronese painters was Padre Marco Medici, whose views as to the importance of this school require a critical revision. Vasari has, I think, done crying injustice to Torbido, and most writers, *more solito*, have followed him blindly, ranking this painter with that superficial artist Pompeo Amalteo.

Torbido, in his early works, such as this portrait at Munich, shows himself to have been a pupil of Liberale as much as an imitator of Giorgione. It is probable, therefore, that, after a short time spent in the workshop of Giorgione, he entered that of Liberale, where he was the fellow-student of Giolfino and the two Carottos. His later works recall Bonifazio the elder—his fellow-countryman—for instance, the altar-piece in the Church of S. Fermo at Verona, the Madonna and Child enthroned on clouds and surrounded by angels. The lower part of this picture, with Raphael and Tobias in a beautiful and poetic landscape, more especially reminds us of that master. His latest works—the frescoes in the cathedral at Verona—show how the pernicious influence of Giulio Romano affected this otherwise independent Veronese painter. We find other works by him at Verona. In the gallery—a "Madonna and Child" (No. 49), the "Angel and Tobias" (†), there ascribed to Moretto—a confusion which we may suppose to have

originated in the similarity of the names Moretto and
' il Moro '—and a " Madonna with Saints and the donor "
(No. 210), finely conceived but in a very bad condition.
In the Church of S. Maria in Organo the fresco of the
" Annunciation," and in S. Zeno an altar-piece in the first
chapel on the right. A much-damaged work under the
name of Moretto is in the Church of Limone, on the
Lago di Garda (†), and a " Transfiguration," mentioned by
Vasari,[1] is now in the gallery at Augsburg.

It would, I think, be an interesting task for a young
student of art desirous of winning his spurs, to make
Torbido, who has hitherto been much underrated, the
object of his researches, and to bring his artistic character
more clearly into the light. He should be compared with
the elder Bonifazio. Both were natives of Verona, in-
fluenced by the school of Giorgione—Bonifazio by Palma
Vecchio, Torbido probably by Giorgione himself. Not-
withstanding this, however, Torbido always remained true
to Liberale—his real master—until the death of that
painter in 1536.

I only know of two or three other portraits by Torbido ;
one, much damaged but nobly conceived, is in the gallery
at Padua (No. 659) ; and an excellent likeness of a man,
with the signature of the artist, is in the Brera ; the Naples
Museum contains a signed portrait by him, which is, how-
ever, heavy and unattractive. The portrait in the Uffizi
(No. 571), which passes for that of Gattamelata by
Giorgione, is decidedly not, as Messrs. Crowe and Caval-
caselle affirm, ' an unmistakable work of Torbido.'[2] In
another place[3] they observe : ' There is some excuse for
substituting Giorgione for Torbido, as is done here ' (in the
Uffizi),' that is, for substituting the master for the pupil.'

Mr. Mündler ascribed the picture to Carotto, and

[1] ix. 182 (ed. Milanesi, v. 293).   [2] i. 511.   [3] ii. 168.

in attributing it to a Veronese painter who had no connection with Giorgione he certainly approached nearer to the truth than Messrs. Crowe and Cavalcaselle. If I am not greatly mistaken, it is by Michele da Verona, a painter who was closely connected with Cavazzola at one period of his career, and who must even have worked with him, of which we have proof in two pictures in the gallery at Verona: No. 298, SS. Michael and Paul—there ascribed to Cavazzola —and No. 301, SS. John the Baptist and Peter (†). Signed frescoes by this little known painter are in the Church of Santa Chiara at Verona. Like Cavazzola and Francesco Morone, Michele proceeded from the school of Domenico Morone, and it is difficult to distinguish his works executed between 1509 and 1514 from those of Cavazzola. In the sacristy of the Church of St. Anastasia at Verona he is confounded with that master in a picture representing St. Paul and other saints; in the lunette fresco above Giolfino's altar-piece in the same church, with Francesco Morone; while in the frescoes of the celebrated side-chapel of SS. Nazzaro e Celso, he is confused with both these painters (†). In the public gallery in the same city works by him are attributed either to Bartolommeo Montagna (†) (a "Pietà," No. 117, Bernasconi collection) or to Falconetto (†) (Nos. 107, 188, 190, 191). Michele's forms—the hands, the folds of the drapery, &c.—are more pointed than those of Cavazzola, his younger contemporary and fellow-pupil, who was far superior to him in composition and in refined and noble drawing. A large and much damaged picture by Michele is in the Brera, signed and dated as follows: 'Mccccci Die II Ivnii Per me Michaelem Veronensem.'[1] A much repainted picture of Samson and

---

[1] A modified replica of this picture is in the church belonging to the Episcopal Seminary at Padua. It is inscribed: 'Die XXVIII. Martii MCCCCCV opus MICHAELIS VER.'

Delilah by him (†), bearing the forged signature, 'Victor Carpatius,' is in the Poldi-Pezzoli collection at Milan. This palpable forgery deceived even the practised eye of Dr. Bode. The picture in the English National Gallery — the "Meeting of Coriolanus with Volumnia and Veturia" (No. 1214)—is the only work I know of by Michele out of Italy.

In Room VIII. we find a picture (No. 1085) representing St. Nicholas in episcopal garb between SS. John the Baptist and Philip. It is dated 1530, and inscribed 'F. SEBASTIAN F. per AGOSTINO CHIGI.' The whole inscription is evidently spurious, for Agostino Chigi died in 1520, and the painting points to Rocco Marconi, a pupil of Paris Bordone. Messrs. Crowe and Cavalcaselle are also of this opinion, which will doubtless be shared even by those who are but superficially acquainted with the Venetian school. The authorities of the gallery have now accepted it as a work by Rocco Marconi : I cannot, however, agree with the catalogue, that it shows as many traits of Ferrarese as of Venetian style.

A portrait of the Emperor Maximilian was once doubtfully ascribed to another and earlier Venetian master ; it has now, however, been recognised as the work of Bernhard Strigel, a painter of Memmingen, and has been removed to Cabinet V. and numbered 191.

There is another Venetian portrait in Room IX. (No. 1119), about which I should like to express an opinion. Dr. Marggraff, in the preface to his catalogue, drew attention to the painter Domenico Caprioli of Treviso, who is little known in Germany. To judge by his pictures, he must have formed his style on the works of Lotto and Giorgione, and, according to documents recently published by Signor Bampo,[1] Caprioli is even to be regarded as the

---

[1] *Spigolature dall' Archivio di Treviso.*

pupil of Lotto. In the new catalogue of the Munich gallery he is called an imitator of Giovanni Bellini, and is still more erroneously held to be identical with Francesco Mancini. A comparison between Mancini's signed altarpiece in the church at Lendinara,[1] and Caprioli's pictures in the gallery at Treviso, and in the Giovanelli collection at Venice—the latter signed with his monogram—seems to prove that this portrait at Munich is merely an old copy. The original I saw some years ago in the collection of the late Mr. Edward Cheney, in London. The Munich copy is a kind of caricature of Giorgione. It is much disfigured by repainting, and would be improved by cleaning.

According to the catalogue, the gallery contains a number of pictures by Paul Veronese. They, however, appear to me for the most part works of his school. I can only accept as possibly genuine the female portrait, No. 1135, and the "Holy Family," No. 1137, and even of these I cannot but entertain great doubts, for on examining the pictures a second time it struck me that the colouring of the portrait was not sufficiently transparent for Paolo, and that it was more probably by Battista Zelotti,[2] while the "Holy Family" looks more like a copy than an original. The director would, I think, have done better had he ascribed the "Jupiter and Antiope" (No. 1133) and the "Cupid" (No. 1134) respectively to

[1] It represents the Madonna enthroned, with the Infant Saviour standing on her knee; at the foot of the throne is an angel playing a musical instrument. Signed: 'OPUS DOMINICI MANCINI VENETI,' p. 1511.

[2] Battista Zelotti was the contemporary and fellow-pupil of Paul Veronese in the school of Giovanni Carotto. According to Vasari (xi. 134; ed. Milanesi, vi. 369), he also studied for some time in Venice under Titian. Later he worked with Paul Veronese, who was his intimate friend, in the service of Conte Tiene, of Vicenza, and in that of the Soranzo family at Castelfranco. Zelotti's pictures are often ascribed to Paul Veronese, though his colouring is never so brilliant and transparent, nor has it that silvery tone so characteristic of the works of that master. (See vol. i. of these 'Studies p. 238.)

imitators of Titian and Paul Veronese. The novel theory,
which we find in the present catalogue, that Paolo Morando,
called Cavazzola, influenced Paolo Caliari (perhaps it was
the similarity of their christian-names which misled the
author), is one which I cannot accept. Paolo Caliari belongs
to a totally different branch of the Veronese school to
that represented by Cavazzola. The compiler of the cata-
logue would, I think, have come nearer the truth had he
substituted the name of Domenico Riccio, known as
Brusasorzi,[1] for that of Cavazzola. Paul Veronese appears
to have settled in Venice in 1555, for in that year he
painted the ceiling of the sacristy of S. Sebastiano in that
city. Shortly after he probably began to decorate the
Villa Barbaro at Masér.

The Munich gallery can, I think, claim to possess a
good example by a later Veronese master, the admirable
portrait-painter Bernardino India, though I may be mis-
taken in this attribution. It hangs in Room IX., No. 1146,
and represents a lady in black seated in an armchair with
a boy beside her. It is certainly not painted in the manner
of Tintoretto, as stated in the old catalogue ; the new one,
with praiseworthy discretion, places it in the school of
Verona.

The Venetian school, as our hasty survey has enabled us
to perceive, is very insufficiently represented in the Munich
gallery. We have met with no works by the painters of
Murano, by the Bellini, by Carpaccio, or by Antonello da
Messina ; and we have sought in vain for Giorgione, Sebas-
tiano del Piombo, Mantegna, and Bartolommeo Montagna.

[1] Some admirable heads of saints
in fresco, by Brusasorzi, are in the
large hall on the upper floor of the
episcopal palace at Verona, some of
them being quite worthy of Paul
Veronese himself. The forerunners
of the latter master, such as Antonio
Badile, Domenico Brusasorzi, Tullio
India (the portrait-painter), and
Paolo Farinato, were all excellent
artists, and deserve to be better
known.

The Veronese, too, are few and far between, while of Brescian masters—Foppa, Moretto, Romanino, and Savoldo —we find not a single example. There are, however, some fair specimens of late Venetian art, such as good pictures by the Veronese Rotari (Nos. 1274, 1275), and four works [1] which in the new catalogue are rightly ascribed to the school of Bernardo Bellotto, instead of, as formerly, to that of Antonio Canale. The so-called portrait of Vesalius (Room IX., No. 1127) is not, I may add, by Jacopo Tintoretto, but by his son Domenico Robusti, and the "Scourging of Christ," No. 1158 (Cabinet XX.), should be attributed to Palma Giovine. The last-named picture is now catalogued as the work of that master; but the portrait still passes as the work of the elder Robusti, though the landscape background alone should have convinced the authorities of the gallery that it was by his son Domenico.

In conclusion, I have still to mention two pictures which in the new catalogue are classed with Venetian works. One (No. 1020, Room VIII.) represents the "Judgment of Solomon," and is said to have once borne the forged signature: 'JACOBUS BELLINVS.' Messrs. Crowe and Cavalcaselle (I, 116, 1) pronounced it to be 'in the style of the declining years of Cariani of Bergamo, or of the Veronese Torbido.' The director of the gallery rejected Cariani probably on account of 'his declining years,' and assigned the picture not to Torbido indeed, but to the school of Verona, of about 1480. It would have been wiser, I think, to have left the picture in its retirement at Schleissheim. To the Veronese school it certainly does not belong, and if a name is to be proposed for such a production, that of some feeble imitator of Cima da Conegliano would be more appropriate. The other picture, a "Concert" (No. 1084), has, at the suggestion of Messrs. Crowe and Cavalcaselle,

[1] Nos. 1267 to 1270, in **Cabinet XX.**

been ascribed to the Friulian Sebastiano Florigerio.
Again I am forced to disagree with them, for this uninter-
esting picture shows none of the qualities of Florigerio's
large and spirited altar-piece in the Church of S. Giorgio
at Udine. It does not even seem to be by an Italian. If
I am not greatly mistaken, it is merely a so-called *pasticcio*
by some Fleming who worked in Italy [1] (†). The director
has, I think, committed a mistake in ascribing to Leandro
Bassano the "Madonna and Child" enthroned between
St. Anthony the hermit and a bishop (No. 1151). It was
once rightly attributed to Giacomo Bassano, the father of
Leandro, and it appears to me to be an excellent and indis-
putable work by him. It is of his middle period, when,
like many of his contemporaries, he was influenced by the
engravings of the elegant Parmegianino. [2]

We will now turn to the schools of Ferrara and Bologna.

THE SCHOOLS OF FERRARA AND BOLOGNA.

The province of Polesina is only divided from that of
Ferrara by the Po, and even a foreigner will have no
difficulty in detecting in the Romagnole dialect of Ferrara
an admixture of the Venetian.

In my 'Critical Studies in the Borghese and Doria
Galleries' I touched briefly, as is my wont, upon the close
connection existing between the Paduan-Venetian schools
and those of the Romagna in general, but more especially
that of Ferrara. I then mentioned the names of Cosimo

[1] The idea for this picture was
probably taken from a drawing by
Domenico Campagnola, now in the
Uffizi (No. 683), and ascribed to
Giorgione. The design, therefore,
is Italian, though the execution is
Flemish. I am acquainted with
various compositions of this descrip-
tion by Venetian masters; for ex-
ample, the "Concert" by Lotto, at
Hampton Court; that by Giacomo
Bassano in the Uffizi; and others.

[2] See Vasari, ix. 120 (ed. Milanesi,
v. 218).

Tura, Francesco del Cossa, Ercole Roberti, Marco Zoppo of Bologna, Lattanzio da Rimini, Niccolò Rondinelli of Ravenna, Dosso Dossi and Scarsellino of Ferrara, and Antonio Allegri of Correggio.

The constant intercourse between the Venetians and the inhabitants of the Romagna is easily accounted for. It was due to natural causes and relationships. In the beginning of the sixteenth century, however, this intercourse was suddenly interrupted. All Italy was then ringing with the fame of the works of Raphael and Michelangelo in the Vatican, and many of the painters of the Romagna were, in consequence, induced to repair to Rome. The first of those who did so, and the greatest among them, was the Ferrarese Benvenuto Tisi, called Garofalo. His example was followed later by Battista Dossi, Ramenghi of Bagnacavallo, Girolamo Marchesi of Cotignola, Jacopo da Faenza, and others. Garofalo, however, notwithstanding a sojourn of two years in Rome—from about 1509 to 1511—always preserved his Ferrarese character. There are several pictures by him in the Munich gallery, though none of much importance.

No. 1081 (Cabinet XVIII.) represents the Madonna and Child between SS. Michael and John the Baptist, and is an early work by Garofalo ; unfortunately much disfigured by restoration, the Madonna and Child having suffered most severely. It is one of that group of the master's pictures which Dr. Bode first ascribed to Ortolano, and afterwards to the ' Master of the Borghese Descent from the Cross.' The influence of Dosso is very apparent in it.[1] A male portrait, formerly exhibited as Garofalo's portrait of himself, which I pronounced to be the work of a Fleming, has

[1] For an account of Garofalo's characteristics, which may be found in this picture, I refer my readers to my *Critical Studies in the Borghese and Doria Galleries*, pp. 205, 206.

now been transferred to the early school of the Netherlands, and is hung in Cabinet II. (No. 166). Another work by Garofalo—" A Madonna and Child "—is in Cabinet XVIII. (No. 1082). It is of no great merit, and must have been painted between 1520 and 1530. The " Pietà " in Room VIII. (No. 1080) is a feeble specimen of his art.

There is a genuine but unattractive work in Cabinet XVII. (No. 1024) by a younger fellow-countryman of Garofalo, Lodovico Mazzolino. This painter always signs himself ' L. Mazzolinus,' which was his family name and not a nickname, as the former catalogue of the Munich gallery assumed. He should, I think, be regarded as the pupil of Domenico Panetti or Ercole Roberti rather than of Lorenzo Costa. The other picture in this cabinet is more likely to be a feeble copy after Garofalo than an original by Mazzolino, and the catalogue, with proper caution, only places it in the ' Ferrarese school.'

We now come to Francesco Raibolini, called Francia,[1] a noble artist who, as a painter, was much influenced, it appears to me, by his fellow-student Lorenzo Costa. There are two good works by him in Room VIII. One (No. 1039) is the well-known " Madonna in the Rose-garden adoring the Infant Saviour." In the other (No. 1040) the Child is standing, supported by his mother, upon a table which is covered with a gold-embroidered cloth. This is a work of the master's early period, of about 1494, in which period he produced the " St. George and the Dragon " in the Corsini gallery at Rome (there attributed to Ercole Grandi di Giulio Cesare), and the small " Crucifixion " in the Archiginnasio at Bologna. In all these pictures the form of hand and ear is very characteristic of the master.

Even the new catalogue adheres to the view that

[1] Francia is a contracted form of Francesco. The Florentines had the forms Francione and Franciabigio—that is, Francesco Bigi.

Francia was influenced by Perugino, but this supposition is not justified by one of his works. Both masters belonged to the same period, but beyond this there was no connection between them. Nor was Francia the pupil of Marco Zoppo, as most books on art state. There is nothing, either in his nielli or in his pictures, to confirm this view, while the technic of his painting points very decidedly to Lorenzo Costa.[1]

In Room VIII. we find a very good picture (No. 1060) by Innocenzo da Imola, a painter who was influenced both by Francia and by the Florentine Mariotto Albertinelli. It represents the Madonna in a glory of angels and cherubim. Below are SS. Petronius, Clara, Francis and Sebastian, and two donors, all life-sized figures.

[1] Francia's workshop at Bologna was divided into two parts. In the upper storey, paintings were produced under the guidance of Lorenzo Costa; in the lower, Francia himself presided, and there coins were struck and the goldsmith's art was practised.

The legend that Francia was a pupil of Marco Zoppo probably originated in Bologna as late as the seventeenth century, and is due to local patriotism. It was assumed that Francia, who belonged to Bologna, must have been a pupil of a painter of that city. Malvasia, in his *Felsina pittrice*, enlarged upon this theory, and made out that Marco Zoppo derived his art from Lippo Dalmasio, that Francia was taught by Marco Zoppo, while Lorenzo Costa was a pupil of Francia. All this, it is scarcely necessary to observe, is a mess served up by a cook full of zeal for the honour and glory of his native city. It appears to me more probable that Francia learnt the elements of drawing from some goldsmith at Bologna. Later, he perhaps became the pupil of Francesco Cossa, who was already settled at Bologna in 1470. The two 'Paci' (works in niello), still preserved in the gallery at Bologna, which Francia executed between the years 1480 and 1485, recall Cossa, more especially in the drawing and in the manner of treating drapery. Marco Zoppo, a pupil of Squarcione and an imitator of Tura, was of no importance as an artist, and, moreover, spent most of his life at Venice. Be this as it may, one thing is certain, that Francia derived nothing from Perugino, nor was he influenced by the youthful Raphael, as many writers on art maintain. On the contrary, more exhaustive research will probably show that Raphael, in his early works, was indirectly influenced by the school of Francia-Costa through his fellow-countryman, Timoteo Viti, who was a pupil of Francia. On a future occasion I shall hope to prove this.

The later painters of Bologna—the 'academic' or 'eclectic' masters so-called—are well represented at Munich, such as Lodovico and Annibale Caracci, Albani, Guido, Guercino, Simone da Pesaro, Tiarini, Cavedone, and Domenichino. This celebrated school may thus be studied in all its phases in this gallery. I cannot, however, close this chapter on the school of Bologna-Ferrara without mentioning its principal representative, one who may be termed its Michelangelo, viz. Correggio. Half-a-dozen pictures are assigned to him in the Munich gallery. The most important work as regards size and artistic merit which is attributed to him, though only doubtfully, is in Room VIII. (No. 1096). It represents the Madonna and Child enthroned on clouds. Below are SS. James and Jerome with the donor. Girolamo da Carpi is certainly not the author of this picture, which might be by Michelangelo Anselmi; but, on the whole, it would be wiser to ascribe it only to the school of Correggio. Thus I wrote ten years ago, and the director of the gallery has since then assigned it to that school. On seeing the picture again, however, I felt convinced that it must be by Anselmi [1] (†).

Another work which the new catalogue ascribes to the 'School of Correggio' is in Cabinet XIX. (No. 1095), the Madonna and Child seated under a tree, with an angel and SS. Jerome and Ildefonso. It may once have been the work of Rondani, but scarcely of Correggio; in its present condition it is so repainted as to be unworthy of a place in a collection of such importance as the Munich gallery.

In the same cabinet is a copy (No. 1098) of Correggio's well-known picture in the English National Gallery, the "Education of Cupid." The new catalogue has accepted it as such.

[1] In the Naples Museum Anselmi is also, I think, confounded with Correggio in a picture known as the "Sleep of the Infant Saviour," No. 6.

The head of a young Faun, formerly in Cabinet XXIII.,
is now no longer there. It has probably been removed to
Schleissheim, the most suitable place for it. The "Ecce
Homo" in Room X. (No. 1238), formerly ascribed to Barocci,
is now rightly attributed to Domenico Feti. I have already
expressed my opinion about the attractive little picture
usually known as the "Faun," [1] and I then rectified the
mistake into which I fell in dealing with it ten years ago.
I have long since come to the conclusion that it is a price-
less early work by Correggio, and, together with his little
picture in the Uffizi,[2] it affords further proof that this
master must have perfected his technic by studying the
works of the Giorgionesque school, and more especially
those of Palma Vecchio and Lotto.

THE LOMBARDS.

We will now turn to the school which writers on art
are wont to term the Lombard school of Parma, and in
which they include the painters of Modena, Parma, and
Carpi. Correggio's imitators, Michelangelo Anselmi and
Rondani, I have already mentioned; Parmegianino,[3]
Bedolo, Pomponio Allegri, Gandini, and others are not
represented in this collection, but there are a few pictures
by Bartolommeo Schedone, who, though educated in the
school of the Caracci, subsequently took Correggio and
Parmegianino as his models. Two pictures by him are
in Cabinet XX., a " Magdalen " (No. 1101), and " Lot and

---

[1] Cabinet XIX., No. 1094.

[2] No. 1002, wrongly assigned to
Titian.

[3] The unpleasing " Madonna "
(Room VIII., No. 1091), which was
ascribed to this painter in the old
catalogue, is by a Florentine of the
school of Vasari, and is accepted as
such in the present catalogue. It
has no connection with Parme-
gianino.

his Daughters" (No. 1102) ; and in Cabinet XIX. there is another "Magdalen" (No. 1103) by this painter. The " Riposo," formerly ascribed to Schedone, has now, at my suggestion, been transferred to the ' School of Rembrandt,' and is placed in Cabinet VIII. and numbered 334.

In Cabinet XVIII. we find a " Salvator Mundi" (No. 1029), to which the former catalogue devoted some space. It belongs to the school of Boccaccino of Cremona, and is perhaps by his brother Bartolommeo or by another of his assistants. All Boccaccino's frescoes in Rome and else-where, with the sole exception of those in the cathedral at Cremona, have perished. His panel pictures are also few in number. The brothers Boccaccino must at one time have worked at Genoa.[1]

We need not devote any further space to these pseudo-Lombards, but will proceed to discuss the true representa-tives of this school which flourished in the district between the Po and the Adda, at Lodi, Pavia, Vercelli, and other places, its intellectual focus being Milan.

The school of Lodi is little known in Italy, even in Lombardy itself. Its principal representatives were Albertino and Martino Piazza, and the sons of the latter, Calisto and Scipione. There are no examples of this school in German or Russian collections. In the English National Gallery, however, there is a " St. John the Baptist" (No. 1152), by Martino Piazza, signed with his monogram.

The Munich gallery contains no works by Vercellese masters such as the Oldoni, Gaudenzio Ferrari, the Giove-noni, Defendente Ferrari, Grammorséo, Lanini, and others. By Giovan Antonio Bazzi, known as ' il Sodoma,' there is, however, a genuine and very refined little picture of his early period. It is in Room VIII. (No. 1073), and repre-sents the " Holy Family."

[1] See *Notisie dei Professori del disegno in Liguria*, by Federico Alizeri

Sodoma is sometimes dignified with the name of ' de' Tizzoni,' from an old patrician family of Vercelli. The Tizzoni may have been his patrons, but there was certainly no relationship between them, the painter's father having been a shoemaker. After his training under Spanzotti, a glass-painter of Vercelli, was completed, Sodoma appears to have removed about 1497 to Milan, where he continued his studies and was influenced by Leonardo da Vinci. In 1501 we find him at Siena. In course of time he founded a school in that city, where Beccafumi, Riccio, and Baldassare Peruzzi became his imitators.

A picture similar to the " Holy Family " in the Munich gallery is in the Pinacothek at Turin. The director at Munich doubtfully ascribes another picture to the master, a small head of St. Michael, in Cabinet XIX. (No. 1074). Few connoisseurs of Sodoma's manner will be disposed to share this opinion. The picture is a mere fragment, and it is wiser to express no opinion upon works of this description, which afford so little clue to their authors. It reminds me of the Bolognese school of Lorenzo Costa rather than of Sodoma, and recalls Ercole Grandi di Giulio Cesare.

Fifty years ago Sodoma was scarcely known out of Siena. As most writers of that day derived all their knowledge of Italian art from books, they would, of course, hear nothing in praise of Sodoma. Works by him, moreover, are not found in the galleries of Madrid, Paris, Dresden, and Vienna. Even the English National Gallery can only boast of one small picture (No. 1144) by this gifted painter, which has been recently acquired. In private collections in England he is more frequently met with—in those of Lord Wemyss, Mr. Holford, Mr. Mond, Sir Francis Cook, and others; a further proof that Englishmen have been

independent of foreign influence in their estimate of works
of art.

Vasari's biography of Sodoma is not without interest
from a psychological point of view. He evidently began
with a strong prejudice against this painter. Sodoma was
not a Tuscan; he had, moreover, completely eclipsed
Vasari's personal friend Beccafumi (Mecherino); again,
Vasari idolised Michelangelo, and Sodoma had never been
betrayed into letting his own small skiff be drawn into the
mighty current of Michelangelo's influence. The bio-
grapher may also have been indignant at the insult offered
by him to the Florentines, in bestowing upon his horse, the
winner of the races in their city, the vile name of Sodoma,
to be proclaimed, as was customary, by all the young roughs
of the city.

From the outset, therefore, we see that Vasari was
biassed against Sodoma. He accuses him of leading a
grovelling (*bestiale*) life, and of working only for gain
instead of for honour and renown, and he stigmatises him
as a reprobate and a fool. When, however, in the course
of his narrative, Vasari begins to speak of Sodoma's
works, his sense of justice and his right perception of art
get the better of his personal feeling, and he shows a true
appreciation of this gifted artist. A painting of a head by
the master he characterises as 'marvellously beautiful'
('meravigliosa'), and he draws attention to the 'grace
and wondrous divinity of expression' ('la grazia e la
meravigliosa divinità') in a "Head of Christ" by Sodoma.
No one, he observes in another place, was able to paint
such exquisite female types as he; and he praises one of
the master's works as the most beautiful in Siena: 'Ed io
credo che sia la più bella che si possa trovare.' In a word,
notwithstanding his enmity to the Lombard painter, Vasari
was forced to admit his great merits. At the beginning of

FEMALE PORTRAIT. BY SODOMA.
(In the Staedel Institute, Frankfurt.)

To face p. 83.

his biography,[1] he tells us that Sodoma painted many portraits during the first years of his sojourn at Siena. Yet the master is scarcely known as a portrait-painter in the present day, and the few works of this class which may, I think, be ascribed to him all pass under the names of more renowned artists. In the Albertina at Vienna there are two drawings in charcoal by Sodoma. One, " Christ crowned with thorns " (Braun, 90), is assigned to Leonardo. The other, the portrait of a man, is attributed to Raphael. Another beautiful drawing by him—the portrait of a man in a black cap—is in the British Museum (Braun, 94). It is there regarded as the portrait of Timoteo Viti by Raphael—an idea which probably dates back to the time when the drawing was in the Antaldi collection at Urbino. The attribution was purely arbitrary, like that of so many other drawings in this collection.

The most admirable of all Sodoma's portraits from life is that of a young and refined woman in the Staedel Institute at Frankfort. The painter must have enjoyed portraying this bright and attractive countenance, and I know no other portrait by the master showing such evident pleasure in its execution and so much care and finish. Though not ascribed to Raphael at Frankfort, it is looked upon as the work of another celebrated portrait-painter, Sebastiano del Piombo. It is certainly one of the gems of this interesting collection.

Dr. Bode has publicly questioned my opinion as to this portrait. In his eyes it is not by an Italian at all, but by a Dutchman—Jan Scorel—the painter of a female portrait once in the second corridor of the Doria-Pamfili gallery at Rome.[2] Under these circumstances I think it

---

[1] See Vasari, xi. 142 (ed. Milanesi, vi. 380).

[2] See *Repertorium für Kunst-* *wissenschaft*, xii. Heft i. p. 72. The good and lifelike portrait in the Doria gallery is there ascribed

desirable to deal more fully with the Frankfort portrait, in the hope that some at least among my readers, who have a more refined feeling for art, will be disposed to accept my views, and to restore to Sodoma what is, in point of fact, one of his finest works. I should first advise all who have not seen the picture itself to study the admirable photograph of it published by Braun (No. 42) under the name of Sebastiano del Piombo.[1] In my ' Critical Studies in the Borghese and Doria Galleries ' I mentioned the following as characteristics of Sodoma :—

1. The hands have tapering fingers, the knuckles being often only indicated by a kind of dimple. The hand

SODOMA'S FORM OF HAND.

in the Frankfort portrait should be compared with the hand of the young king on the right in Sodoma's fine altar-piece—the " Adoration of the Magi "—in the Church of S. Agostino at Siena ; with the hand of Eve in the fresco of the " Descent into Hades," in the public gallery at Siena ;[2] and with the hand of the Madonna in two other pictures, one in the possession of Mme. Ginoulhiac at Milan, the other in the Morelli collection.[3]

2. The eyes are almond-shaped. This characteristic is met with in all Sodoma's pictures ; in the portrait at

to Holbein. The technic of this painting is totally different to that in the portrait at Frankfort ; so, too, is the form of the hand ; while the modelling of the mouth and of the eyes is much coarser in character We see that the artistic personality of Scorel is as alien as possible to that of Sodoma.

[1] In order to invest the portrait with greater interest, the name of one of the Medici has been bestowed upon it by the catalogue. I think it more probable, however, that the lady represented belonged to a noble family of Siena. The form of her earrings is characteristic of the Sienese goldsmith's art.

[2] These two works have been photographed by Lombardi at Siena.

[3] Now at Bergamo.

Frankfort, in the Madonna with St. Leonard in the Palazzo Pubblico at Siena, in the "Adoration of the Magi" in S. Agostino, and in the fresco in S. Domenico, both in that city; in the so-called "Madonnone" at Vaprio, and in the frescoes in the Farnesina at Rome; as also in the following drawings: the head of a young man crowned with laurel, and the Madonna with the Child, who holds a cat in his arms—both in the Uffizi,[1] the last named being ascribed to Leonardo—and the study for the head of Leda—a pen drawing at Windsor (Grosvenor Gallery Publication, No. 50).

3. His landscape consists generally of a broad, well-watered plain, with groups of low trees. He often introduces on one side a hill, with buildings, towers, Roman temples and arches. Landscape backgrounds of this description occur in the female portrait at Frankfort, in the picture with the Madonna and St. Leonard in the Palazzo Pubblico at Siena, in the "Adoration of the Magi" in S. Agostino, in the St. Sebastian of the Uffizi, and elsewhere. I may supplement the characteristics of Sodoma which I have just mentioned by a few more; *quod abundat non viciat.*

4. The ear in the female portrait at Frankfort is similar in form to those in his other works. It should be compared with the ears in the following pictures: with those of St. Leonard in the Palazzo Pubblico at Siena, of St. Joseph in S. Agostino, of

SODOMA'S FORM OF EAR.

a halberdier with his back to the spectator in the "Crucifixion" in the public gallery at Siena, and with those of one of Alexander the Great's attendants in the fresco in

[1] Case 166, No. 566, and Case 105, No. 421; Braun, No. 448.

the Farnesina. The children in Sodoma's pictures have
always, however, a more rounded form of ear.

5. Sodoma's treatment of hair is also peculiar to
himself. In female heads it is often arranged in crisp
waves on the temples, as in the portrait at Frankfort. We
meet with this characteristic in the following works : the
" Lucretia " in the Kestner Museum,[1] the " Roxana " in
the Farnesina, the " Madonnone " at Vaprio, the Madonna
belonging to Mme. Ginoulhiac at Milan, the pen drawing
for the head of " Leda " (Grosvenor Gallery Publication,
No. 50), and the pen drawings, under the name of
Leonardo, at Chatsworth (Braun, 51), and in the Uffizi
(No. 421 ; Braun, 448).

Even the long stiff folds in the dress of the lady re-
presented at Frankfort correspond with those in Sodoma's
pictures ; as, for instance, in the drapery of the beautiful
female figures in the frescoes in the Farnesina.

I could sustain my reasons for ascribing this portrait to
Sodoma by further proofs, but I fear that I may have
already overtaxed the patience of my reader. My object
has been to reinstate this gifted Lombard master in his
rightful place, as he has been both maligned and misun-
derstood. I trust, therefore, that I may be pardoned for
this digression. It is incomprehensible to me how Dr.
Bode could have thought of attributing the Frankfort
portrait to a Dutch painter of the first half of the sixteenth
century. The forms and the landscape are wholly Italian,
and of a totally different character to those in Flemish and
Dutch pictures. But, apart from this, what northern
painting of that date can show such spirited and flowing
lines, such breadth and freedom of touch, or a like fresh-
ness and charm both of conception and representation?—
qualities which we find brilliantly exemplified in this.

---

[1] Now in the gallery at Hanover.

splendid portrait. As to its being by Sebastiano del Piombo, the colouring, which is not Venetian in character, sufficiently disproves this; while neither the landscape background nor the forms of the hand and ear are those peculiar to that master.

In the old catalogue of the Munich gallery several pictures were assigned to Leonardo da Vinci. One, representing St. Cecilia, must now have been removed to Schleissheim, as I was unable to find it in the collection. Ten years ago I pronounced it to be a feeble copy of Raphael's portrait of Giovanna d'Aragona in the Louvre, and, like the picture of the same subject in the Doria gallery at Rome,[1] by a Fleming. The director appears, in this instance, to have accepted my opinion. A second work, formerly attributed to the great Florentine, is now held to be a copy, or an imitation, of the master, and hangs in Cabinet XVIII. (No. 1041). A third—a "Madonna," in Room VIII. (No. 1042)—is described in the present catalogue as the work of a Fleming, probably of Bernard van Orley. But why Van Orley in particular? It seems as likely to be by Crispin van der Broeck, or any other painter of the school of Antwerp, as by Van Orley. Flemish imitations of Italian originals are very frequently met with, and it is a great satisfaction to me to find that several of them have now been accepted as such in Munich.

It is deplorable that Leonardo is still so little understood. At St. Petersburg, pictures by Cesare da Sesto and Bernardino de' Conti are attributed to him. There is some excuse for this, as both were Italian artists belonging to his immediate school. But at Augsburg and at Berlin, incredible as it may appear, the inferior productions of Flemish imitators are actually exhibited as the work of Leonardo and his pupils, and it behoves students of art

[1] See my *Critical Studies in the Borghese and Doria Galleries*, p. 311.

to protest emphatically against such profanation of the master's name. The director at Munich, however, deserves the gratitude of all who value the great Florentine's art for having removed one of these pseudo-Leonardos to Schleissheim, while he has, at my suggestion, transferred the other two to the Flemish school.

According to Dr. Marggraff's catalogue, there was a genuine and also a doubtful work by Bernardino Luini in this gallery, as well as a copy after him. This painter came from Luino or Lovino, on the Lago Maggiore. He was a pupil of Ambrogio da Fossano, called Borgognone, and became, at one period of his career, an imitator of Leonardo.

The so-called genuine work is now attributed to Gian-pietrino. It is in Room VIII. (No. 1047), and represents the Madonna with the Infant Saviour, who holds a gold-finch. A landscape forms the background. I must here repeat what I said formerly with regard to this picture, that it is an inferior and repainted copy of one by Gian-pietrino in the Borghese gallery at Rome.

Gianpietrino, or Gianpedrino—not ' Giovanni Pedrini,' as in the catalogue—was not only an imitator of Leonardo, but also his actual pupil, as every student who examines his genuine pictures and drawings will admit. The sweet smile which characterises all Gianpietrino's female heads he derived from his master, and, with the exception of Sodoma, he was more successful in reproducing this ex-pression than any of Leonardo's pupils. He usually painted half-length figures, some of which have been ascribed to his master.[1] He is often confounded with Sodoma, and sometimes even with Luini and Marco d'Oggionno. In the Turin gallery, for example, a picture

[1] A large number of these half-length figures by Gianpietrino have passed out of Italy under the names of more renowned painters.

PICTURE BY GIANPIETRINO.

(In the Borromeo Collection at Milan.)

To face p. 88.

of "Christ bearing the Cross" (No. 107), by him, is attributed to the latter painter. Gianpietrino is, however, easily recognised by his form of hand and ear, by the cold flesh-tints, and by the golden-red colour of his draperies. Portraits by him are extremely rare. One is in the possession of the Marchese Emilio Visconti-Venosta at Milan. It is a very refined work, and represents Cardinal Ascanio Sforza, the brother of ' il Moro.' Gianpietrino's workshop must have been one of the busiest and most frequented in Milan between the years 1520 and 1530.[1]

The feeble production which Dr. Marggraff described as a copy after Luini is now in Cabinet XIX. (No. 1046), and the picture once doubtfully assigned to the master is in Room VIII. (No. 1045). The last named represents St. Catherine holding a palm branch, a wheel lying beside her, with a landscape background. The picture has suffered greatly from repeated restoration, so that it is difficult to recognise its true author. The whole of the right hand is new, and I can detect in it the manner of the late Signor Molteni, the picture-restorer at Milan. Dr. Marggraff, as I have already observed, ascribed the picture doubtfully to Luini, and the author of the present catalogue, by assigning it unconditionally to that master, has, I think, made a step in the wrong direction. Even students who have but a slight acquaintance with the types and forms of this characteristic master will see that the attribution in the catalogue is incorrect. Notwithstanding the injury which the picture has sustained, Messrs. Crowe and Cavalcaselle,[2] with more discernment, recognised in it the manner of Andrea Solario. I also believe it to have been originally by him. The red and violet tones of the mantle and robe of this St. Catherine are characteristic of Solario, but differ

---

[1] See my *Critical Studies in he Borghese and Doria Galleries*, p. 162.
[2] ii. 60, 61.

altogether from Luini's scale of colouring; the left hand,
which has retained its original form, is unlike that dis-
tinctive of Luini, and the landscape has no connection with
that master, but resembles the landscapes in Solario's pic-
tures.   As far as I know, there are no works by Solario in
German collections.[1]   It is, therefore, pardonable that the
master should be little known to the majority of art-critics
in Germany.   Most of his works are at Milan and Paris,
and there this refined and conscientious painter may best
be studied and appreciated.   The English National Gallery
also contains some excellent portraits by him.

  Luini, on the other hand, is well represented in foreign
galleries.   The Louvre contains three good frescoes and
three easel pictures by him.   Among the last named, the
"Madonna with the Infant Saviour asleep' (No. 1354) and
the "Salome" (No. 1355) are especially noticeable.   In
the Museo del Prado at Madrid there is a fine "Holy
Family" (No. 290) by him, and a genuine though much
repainted "Daughter of Herodias" (No. 291).   In the
public gallery at Vienna there are two works by this
attractive Lombard master, one being also a "Daughter
of Herodias," the other a "St. Jerome as a Penitent."
Another picture in the same gallery, which at first sight
recalls Luini, is a "Christ bearing the Cross."   The
catalogue places it only in the school of Leonardo.   If I
am not mistaken, it is again the work of a Flemish imitator,
who this time chose Luini for his model instead of Leonardo
or Verrocchio, as was usually the case (†).

  In the Esterhazy gallery at Buda-Pesth, which contains
so many rare Italian pictures, we find quite a colony of
Milanese artists: two admirable "Madonnas" by Luini; one

[1] The "Christ bearing the Cross" at Lützschena, and the "Daughter of Herodias" at Oldenburg, both ap-peared to me to be Flemish imita-tions of Solario (†).

SUSANNA. BY BERNARDINO LUINI.

(In the Borromeo Collection. Milan)

To face p. 90.

STUDIES OF CHILDREN. DRAWING BY LUINI.

(In the Ambrosiana, Milan.)

To face p. 90.

THE ADORATION OF THE MAGI. DRAWING BY CESARE DA SESTO.
(In the Venice Academy.)

To face p. 91.

by Boltraffio (†),[1] and one by Cesare da Sesto; a work by Gianpietrino, and another by Ambrogio Borgognone. There is only one picture by Luini in the English National Gallery—"Christ among the Doctors," formerly ascribed to Leonardo—but in several private collections in London he is represented. A "Madonna" is in that of the late Sir Richard Wallace; a picture, under the name of Leonardo, representing the Infant Saviour embracing the little St. John, is in the Ashburton collection; a recumbent Venus, much repainted, in that of Lord Dudley;[2] a "Madonna," also much restored, in that of Sir Francis Cook; and another picture, equally injured—"Joseph and Potiphar's Wife"— belongs to Lord Wolseley.

We will now turn from this Lombard master, who in Munich, as in other places, is less known than he deserves to be, and continue our survey in Room VIII.

Under No. 1044 we find a "Madonna" which the director deemed worthy to be brought from Schleissheim and to be placed in the gallery. On the authority of Messrs. Crowe and Cavalcaselle this feeble copy is now attributed to Bernardino de' Conti. It would, I think, have been wiser to have left it in retirement at Schleissheim. The country air would have been equally beneficial to another picture in this room (No. 1048), which has also been removed from Schleissheim into the more aristocratic but less congenial atmosphere of the Pinacothek. It has been hung high, and as far removed as possible from the scrutiny of students. In the catalogue it bears the alluring name of Cesare da Sesto, though Cesare *da Sezzo* would have more accurately described its true author. If I am not mistaken, this is again

[1] This very characteristic work by Boltraffio—vividly recalling the " Madonna " by the same master in the English National Gallery—is ascribed by Dr. Bode to Bernardino de' Conti. How little even the most renowned art-critics of Germany seem to know of the Milanese school!

[2] Now in the collection of Mr. Mond.

the work of one of the many itinerant Flemings who came to Milan in the course of their wanderings (†). The picture is coarse and lifeless throughout, the face is expressionless, and the folds on the upper part of the red sleeve of the Madonna are distinctively northern in character. Her present sur-roundings are clearly distasteful to her, and though she seeks to disguise her feelings beneath a set smile, it is evident that she is pining for the seclusion of Schleissheim. The director could not do better than gratify her modest wish.[1]

Two pictures of Lombard origin in Room VIII. still remain to be mentioned. They are numbered 1027 and 1028, and represent respectively SS. Ambrose and Louis of Toulouse. Dr. Marggraff assigned them doubtfully to Andrea Solario, called 'lo Zingaro,' but they are now rightly ascribed to a Lombard of the close of the fifteenth century or the early part of the sixteenth. Messrs. Crowe and Cavalcaselle consider them to be by a Lombardo-Pavian artist, and I am also of this opinion. It is evident that the painter was closely connected with Pier Francesco Sacchi, though I should not venture to affirm, as the above-named writers have done, that they were the work of Cesare Magno, a pupil and imitator of that master.

THE TUSCANS.

Our survey has taught us that, with the exception of Sodoma, the great masters of the Lombard school are hardly at all represented in the Munich gallery. The

[1] In the Museo del Prado at Madrid we find a Flemish copy of Leonardo's "St. Anne" in the Louvre. Don Pedro Madrazo, in his catalogue, rightly alludes to it as a *pasticcio* by a Fleming. I only know of two works by Cesare da Sesto in German collections—the "Madonna" in the gallery at Buda-Pesth, and the "Daughter of Hero-dias" at Vienna. A fine red chalk drawing, with the study for the hand

THE ADORATION OF THE MAGI. BY CESARE DA SESTO.

(In the Borromeo Collection, Milan.)

To face p. 92.

earlier Florentine painters, on the other hand, are better exemplified here than either the Ferrarese or the Lombards.

Four small panels in Cabinet XVII. (Nos. 989–992), with scenes from the legend of SS. Cosmo and Damianus, are by the monk Giovanni da Fiesole, known as Fra Angelico. They may unquestionably be classed among the better works of this amiable master, whose genius manifests itself in the very simplicity of his creations. In his mode of conception he belongs wholly to the fourteenth century, and had no part in the change which Florentine art underwent in the first half of the fifteenth century. His works are imbued with a spirit of devout piety, and in this respect he might be termed the ' St. Francis ' of Italian art.

The new catalogue names Orcagna as one of the painters from whom Fra Angelico derived his style. We need not discuss this theory at present; suffice it to say that it finds no confirmation either in documents or in the master's own works. It appears to me more probable that in his youth Fra Angelico worked as a miniaturist, and that it was only in his later period—after 1420—that he increased his knowledge of painting by studying the frescoes of Masolino and Masaccio in the Brancacci Chapel.

He died at Rome in 1455, and was buried in the Church of S. Maria sopra Minerva, where a tablet, which the brothers of his order erected to his memory, still marks the resting-place of this devout and noble artist. His unpretending tomb is not designed to attract attention, and will doubtless be regarded with a contemptuous smile by those who contrast it with the ostentatious marble statues commemorating many of the pseudo-great of our own day.

of the executioner in this picture, is at Windsor under the name of Leonardo. (Braun, 242). The " St. Catherine," ascribed to Cesare da Sesto in the Staedel Institute at Frankfort (No. 43) is certainly not by him, but more probably by a Lombardo-Venetian painter.

The panel (No. 998) representing the Almighty surrounded by angels playing on musical instruments, is not by Fra Angelico, but can only be regarded as a copy of a later period. Messrs. Crowe and Cavalcaselle, as well as the authorities of the gallery, are of the same opinion.

Fra Filippo Lippi, a younger contemporary of Fra Angelico, and like him a Florentine, was also a monk, but the Carmelite was a man of a very different temperament to the Dominican. Left an orphan at an early age, the unruly turbulent boy was placed in a Carmelite monastery, and while still quite young was sealed to the monastic vocation, a destiny for which wise mother Nature had by no means fitted him. His reckless and passionate nature often involved him in grievous embarrassments, and it was due to his great artistic gifts alone that he was able to extricate himself from his difficulties.

Masaccio must be regarded as his true master. By studying that painter's epoch-making frescoes in the Church of the Carmine at Florence, Filippo Lippi undoubtedly developed his own art. The modelling of the heads and the form of the hands in his early works vividly recall Masaccio, though he must also have felt the influence of Fra Angelico. The frescoes in the choir of the cathedral at Prato are Fra Filippo's greatest works. On one wall he has depicted the life and martyrdom of St. Stephen; on the other, that of St. John the Baptist. These splendid paintings were begun in 1456 and completed in 1464; they were therefore executed at the same period as Mantegna's equally celebrated frescoes in the Eremitani Chapel at Padua. In order to understand the aims and capacities of art at that date in its highest achievements these two great works should be studied and compared with one another. What strikes us at once irresistibly in the representations of these two masters is the force of character displayed in the art of

each. Fra Filippo carries us away by grandeur of concep-
tion and dramatic vitality, while Mantegna enthralls us by
a more seizing force of representation and by greater perfec-
tion of execution. Both works unquestionably rank among
the finest productions of fifteenth-century art in Italy.

The Munich gallery contains two pictures by Fra Filippo,
both in Room VIII. One (No. 1005) represents the
"Annunciation"; the other (No. 1006), the Madonna with
the Infant Saviour on her knee. The first is a characteristic
example of a subject which Fra Filippo treated several
times; for instance, in the Church of S. Lorenzo at Florence,
in a private chapel at Antella, near that city,[1] and in two
pictures now respectively in the Doria gallery at Rome
and in the English National Gallery (No. 666). There are
two other admirable works by this master in the latter col-
lection, the "Vision of St. Bernard" (No. 248), and St.
John the Baptist with six other saints (No. 667), all fine
and lifelike figures. The Triptych (No. 586),[2] ascribed to
him in the same gallery, is not, I think, by the master
himself, but by some imitator (†). A little picture by Fra
Filippo, which I count among his most exquisite and deeply-
felt works, is the "Marriage of SS. Joachim and Anna" in
the University galleries at Oxford.

Two pictures in the Louvre are attributed to this great
artist. One, the Madonna and Child between two priests
and six angels (No. 1344), is a genuine and characteristic
example. The other, the "Nativity" (No. 1343), is not,
I think, by the master, but recalls the school of Alesso
Baldovinetti (†).

Fra Filippo is not represented in the galleries of Vienna,
Dresden, or Madrid. In the Berlin Museum, however,
there are several good specimens of his art.

[1] Now in the collection of Miss Hertz at Rome.

[2] It represents the Madonna and Child between saints and angels.

Dramatic character in painting, which was first introduced by Masolino and Masaccio, and was developed and perfected by Fra Filippo Lippi, found its most vigorous and spirited exponent in Alessandro Botticelli, Fra Filippo's distinguished pupil. The merits of this great artist have only been recognised again in recent years, and first of all in England. The Munich gallery contains but one work by him, a so-called "Pietà." It represents the Madonna supporting the lifeless body of Christ; St. John is beside her, while two of the holy women bathe the head and feet of the Saviour with their tears. In the background stands a third, holding three nails. An inferior copy of this picture, of smaller dimensions, is in the Poldi-Pezzoli collection at Milan (†). According to the present catalogue of the Munich gallery, Botticelli was influenced in the latter part of his career by Verrocchio, who, be it remembered, had already quitted Florence in 1484. This newly invented theory we may dismiss for the present. Some German critics, indeed, would fain represent Verrocchio, who was undeniably great as a sculptor, in the guise of a sort of 'Mother of Mercy,' sheltering under the folds of her ample cloak all contemporary artists, not only of Tuscany but even of Umbria also. As a creative and original genius, Botticelli appears to me to have been an artist of a very different stamp to Verrocchio. But this is a question of individual taste and æsthetic culture, and one which each student of art must decide for himself. The figures in Botticelli's picture at Munich are nearly life-sized; all are of great vitality and animated by the deepest devotion.

No. 1008 in Room VIII. is a characteristic work by Filippino Lippi, the son of Fra Filippo, and a pupil of Botticelli. It represents Christ appearing to His mother after His resurrection. Another panel picture in this room formerly bore the name of Domenico Ghirlandaio. Messrs.

Crowe and Cavalcaselle with more discernment ascribed it to Filippino Lippi, a name which has been accepted by the director of the gallery. Ten years ago this attribution appeared to me to be the most appropriate. On seeing the picture again, however, and in a better light, I came to the conclusion that Dr. Frizzoni was right in his surmise that it was an early work by Raffaellino del Garbo, the pupil and assistant of Filippino. The type of the angel on the left, in the upper part of the picture, coincides with the angel in Raffaellino's picture at Berlin (No. 90). The head of St. John recalls Raffaellino's types in other pictures; the hands of St. John the Baptist and of the Evangelist with strongly marked finger-joints are characteristic of this master; the landscape with the light brown rocks recalls that in Raffaellino's well-known picture in the Florence Academy, and the scale of colour differs from that of Filippino, but is characteristic of his pupil. Everything, in short, in this picture seems to me to betray the feeling and the hand of Raffaellino di Bartolommeo del Garbo, rather than that of his master and prototype Filippino.

Filippino's pictures are rarely met with out of Italy. There are none at Madrid, Vienna, Dresden, or Paris. At Berlin, on the other hand, there are a few admirable examples. A characteristic picture by him is in the English National Gallery (No. 293), and an exquisite " Tondo" is in the Christ Church collection at Oxford, representing Cupid weeping, a centaur having despoiled him of his arrows. The picture is there ascribed to the Lombard school (†).

Among the more important works by Florentine masters in the Munich gallery, I would mention the three large panels by Domenico Ghirlandaio in Room VIII.: No. 1011 represents the Madonna in a glory composed of rays of flame and surrounded by angels and seraphs; SS. Dominic,

Michael, John the Evangelist and the Baptist, kneel on the
earth in adoration ; No. 1012, St. Laurence, in the rich
garb of a deacon, holding the gridiron and the palm ; and
No. 1013, St. Catherine of Siena. These panels, with
three others by the master now in the Berlin gallery, all
formed part of an altar-piece once in the choir of S. Maria
Novella at Florence. The two pictures in Cabinet XVII.
(Nos. 1014, 1015), ascribed to Mainardi, the pupil of
Ghirlandaio and his brother-in-law, appear to me far too
weak for the master himself, and are more probably by one
of Ghirlandaio's many imitators.[1] One of these feeble
productions represents SS. George and Sebastian, the
other the Madonna and Child. The director now rightly
describes them as works of the school. A place has been
assigned in Cabinet XVII. to another work of the same
class, representing two episodes from the legend of St.
Francis of Assisi. Since Messrs. Crowe and Cavalcaselle
were determined to bestow a name upon it, they did
wisely in selecting that of an almost unknown Umbrian
painter—Matteo da Gualdo. I am also of opinion that
it is of Umbrian origin, and certainly not Florentine, as
the present catalogue informs us. A drawing of the same
subject is in Mr. Malcolm's collection in London, and is
ascribed in the catalogue to Antonio del Pollaiuolo. This
is perhaps the reason why the authorities at Munich were
misled into attributing it to a Florentine painter. The
feeble drawing in the Malcolm collection seems to me to
be of later date than the picture in the Munich gallery.
The question is, however, of no importance, and we
need waste no more time over it—*le jeu ne vaut pas la
chandelle.*

---

[1] See Vasari on the subject of Ghirlandaio's pupils : 'Discepoli, dei quali egli aveva numero grande' 'Disciples, of whom he [that is, Ghirlandaio] had a great number ') (xii. 161 ; ed. Milanesi, vii. 139).

Let us now return to Room VIII., and examine a picture (No. 1077) which, I think, has only recently made its appearance in the gallery. The catalogue describes it as a work of the school of Ridolfo Ghirlandaio. According to Vasari, a great number of painters were employed in the workshop of that master. This picture, however, does not appear to me to have a trace of Ridolfo's manner, but is by some imitator of Raphael not wholly spiritless, though the drawing shows so little individuality that it is impossible to attribute it to any particular painter.

Our attention is next arrested by a panel picture representing three coarse-looking peasants and a boy with crooked legs holding a fish. This gives us a clue to the subject. The painter evidently intended to represent Tobias with the three archangels. To the indignation of all students of art, this picture was once attributed to the great sculptor Verrocchio. In the new catalogue the equally inappropriate name of Pier di Cosimo has been substituted. The picture is little better than a caricature, and can only be ascribed to some very inferior Florentine painter of the close of the fifteenth century [1] (†).

Before proceeding further, I must permit myself to observe that there are many pictures in the Munich gallery which appear to me unworthy of a collection of such importance. In any case, such works should not be placed in the same room with those of the greatest Italian masters such as Raphael, Botticelli, Filippino, Ghirlandaio, Perugino, Francia, Sodoma, Lotto, Palma Vecchio, and others ; for, though the value of everything in this world is relative, and it is always desirable in a large gallery to enhance the merits of the good pictures by contrasting

[1] In the Louvre, Pier di Cosimo is charged with the feeble work of some Florentine (No. 1416), who appears as an imitator, partly of Filippino and partly of Fra Bartolommeo (†).

them with the productions of inferior painters, yet it seems
to me that the practice has been carried too far in Munich.
The contrast between Van Dyck's refined and elegant
portraits in Room VII. and the feeble copies and works
of the school collected in Room VIII. [1] is most unpleasant.
They seem like so many country tramps who should have
pushed their way unbidden into the society of the high
dignitaries of the Crown, and presumptuously taken and
insisted on maintaining a place, for which they are by
no means fitted, on the gilt and velveted chairs of State.
I trust that the director, who has already done so much for
the gallery with which he is connected, will pardon me
for making this remark.

Another picture in Cabinet XVII. (No. 1018), which
was formerly ascribed to Verrocchio, is now said to be a
copy of a picture by Lorenzo di Credi. In point of fact,
it is the copy of a picture in the Borghese gallery, which
is there attributed to Lorenzo di Credi, but which I consider
to be by a pupil whom I have designated as 'Tommaso.' [2]
I believe that the Munich gallery also possesses an original
by this Tommaso. It is in Room VIII. (No. 1017), and,
like all other works of this painter, is attributed to his
master, Lorenzo di Credi (†). I would beg all students to
examine the type of the Madonna, the flowingly curved
opening of the Infant Saviour's ear, the sharp lights, and
the folds of the drapery. All these characteristics are
identical with those to which I drew attention when
speaking of the picture in the Borghese gallery.

In Cabinet XIX. we meet with two characteristic pic-
tures—a "Madonna and Child" (No. 1058) and "St.
Bernardino of Siena" (No. 1059). The former catalogue

---

[1] Such as Nos. 1016, 1020, 1021,
1026, 1027, 1028, 1044, 1047, 1048,
1055, 1072, 1077.

[2] See my *Critical Studies in the
Borghese and Doria Galleries*, pp. 89,
90.

·described them as works of Pacchiarotto. Messrs. Crowe and Cavalcaselle ascribed them, and rightly I think, to another Sienese painter, Girolamo del Pacchia,[1] an attribution which the director has now accepted. They are of similar size, and were probably painted for the adornment ·of a bier, a custom which was exclusively confined to Siena. The finest examples for this purpose were painted by Sodoma; I need only call to recollection here those which he executed for the Confraternities of ' S. Giovanni Battista della Morte ' and of the ' Santissima Trinità ' at ·Siena.

A " Madonna and Child " in Room VIII. (No. 1090) is a fairly good specimen of another Tuscan, Jacopo da Pontormo.

In Cabinet XVIII. is a Madonna seated with the Child upon her lap in front of a green curtain (No. 1075). The late Dr. Marggraff described it as ' in the manner of Fra Bartolommeo.' Messrs. Crowe and Cavalcaselle (iii. 475) were reminded in this picture partly of Michele di Ridolfo, partly of Puligo, and also of the Brescianini of Siena. This uncertainty is, however, pardonable, since in the Turin gallery a " Holy Family " by A. Brescianino (No. 115) is ascribed to Girolamo del Pacchia (†). I believe the picture in Munich to be undoubtedly by the same Andrea del Brescianino (†) or del Brescia,[2] as Vasari calls him. This painter left Siena in 1525 for Florence, accompanied by his brother Raphael, and there studied the works of Fra Bartolommeo, whom he also sought to imitate. The director of the Munich gallery has accepted my

[1] In the Naples gallery Girolamo del Pacchia is confounded with Domenico Ghirlandaio (Sala Toscana, No. 28, a "Madonna and Child ").

[2] His family name was Puccinelli; his father was a Brescian, hence Messrs. Crowe and Cavalcaselle would discern in Andrea del Brescianino's pictures the influence of Civerchio (iii. 401). It certainly requires a remarkably keen sight to detect this.

attribution, and the picture now passes under the name of Brescianino.

In Room VIII. we find four panels of Saints by Francesco Granacci (Nos. 1061, 1062, 1063, 1064). They are of his last period, and are not favourable specimens of his art. . To this master is now ascribed the picture formerly regarded as the work of Fra Bartolommeo. It hangs in Cabinet XVIII. (1065), and represents the Madonna in a landscape kneeling and adoring the Infant Saviour; St. Joseph is seated opposite to her. I should be disposed to consider it only of the school of Granacci. Messrs. Crowe and Cavalcaselle are in doubt whether to attribute it to Michele di Ridolfo or to some other painter (iii. 475).[1]

The Munich gallery, as we have seen, cannot lay claim to a single picture by Fra Bartolommeo, who is so rarely met with out of Italy.[2] His colleague and fellow-pupil, Mariotto Albertinelli, with whom he is often confounded both in paintings and drawings, is, however, represented by an " Annunciation "—a work of his later period (Room VIII., No. 1057).

In treating of the Tuscan masters, I had almost omitted to mention one of their greatest representatives—Giotto da Bondone. According to the catalogue, there are three interesting pictures by him in Cabinet XVIII. (Nos. 981, 982, and 983). They belonged to a series which, according to Vasari, Giotto painted as panels for the presses in the sacristy of S. Croce at Florence. Most of them are in

[1] [Another picture formerly attributed to Fra Bartolommeo, to which Signor Morelli refers, has now been removed from the gallery.]

[2] There are no works by Fra Bartolommeo in the public galleries at Berlin, Dresden, or Madrid, nor in the English National Gallery. There are three, however, in the Louvre: the "Annunciation," No. 1153; a "Holy Family," No. 1154; and the "Noli me tangere," No. 1115, an excellent work, falsely ascribed to Albertinelli (†). In the public gallery at Vienna there is both a genuine work by the master and one of his school.

the Academy at Florence, two are said to be in the Berlin gallery, and the remaining three are those just mentioned at Munich, which represent the "Crucifixion," "Descent into Hades," and the "Last Supper." Baron Rumohr thought that these pictures, like those in Florence, were executed by Giotto himself. Messrs. Crowe and Cavalcaselle (i. 342) consider the "Last Supper" to be merely a work of his school: respecting the other two, they unfortunately express no opinion, but mention them only in a general way as damaged works. They appear to me to be by some good pupil of Giotto—the "Crucifixion" being especially careful in execution, and nearly approaching the master himself. In order to become thoroughly acquainted with this gifted artist, he should be studied in the frescoes of the Arena Chapel at Padua, in those of the Lower Church at Assisi, of the Capella Peruzzi in S. Croce at Florence, and in the large Madonna of the Florence Academy.

The fourth work, ascribed to Giotto in the old catalogue, is a male portrait in Cabinet XVII. (No. 996). The name—FRANCISCVS BRACIVS—inscribed on the upper part of the picture, is of a character which points to the seventeenth century. In the new catalogue, though no longer ascribed to Giotto, this absurd portrait is still, to my surprise, attributed to a Florentine painter of the fifteenth century. Leaving the modelling of the head and of the hands altogether out of the question, the heavy quality of the oil painting should alone have proved that this is impossible. I am as fully convinced as formerly that it is not the work of an Italian, but of some inferior Flemish or German painter. Many such botches by northern hands, which were once regarded as Italian works, as, for example, Nos. 166, 191, 334, 1041, 1042, the "St. Cecilia," and the so-called "Portrait of Giovanni Bellini by himself," have, at my suggestion, been either removed to Schleissheim or transferred to suitable cells in other parts of the Munich gallery. I venture to hope, therefore, that before long a like fate may befall this wretched Franciscus Bracius. He certainly has no part nor lot with the Florentines (†). The "Miracle of St. Anthony" in Cabinet XVII. (No. 1022), which is catalogued as 'unknown,' is a modern copy of a picture by the Sienese Francesco di Giorgio, and is nothing more nor less than an imposture. Messrs. Crowe and Cavalcaselle [1] regard it as an original by that painter, but a closer study of it will, I think, convince them that it is what I have described it to be. The drawing of the hands and of some of the heads is extremely careless, the treatment of the architecture is defective, and the blue of the sky looks suspiciously fresh. Francesco di Giorgio, as we see him in his small pictures in the Palazzo Pubblico at Siena and in his predella in the Uffizi (No. 1304), is an artist of a very different stamp. Dr. Bode, indeed (ii. 589), would ascribe the last-named picture to another Sienese—Neroccio Landi. I have, however, proved on former occasions that the Berlin critic, in his well-meant efforts to rename Italian pictures, has not been so successful as in his reattributions of German and Dutch paintings.

Dr. Marggraff observed of the four small pictures in *grisaille* in Cabinet XIX. (Nos. 1067, 1068, 1069, 1070, and 1071) that they were Andrea del Sarto's original sketches in oil for some of the frescoes in the cloister of the Scalzo at Florence. Had he not repeated the statement in the revised edition of his catalogue I should not have thought it necessary to mention that, like the sketches presented by Professor Santarelli, the sculptor, to the Uffizi, they are late copies from the frescoes. The present director of the Munich gallery has now accepted them as

[1] They first speak of this picture as by 'a weak imitator of Pesellino' (i. 548); later, however, they assign it to Francesco di Giorgio (iii. 68).

such. The collection can boast of no original work by Andrea del Sarto. According to the new catalogue, his hand may still be traced in the "Holy Family," No. 1066, Room VIII. This may originally have been the case, but the picture, in its present deplorable condition, cannot give us the slightest idea of the great Florentine's art, and I should certainly advise the director to have it banished to Schleissheim. As we are not able to study this attractive painter at Munich, I will avail myself of this opportunity to name a few characteristic drawings by him. Like those of the great Venetian colourists—Titian, Bonifazio I., Tintoretto, and Paul Veronese—many of Andrea del Sarto's finest chalk drawings aim primarily at pictorial effect, yet at the same time the proportions are so faultless, the lines are so flowing and full of grace, that his drawings afford me more pleasure than those of any other Italian master, with the sole exception of Leonardo. He is represented in the Louvre by six typical examples. In the Uffizi at Florence are also a number of his drawings, including some admirable specimens.

THE UMBRIANS.

In conclusion, we have still to examine the works of the Umbrian school in the Munich gallery, or, more correctly speaking, those of the school of Perugino. The Madonna in Room VIII. (No. 1036) strikes us at once as a work of this master, though the late Dr. Marggraff seemed disposed to cast doubts upon its genuineness. It is a feeble picture, and much overcleaned; but none acquainted with the later works of this very unequal painter will deny that the forms and characters peculiar to him are as apparent in it

as in the other two which are attributed to him in this
room (Nos. 1034 and 1035).[1]   And inasmuch as my view
of these three works by Perugino coincides with that of
Messrs. Crowe and Cavalcaselle and of the present
director, I may congratulate myself on being this time at
least in accord with the most reputed art authorities.

Once more, I entirely agree with Dr. Marggraff with
regard to Perugino's beautiful picture, No. 1034.   It is an
admirable work, and, with the exception of some injuries,
due to overcleaning, is well preserved.   It represents the
Madonna, attended by two angels, appearing to St. Bernard,
who is seated at a desk in an open colonnade.   Behind him
are SS. Bartholomew and John the Evangelist.   Vasari
erroneously ascribed this picture to Raffaellino del Garbo.[2]
The mistake was probably accidental, but his Florentine
commentators, in consequence, at once denied Perugino's
authorship, and attributed it, with their author, to Raffael-
lino.   Such a method of proceeding is not allowable in
dealing with the history of art, and only writers who
give their opinion of things they have never seen could
have fallen into such absurd mistakes.

Raffaellino certainly treated this subject, for a good draw-
ing by him, washed in colour and heightened with white,
is in the British Museum.[3]   It represents the Madonna,
attended by two angels, appearing to St. Bernard, who is
seated at a desk.   But whether the master ever painted a
picture from this drawing, and whether it be still in existence,
I am unable to say.   This subject, however, was first treated
by Fra Filippo Lippi, as is shown by a picture in the
English National Gallery.   Later, Filippino made use of

---

[1] This picture represents the
Madonna adoring the Infant Saviour,
who lies on the ground between SS.
John the Evangelist and Nicholas.

[2] (Ed. Le Monnier, vii. 193; ed.
Milanesi, iv. 237.)

[3] Photographed by Braun (No. 28),
under the name of Filippino Lippi.

his father's idea, and produced the splendid work in the Badia at Florence, which is one of the masterpieces of Florentine art. This picture, in turn, must have inspired Fra Bartolommeo's "Vision of St. Bernard," now in the Florence Academy.[1] Messrs. Crowe and Cavalcaselle (iii. 255) of course accept the Munich picture as the work of Perugino, though they consider that it was probably copied [2] from the painting which Vasari describes as by Raffaellino del Garbo. As though all Vasari's statements were to be accepted without question!

No. 1035 of the Munich gallery is a late and feeble work by Perugino, superficial alike in conception, drawing, and execution. The catalogue speaks of Perugino unconditionally as the pupil of Verrocchio. This is, I think, a mistake. In all probability he was first trained at Perugia under Fiorenzo di Lorenzo, and then at Arezzo under Piero della Francesca. He was already a finished artist when he went to Florence soon after 1470.[3] The "Tondo," in the Salon Carré of the Louvre (No. 1564), clearly recalls Fiorenzo di Lorenzo; while in the large altar-piece in the Church of the Calza at Florence, and in the "Pietà" in the Academy in that city, the influence of Signorelli is apparent; but in none of his early works is the influence of Verrocchio discernible (†).

We now come to the two predellas in Cabinet XIX. (Nos. 1037 and 1038), which have attracted so much attention among German, Italian, and English art-critics.

[1] Two drawings for this subject —referred to by Vasari's commentators—are in the Uffizi. One is ascribed to Perugino, but appears to me to be a copy. The other (Case 436) is attributed to Raffaellino del Garbo, but is, I think, only another copy of Perugino's picture.

[2] 'There is a copy of this vision of St. Bernard in S. Spirito at Florence, the original being given by Vasari to Raffaellino del Garbo.'

[3] See Vasari, iv. 23 (ed. Milanesi, ii. 500) in the *Life of Piero della Francesca.*

The late Baron Rumohr, one of the greatest German authorities on Italian painting, considered them to be early works of Raphael.   Messrs. Crowe and Cavalcaselle pronounced them to be by Perugino; while Passavant, another Raphael connoisseur, ascribed them only to the school of Perugino (ii. 823).   I, of course, make no claim to be considered an authority, but it seemed to me, ten years ago, that they were by the hand of Giovanni Spagna, from drawings by his master, Perugino.   On seeing them again, however, I had the rare satisfaction of being able to confess myself a convert to the view of Messrs. Crowe and Cavalcaselle, and consequently of the present director of the gallery.

Let us now pass on to the pictures bearing the name of Raphael.   One in Cabinet XIX. (No. 1078) is the portrait of a youth with a swollen nose, wearing a black cap. His costume (and possibly, too, his large nose) led Herr Passavant, the great Raphael connoisseur, to infer that this young man must have belonged to a patrician family of Florence.   Hence he concluded that Raphael painted the portrait during his first sojourn in that city.   Other connoisseurs—for instance, Ignatius Hugford, an English artist, and Raphael Mengs, the celebrated Saxon painter and art-critic—pronounced it to be genuine, and, to crown all, it is signed

'RAPHAELLO (*sic*) VRBINAS. FEC.'

Whether, before being restored, this picture could lay claim to so distinguished a parentage, I am unable to say. In its present condition it certainly shows not a trace of Raphael's hand.

The signature is undoubtedly forged. This Dr. Marggraff admitted, and, on the whole, his opinion of this feeble portrait coincided with my own.   It has certainly no connection with Lorenzo Costa—which is the view expressed in the new catalogue—but is an Umbrian production.   The

statement that it is by the same hand as the so-called
Raphael at Hampton Court (No. 70) is, I think, very un-
likely. Then, as now, inferior painters were plentiful
enough, and as far as mediocrity goes, the Hampton Court
portrait is a worthy pendant to the one in Munich.

Another so-called Raphael in Cabinet XVIII. (No. 1053)
appears to me of very doubtful authenticity. It is a head
of St. John painted in fresco upon a tile. Dr. Marggraff
was undecided, whether to ascribe it to Raphael or not.
Passavant [1] regarded it as one of the master's first attempts
in fresco, executed prior to his painting on the wall of
S. Severo at Perugia. The director is of the same opinion,
and ascribes it to Raphael. The theory would be plausible
enough if the painting itself testified to the hand of that
master. But, on examining this insignificant head more
closely, we are struck by the hard, ungraceful modelling of
the neck, by the awkward, tasteless treatment of the hair,
by the total absence, in short, of all Raphaelesque feeling.
Altogether the work seems to me extremely suspicious, and
I should not be surprised if this 'first attempt at fresco
painting by Raphael' proved after all to be a modern forgery.

In Cabinet XIX. is the world-renowned "Madonna de'
Tempi," once in the Casa Tempi at Florence. Passavant
considered that it was painted in 1506, and that it was con-
sequently of the same period as the "Madonna nel Prato,"
now at Vienna. It appears to me, however, to belong to
that earlier period of the young master's career during which
he produced the "Madonna del Granduca," now in the
Pitti. It was certainly painted some time before the
"Madonna nel Prato," the "Madonna del Cardellino," and
the "Madonna" belonging to Lord Cowper. For many
years, when in the Casa Tempi, it was altogether forgotten,
and the injury it afterwards sustained through unskilful

[1] i. 72.

restoration has nearly deprived it of all its charm. The landscape background has been much overcleaned ; the mouth of the Madonna has been so disfigured that she looks as though she were suffering from toothache, the left eyelid is damaged, and the original outlines of the brow and of the nose are lost. The left arm of the Infant Saviour has also suffered, but his head, with the exception of the contour of the left cheek, is well preserved. The hands resemble those of the " Madonna del Granduca " in the modelling, but have also been much damaged by the restorer. Yet, notwithstanding its bad state of preservation, the "Madonna de' Tempi " is, in my opinion, the most Raphaelesque of all the works ascribed to the master at Munich. The cartoon for this picture—a black chalk drawing on green paper heightened with white—is in the Musée Fabre at Montpellier, but in such a deplorable condition that it is now of little value.

On the opposite wall is the " Madonna della Tenda " (No. 1051), so-called on account of the green curtain forming the background, which has also been cruelly treated by iconoclasts and picture-restorers. It represents the Madonna in profile. Her right arm is round the Infant Saviour, who is seated on her knee, while her left hand rests tenderly on the neck of the little St. John, who stands by with his cross. The picture is in reality nothing more than a modified version of the " Madonna della Seggiola " in the Pitti, and shows the manner of Giulio Romano, especially in the heavy upper lip of the Madonna and of St. John. It should be compared with the " Madonna della Catina " by Giulio Romano in the Dresden gallery, in which the same characteristic treatment of the upper lip may be observed. The form of the Madonna's ear also differs from that in Raphael's genuine works. An old copy of this " Madonna della Tenda " is in the Turin gallery, where it passes for a Raphael.

In order to study the other two pictures ascribed to Raphael, we must return to Room VIII. One (No. 1049) is known as the " Madonna di Casa Canigiani " at Florence. Passavant considered that it was executed in 1506. Raphael was at that time in Florence, engaged in preparing the cartoon for the " Entombment," a picture [1] which he executed for Atalanta Baglioni of Perugia. The Madonna just mentioned, the " Entombment," and the small " Holy Family " in the Madrid gallery, all belong, therefore, to the same period—1506 to 1507. Before the Munich picture was unfortunately cleaned and repainted, the date (1506) was said to have been legible on the hem of the Madonna's robe, where the painter's signature is still preserved. The original drawing for this picture I believe to be in the Albertina (†), and not, as stated in the catalogue, in the collection of the Duc d'Aumale. There are several other copies of this study, of unequal merit, at Oxford and at Windsor. Passavant rightly observed that the drawing of the picture most recalled that of the " Entombment," though both drawing and modelling appear to me much weaker than in the celebrated work in the Borghese gallery. An old copy of the Munich Madonna is in the sacristy of S. Frediano at Florence, and another is in the Corsini gallery. [2] The hard and lifeless drawing of the last-named copy, and the treatment of the landscape, prove that it is the work of a Fleming. In the catalogue of the Corsini collection, compiled by Signor Milanesi, one of the commentators of Le Monnier's ' Vasari,' the Flemish copy is extolled as the original, while the original is cited as a copy.

The " Madonna di Casa Canigiani " at Munich has been so entirely disfigured by restoration that one is almost inclined at first to doubt its authenticity. A closer examina-

---

[1] Now in the Borghese gallery at Rome.

[2] This picture now belongs to the heirs of the Marchese Rinuccini.

tion of the forms, however, proves that the work has not only been designed by Raphael, but in part also painted by him. It must, therefore, be classed with those works which were executed with the help of assistants, such as the "Entombment," the " Madonna di Casa Colonna " at Berlin, the " Madonna Nicolini " in Lord Cowper's collection, and others. The colours have lost all brightness and transparency, and many parts have been so defaced and overcleaned that it is almost impossible to discern in it the hand, and still less the spirit, of the master. Those portions which have suffered most severely are the body of the Infant Saviour, the feet, the right arm, the hair of St. John, and the hand of St. Anne, which, more especially in the thumb, is wholly un-Raphaelesque in modelling. Her right foot is out of drawing, so, too, are the feet of St. Joseph. The part which most recalls the feeling and the character of the master is the head of the Infant Saviour. The picture was brought to Germany by Anna Maria de' Medici, who had received it as a bridal gift from her father, the Grand Duke Cosimo III.[1]

There is yet one other picture to mention which bears the name of Raphael in this room (No. 1052)—the celebrated portrait, so-called, of Bindo Altoviti of Florence. Vasari mentions it in the following terms: ' ed a Bindo Altoviti fece il ritratto suo, quando era giovine, che è tenuto stupendissimo' (' and for Bindo Altoviti he painted his portrait when he was young, which is held to be very fine '). From this it is evident that Vasari had not seen the picture himself. Let us first see what more recent writers on Raphael have to say about it. Baron Rumohr[2] devotes some space to it, and pronounces it to be Raphael's por-

---

[1] The picture has not long since been carefully restored, and has gained much by the process.

[2] *Italienische Forschungen*, iii. 109.

trait of himself, and one of his best works. His opponent, Missiri, regarded it as the portrait of Altoviti, and, referring to this, Rumohr observes : 'Had it been the portrait of Bindo, Vasari would have said, "il ritratto di lui," and not "suo," as, in Italian, the possessive always refers to the subject of the sentence.'

The criticisms of this gifted writer usually met with the unqualified approval of most of his contemporaries in Germany, and they accepted his grammatical interpretation of this passage without question. Now I myself have the greatest respect for learning. In this particular instance, however, I cannot help thinking that the German critic would have acted more discreetly had he not taken upon himself to instruct the Tuscan Missiri in the grammar of his mother-tongue. Vasari expressed himself exactly as every Tuscan would do in ordinary conversation. Had he meant Raphael, and not Bindo, by this ' suo,' he would probably have said ' suo proprio.' He uses the same form in other cases. Thus, in the ' Life of Titian,' [1] he says : 'Dopo in casa di M. Giovanni d' Anna gentiluomo e mercante fiammingo, suo compare, fece il suo ritratto, che par vivo ;' and in another place : ' E l' anno che fù creato doge Andrea Gritti, fece Tiziano il suo ritratto, che fù cosa rarissima.

Passavant, another writer on Raphael of great renown, affirms that it could not have been painted before 1512, and that it represents a young man of about twenty-two. As Bindo Altoviti was born on September 26, 1490, he was exactly twenty-two in 1512, and Passavant therefore inferred that this must be his portrait. He also extols the excellent preservation of the painting. I must beg all students of art who have been in Rome to compare it with the admirable portrait of the donor in the so-called

[1] xiii. 20, 27 (ed. Milanesi, vii. 429, 437).

" Madonna di Foligno." According to Passavant,[1] Raphael executed this picture for Sigismondo Conti between 1511 and 1512. The breadth and fulness of touch in the portrait of Conti are of a very different quality to the cold conventionality of the technic in the picture at Munich. There is no proof that the youth there represented is only twenty-two ; it is as likely that he had already attained the age of twenty-five or twenty-six. This is of little importance. A more interesting question to solve is, whether it be really by Raphael or only an old copy of some merit. Ten years ago I observed that the over-smooth violet-red tone of colouring in the face seemed to indicate the touch of a picture-restorer of the last century, and certainly did not recall Giorgione, as some critics considered. Since then the picture has been carefully cleaned, and these violet-red flesh-tints—which mainly, I fear, induced several critics to regard it as one of Raphael's finest works—have disappeared. Dr. Bayersdorffer, the inspector of the gallery, has ascribed the portrait to Giulio Romano, but I think erroneously. The touch is not that of the school of Raphael, and neither the form of the ear nor the treatment of the hair and of the eyebrows resembles the manner of Raphael or of his pupils. Either I have made a great mistake, or all former critics have been deceived in this portrait ; which latter contingency, though of course not very probable, is still within the range of possibility.

In the preceding pages I have been often forced to dispute universally accepted opinions, and my readers have, I doubt not, grown weary of the process. I must confess that the task was far from pleasant to myself, for it is infinitely more agreeable, especially at my age, to live at peace with all the world, instead of placing stones in the pathway of common opinion, and so checking it in the traditional security of its march.

[1] ii. 111.

ORIGINAL DRAWINGS BY ITALIAN MASTERS
IN THE PRINT ROOM.

The celebrated collection of drawings and engravings in the Munich gallery is arranged in several rooms on the ground floor. With the exception of the Albertina at Vienna, no other German collection can show so many good drawings by Italian masters. I shall confine myself to mentioning those which appeared to me to be genuine. I should have preferred to have followed the same plan which I adopted in speaking of the pictures; that is, to have mentioned them according to their schools. The drawings are, however, distributed through sixteen volumes without system, method, or classification, and on reflection it appeared to me that I should add greatly to the difficulties of those who might desire to verify my attributions if I obliged them to turn continually from one volume to another. I am now speaking of things as I found them ten years ago. It is possible that a more systematic arrangement has now been adopted, but I was unable, during my recent short visit to Munich, to examine the collection again.

The following are the drawings of importance which I found this time exhibited in the ante-room leading to the department of prints and drawings:—

Raphael: two drawings on one sheet representing a bishop with uplifted hands looking upwards—a study for the "Disputa"—and on the reverse, a kneeling youth with folded hands also looking up. Both were executed by Raphael in charcoal, but have been worked over with the pen, apparently by a later hand, and disfigured. In their present condition they have almost lost all value.

Fra Bartolommeo: two excellent drawings in charcoal, representing the heads of two monks.

Domenico Campagnola (†): a good pen drawing, representing a landscape, such as he usually treated. It was ascribed to Titian, and numbered 4148.

To my great satisfaction I noticed that the historical drawing for the equestrian statue of Francesco Sforza has now been ascribed to its true author, Antonio del Pollaiuolo (†). This most interesting study would be more advantageously seen if placed where a drawing wrongly attributed to Paul Veronese now hangs. Students of art would then be enabled to examine it more closely.

The drawings ascribed in this room to Domenico del Ghirlandaio, Michelangelo, Leonardo da Vinci, and Titian appear to me of doubtful authenticity. The German masters, on the other hand, are well represented.

Of the many more or less interesting drawings by Italian masters of the fifteenth century, which are to be found in this Munich collection, I will only mention the most important.

Ten years ago Volume 50 contained the following: A sheet with studies for machinery, by Leonardo da Vinci, accompanied by a written explanation. Drawn with the pen, the shading being from left to right. Drawing by Mantegna, in pen and wash, "Christ between SS. Andrew and Longinus," with the inscription: 'Pio et Immortali Deo.' Probably this was the drawing for the well-known engraving of that subject. A *grisaille* drawing on canvas, representing Mucius Scaevola, also appeared to me to be by Mantegna, while a study in pen and ink for the figure of an Apostle, likewise attributed to the master, seemed to me by Liberale da Verona (†).

A sheet with studies of the different proportions of one of the bronze horses of St. Mark's at Venice was ascribed to Verrocchio. It is difficult to say whether they are by him, by Leopardi, or by some other sculptor of that date.

The same must be said of the study of a horse in the
Louvre, which is also attributed to Verrocchio. A pen and
wash drawing, representing David about to cut off the head
of Goliath, passes under the name of Titian. It appeared
to me to be by Carpaccio (†). Lastly, I may mention an
excellent drawing by Domenico Ghirlandaio. The subject
appeared to represent a baptism (?) in a temple with
several spectators.

Volume 51. Among these drawings I was fortunate
enough to discover an admirable example, washed with
water-colour, by Sodoma, which was there ascribed to
Maturino. It represented Diana, surrounded by her com-
panions, and chasing into the forest a satyr and his nume-
rous family. It is one of Sodoma's finest drawings (†).
On the other hand, the " Assumption of the Magdalen," a
washed drawing by the same master, is unpleasing owing
to excessive restoration.

Volume 52 contains about twenty good and genuine
drawings by Fra Bartolommeo, among them some very
fine examples. With the exception of the Uffizi, Munich
possesses more drawings by this master than any other
collection in the world. Among them I discovered one by
Bartolommeo Montagna (†), the Madonna with outstretched
arms between two angels, a washed drawing on blue paper.

As the drawings of this latter severe and noble master
are not sufficiently appreciated, and are, moreover, rarely
met with either in public or private collections, I will take
this opportunity of directing attention to a few of them.

At Lille, a " Madonna and Child," attributed to Giovanni
Bellini; a drawing washed with water-colour and heightened
with white (Braun, 12) (†).

At Oxford, in the Library at Christ Church, the head
of the Madonna in black chalk. This drawing by Mon-
tagna (†) is ascribed by Sir J. C. Robinson to Francia.

At Windsor,[1] a seated figure of the " Salvator Mundi,"
and a head of the Madonna, both in black chalk (†).

At Cassel, in the choice collection of Herr Edward
Habich, there is a black chalk drawing by Montagna. It
is the study for his picture in the Louvre, representing the
" Ecce Homo " (No. 1393).[2]

In order not to try the patience of my readers too
severely, I will now bring this notice to a close, though
there are other drawings in this collection deserving of
attention. It is most desirable to study the painters in
their sketches and drawings, and those who neglect to do
so can form but a very inadequate idea of the character of
each master. This study, however, can only benefit those
who have already attained to a certain proficiency in the
knowledge of pictures ; for drawings are a snare to a mere
beginner in art-criticism, and would both perplex and
mislead him. *Exempla sunt odiosa.*

[1] *Old Masters*, vol. iii.

[2] See *Drawings by the Old Masters in the Habich Collection at Cassel*, edited by Dr. O. Eisenmann, director of the Royal gallery at Cassel (Lieferung 1, Lübeck, Nöhring, 1890).

THE DRESDEN GALLERY.

PREFACE.

THE post of director of the Dresden gallery, formerly occupied by Professor Hübner, is now held by Dr. Karl Woermann, a gentleman who is much respected in his own country and has rendered good services as an art-historian. In a comparatively short space of time he has achieved many radical reforms, not only in the arrangement but more especially in the attribution of the pictures. The new catalogue, which he has issued and practically re-written, challenges comparison with the best and most recent works of the kind. Indeed, as regards its general plan, it surpasses the majority of these publications. Dr. Woermann aims at an historical and chronological classification, and, instead of following the alphabetical order usually adopted, has compiled his catalogue upon logical and scientific principles.

He has accomplished the difficult task of arranging the pictures in a manner which cannot fail to meet with the approval of all intelligent students of art. The large altar-pieces, of which there are an unusual number in this collection, have been hung in those rooms which are lighted from above ; the small easel pictures, on the other hand, have found a place in the cabinets, where the light, falling upon them from the side, enables the spectator to see them to the best advantage.

Unlike some of his colleagues, who consider themselves infallible in their intimate acquaintance with every school of painting, Dr. Woermann is not above listening to the opinions expressed by other critics. In the interests of the gallery with which he is connected, he has travelled far and wide, and has spared neither time nor expense in order to test, by comparative study, the value of many attributions proposed by art-critics for the pictures in the Dresden gallery. With this end in view he has not only visited all the collections in Germany and the Netherlands, but those in Italy also, and has subjected them anew to a critical examination. To my great satisfaction, Dr. Woermann has now, after an exhaustive study of the subject, publicly expressed his conviction that the changes proposed by me in the naming of the pictures are, for the most part, worthy of acceptance. In thus setting aside all prejudice and personal considerations, and making himself responsible for these opinions, the director of the Dresden gallery has shown himself to be a man of liberal and impartial judgment, and animated by a true and unselfish zeal for his subject.

If I am not mistaken, he has accepted forty-six out of fifty-six of my suggestions. Of the remaining ten, he has reserved a part for further consideration, and the rest he has rejected. Unprejudiced observers might be led to infer from this that either Lermolieff was wiser than other students of art, or that the method pursued by him was superior to theirs. The first assumption would, of course, be ridiculous on my part, and in this even my bitterest opponents will agree with me. We are, therefore, driven to the conclusion that these highly satisfactory results are due to the experimental method, which at present is still regarded by many with suspicion.

This conviction has emboldened me to express my

opinion about some of the pictures in the Dresden gallery for the second time. I hope on this occasion to be able to correct some mistakes which I committed ten years ago, for my motto is, and ever will be, ' One day telleth another.'

INTRODUCTORY.

The Dresden gallery, a collection unequalled in its way, owes its existence, in a great measure, to Augustus III. and his eccentric minister, Count Brühl, who were both enthusiastic patrons of art, and employed a number of competent connoisseurs to select pictures for it. The late Dr. Hübner, in his introduction to the catalogue, has left us a pleasant and interesting account of its gradual rise and development.

The great additions made to the collection by the purchase of a hundred of the finest pictures from the gallery at Modena,[1] and by the almost simultaneous acquisition of Raphael's Sistine Madonna from Piacenza and of Holbein's Madonna from the Casa Dolfin at Venice, established the reputation of the gallery. It soon came to be regarded not only as the most magnificent in Germany, but, with the exception of the Louvre, as the richest in the world. It will not be unprofitable, I think, to examine these pictures critically, to classify them chronologically according to their schools, and to compare them with those in other collections—a method of study which will enable us to form a right estimate of their value.

[1] The deed of sale for these pictures was signed at Ferrara on September 17, 1745. (See *Notizie di sei dipinti ad olio di Antonio Consetti Modenese, posseduti e de-* *scritti dal conte Giovanni Francesco Ferrari-Moreni,* Modena, Soldani, 1858, p. 13 ; and also *La Galleria Estense di Francesco I.,* by Cavaliere A. Venturi.)

The gallery at Modena, to which the Dresden collection owes some of its finest pictures, had been only formed by degrees. The works of Titian, Paul Veronese, Dosso, and Garofalo, which it contained, were transferred from Ferrara to Modena by Cesare d'Este in 1598 and 1599. The most important paintings, however, such as the four altar-pieces by Correggio, were carried off by force or by fraud from the churches for which they were painted by Duke Francis I. d'Este, in order to adorn his palace at Modena; for in the last century all the petty princes of Europe sought to emulate Louis XIV., the *Grand Monarque* so-called, in his taste for lavish display, and each one of them sought to possess, not only a Versailles but a Louvre of his own. The collection at Modena was composed principally of works of the schools in its more immediate neighbourhood, such as those of Ferrara-Bologna, Parma, and Venice. We will, therefore, begin our critical studies in the Dresden gallery with the Ferrarese and Venetian schools.

THE FERRARESE SCHOOL.

Among all the inhabitants of the former province of the Emilia, the district lying between the Po, the Apennines, and the Marecchia, none were so richly endowed with artistic gifts as the Ferrarese. In this respect they may rank, as Messrs. Crowe and Cavalcaselle very justly observe, with the Veronese. Yet while we can trace, in works that have been preserved, the development of this latter school from the beginning of the fourteenth century to the end of the sixteenth, we know absolutely nothing of the earlier history of that of Ferrara. The names of the artists of that period have indeed come down to us, but all their works have perished.[1] We are, therefore, forced to pass over the 'heroic' or 'Giottesque' period of this school, and to begin our studies with the epoch of 'character,' that is, the period when it was the principal aim of art to seize and represent the outward appearance of persons and things determined by inward and moral conditions. The principal representatives of this epoch in the school of Ferrara were: Cosimo Tura, Francesco del Cossa, and Ercole Roberti. These three important and characteristic painters may be said to occupy the same position in this school as did Piero della Francesca and his pupil Luca Signorelli in the Umbrian; Andrea del Castagno, Fra Filippo, Antonio del Pollaiuolo, and Sandro Botticelli in the Florentine; the Vivarini in the Venetian; Mantegna, Crivelli, Dario, and Girolamo da Treviso in the Paduan; Liberale, Domenico Morone, and Bonsignori in the Veronese; and Vincenzo Foppa in the Lombard.

Art-historians are wont to speak of this epoch of art in North Italy as the 'Mantegnesque;' the term is sufficiently appropriate if it be taken to signify that Mantegna was the greatest representative of art at that date. If, however, it

[1] There do not appear to have been any artists of importance at Ferrara even in the beginning of the fifteenth century. Otherwise Byzantine painters, such as Giorgias of Constantinople, would scarcely have found occupation there. (See, with reference to this, *Notizie relative a Ferrara*, by L. N. Cittadella, 1864, p. 562.) This painter, Giorgias, appears to have learnt his art at Venice. A picture by him, on a gold ground, representing St. Mark, is in the Brera at Milan, and was probably brought there from Ferrara. All the painters who were employed at the Court of Ferrara in the first half of the fifteenth century came from other parts of Italy; for instance, Pisanello, Jacopo Bellini, a certain Andrea of Padua, an Angelo da Foligno, a Daniele Agresti, a Servadio of Verona, and a Jacopo da Soncino, called Sagramoso. The latter was working at Ferrara from 1419 to 1457. (See *I Pittori degli Estensi nel sec. XV°*, by Giuseppe Campori of Modena.) These last-named painters were of little importance, and must either have been dead or very old before 1455, the period when Tura and Cossa were at the commencement of their career.

be meant to imply that the painters of all the schools in the valley of the Po were directly influenced and guided by him, and became his imitators, I must resolutely protest against it as a shallow and superficial interpretation of the history of art.[1]   In order to understand the course of each

[1] The Veronese painters, Francesco Carotto, Bonsignori, and Giolfino, are frequently spoken of as imitators of Mantegna. With respect to Carotto, I am quite ready to admit that, after studying with Liberale, he went, as Vasari states, while still a youth, to Mantua, and was there influenced by Mantegna. The works which he produced at that period recall that master; for example, a small and unpleasing "Madonna" at Modena (No. 50) and another in the Staedel Institute at Frankfort (No. 145). If we compare these two pictures with an earlier "Madonna" by Carotto, in the Louvre (No. 1318, erroneously ascribed to Girolamo dai Libri), which he executed under the guidance of his master, Liberale, we cannot fail to see that, although when influenced by Mantegna he may have refined his earlier manner of painting, yet he never lost his distinctive Veronese character. On his return to his native city he soon abandoned the style of Mantegna, and gradually developed his own characteristic manner, which was thoroughly Veronese, and to which he adhered to the end of his life.

With regard to Bonsignori, I should advise all unprejudiced students to examine the works which he produced before he settled at Mantua in 1490, in the public gallery at Verona and in the Churches of S. Bernardino and S. Paolo in that city. They will, I think, agree with me that the influence of Aloise Vivarini and Liberale is apparent in them, but that they show no especial connection with Mantegna. Later, when Bonsignori settled at Mantua, he, no doubt, derived much from his great colleague Mantegna—nay, he even approached him so nearly that some of his portraits are ascribed to that master by inexperienced critics; for instance, in the public gallery at Bergamo, where Bonsignori's portrait of Vespasiano (?) Gonzaga (No. 154) is attributed to Mantegna (†). If I am not mistaken, the black chalk drawing for this portrait is in the depôt of the Uffizi. The same confusion occurred in the Sciarra-Colonna gallery in Rome, where a portrait of another Gonzaga (Lodovico ?) by Bonsignori actually bore the forged signature of Mantegna. It was dated 1504. Again, the works of Mantegna's personal friend, Niccolò Giolfino, in the Church of S. Anastasia and in the gallery at Verona, point, not to the influence of the great Paduan, but very decidedly to that of Liberale. It seems incredible that even Florentine painters, such as Pollaiuolo and Botticelli, should have been confounded with Mantegna. In the Duc d'Aumale's collection an allegorical figure representing "Plenty" —a feeble work of the school of Botticelli—was ascribed by Pietro Selvatico to Mantegna. He speaks of it as painted in the master's best manner, and representing one of the

different school of painting in Italy it is necessary to con-
sider it as an organic whole, which, like a living being,
passes through successive stages of development and decay.[1]
The Venetian school had the good fortune to be undisturbed
by foreign influences, and we may therefore trace its course
from the time of the Byzantines, so-called, down to Tiepolo
and Pietro Longhi.

On the other hand, it was not until the second half of
the fifteenth century that the school of Ferrara developed

Seasons (Vasari, v. 193, ed. Mila-
nesi, iii. 422). The same critic,
who enjoyed a considerable repu-
tation in his day in Italy, took
Cossa's "Annunciation," in the
Dresden gallery, for the work of
Mantegna, misled by the forged
signature of the latter master. The
same mistake occurs in the Staedel
Institute at Frankfort, where a pic-
ture by Cossa still passes for one by
Mantegna, on account of its spurious
cartellino. It has been a very com-
mon mistake, due to ignorance, to
ascribe to the greatest representa-
tives of one epoch of art a large
portion of the works produced
during that period. Hence to Man-
tegna, Perugino, Leonardo, and
others have been attributed the
most miscellaneous productions.
What has just been said proves, I
think, that, if the history of Italian
art is ever to be based on any solid
foundation, it must first be sub-
jected to a thorough and critical
revision.

[1] Technical methods may be im-
parted by one school to another, but
the conception and the feeling in a
work of art are inherent and vital
qualities belonging, like speech, to
each individual, to each nationality
and race. Thus Antonello da Messina,
though he learnt the Van Eycks'
system of painting with oil as a
vehicle from a Fleming, always re-
mained an Italian in his mode of
representation; and Dürer, though
he sojourned long in Venice, shows
his German nationality in every
stroke of his brush. I do not, of
course, deny that a Tuscan painter
may at times have influenced a
Lombard or a Lombard a Venetian,
and *vice versâ*; or, again, that
Italians have influenced some Flem-
ish painters, or that Dürer and Van
Eyck, the two great representatives
of art north of the Alps, have been
imitated by Italians. All this is
natural enough, and it would be
absurd to dispute it, but it does not
prove that the development of a
whole school of painting was at any
time interrupted or in the slightest
degree influenced by these accidents.
It appears to me that the principles
upon which the study of art is and
has been conducted ever since the
days of Vasari are radically wrong,
and calculated to impede any real
progress in this line. I have reverted
to this fact several times, as I think
it desirable to warn students against
teaching so misleading.

its peculiar and vigorous character.[1] The Ferrarese were much influenced by the learned school which Squarcione had founded at Padua in 1430. But they must also have received an impulse to develop their art along similar severe and scholarly lines from Piero della Francesca of Borgo S. Sepolcro, the great master of perspective, who had worked for some time in their city. Roger van der Weyden was also employed by the House of Este in 1451, but there is nothing to justify the view of Messrs. Crowe and Cavalcaselle that this painter influenced Galasso Galassi, Tura, and Cossa. It appears to me as untenable as their theory that Lorenzo Costa and the younger Ercole Grandi were influenced by the painters of Perugia.[2]

Art, as already observed, is a living organism exercising its faculties within given limits and regulating its development by stated laws. Unfortunately this fact is constantly

[1] In the public gallery at Ferrara there is a panel representing the Trinity, signed 'G. G.,' and dating from the first half of the fifteenth century. If this coarse picture be the work of Galasso Galassi, to whom it is there ascribed, there must have been two Ferrarese painters of that name—the one just mentioned, who, according to Vasari, painted the frescoes in the Church of Mezzaratta, near Bologna, about 1404, and a younger painter, who was born, according to Vasari, about 1438. To this artist are ascribed two panels in one of the Churches of S. Stefano at Bologna. They represent SS. Peter and John the Baptist, and on one are the letters G. G. To this painter might be ascribed a " St. Apollonia " in the gallery at Bologna, which Messrs. Crowe and Cavalcaselle (i. 349, 4) agree with the director of that collection in attributing to Marco Zoppo. I may here mention another Ferrarese painter of this period, Antonio Alberti of Ferrara, the grandfather of Timoteo Viti. He was for many years at Urbino, and painted there, in 1439, a large altar-piece for the Church of S. Bernardino. It is now in the Academy of Fine Arts in that town. Vasari, for no apparent reason, speaks of Alberti as a pupil of Angelo Gaddi. As a painter he is not altogether without character, and might rank in the artistic scale between the Venetians Jacomello de Flor and Antonio Vivarini.

[2] This absurd theory of 'influences' is in reality a mere delusion, though it may have an outward show of learning. Where, let me ask Messrs. Crowe and Cavalcaselle, have they ever seen authentic works by Galasso Galassi the younger which might have led them to conclude that this painter was influenced by Roger van der Weyden?

overlooked, and the art of painting is regarded as a mere outward and accidental manifestation, standing in no relation to the distinctive character of the people among whom it flourishes. Yet a more careful study of those schools in which art-historians affirm that they can trace the influence of Flemish painters and of Umbrian, Florentine, or other masters, will prove that they ever preserved their essentially local character.

Many Italian painters besides Antonello da Messina no doubt learnt the method of oil painting employed by the Van Eycks from Flemings sojourning in Italy; this I am quite ready to admit, and such was also the case in Germany. Again, it is highly probable that Italian painters copied and sought to imitate the works of Jan Van Eyck, Hugo van der Goes, and Hans Memling, for the works of these masters were highly prized by all patrons of art in Italy. But this hardly appears to me to justify the view of Baron Rumohr, that the Flemings taught the Italians naturalism or realism, a theory totally without foundation. In Italy, as in Germany and the Netherlands, it was the development of art itself which involuntarily led to a closer study of nature.[1]

Let us now return to the Ferrarese. The more important masters of the second half of the fifteenth century were Cosimo

[1] Vasari, in the *Life of Paolo Uccello* (iii. 92, ed. Milanesi, ii. 209), writes as follows: 'Ma fù bene assai che Paolo con l' ordine della prospettiva gli andò diminuendo e ritraendo (i paesi) come stanno quivi appunto, facendovi tutto quel che vedeva, cioè campi, arati, fossati, ed altre minuzie della natura,' etc. And in the *Life of Alesso Baldovinetti* (iv. 104; ii. 595): ' E di tutte le minuzie, che la madre natura sa fare, si sforzò d' essere imitatore. Dilettossi molto di far paesi, ritraendoli dal vivo e naturale, come stanno appunto' ('Paolo continued to draw and to represent the landscapes admirably, according to the laws of perspective, and to delineate everything as he saw it; that is to say, fields, ditches, trenches, and other details of nature '). (' And he [Baldovinetti] set himself to imitate every detail as it is produced by nature. He took pleasure in representing landscapes from nature, and in depicting them exactly as they are in reality.')

Tura, known as Cosmé,[1] a hard, dry, and angular painter, but often very impressive; Francesco Cossa, serious with an occasional tendency to moroseness in feeling akin to Tura, though never so grotesque; Ercole Roberti, few of whose works have been preserved; Ercole Grandi di Giulio Cesare, Francesco Bianchi, known at Modena as Frarè, Coltellini, Domenico Panetti, and Lorenzo Costa.

This group of painters after a time separated into two divisions, one remaining at Ferrara with Tura, Panetti, and Coltellini; the other, with Cossa, Ercole Roberti, and Lorenzo Costa, migrating to Bologna at the instance of the Bentivogli, worked there for the greater part of their lives. Francesco Bianchi settled at Modena between 1480 and 1490. Francesco Cossa went to Bologna as early as 1470, Lorenzo Costa about 1483.[2]

[1] In 1458, Tura was appointed to he post of Court painter to the Duke Borso, and was employed to complete the frescoes in the castle of Belfiore, which had been begun by Angelo da Siena. According to a document published by Signor Alfredo Venturi, Tura was in bad circumstances in 1490 and in ill-health. In addition to his other misfortunes, he had debtors who refused to pay him.

[2] As early as 1456, Francesco Cossa is mentioned as a painter in connection with works which he executed with his father for the cathedral at Ferrara (see *Cittadella*, *op. cit.* p. 78). On March 25, 1470, after he had completed three of the principal frescoes in the hall of the Schifanoia palace, he addressed a letter to Duke Borso, which has been published by Signor Venturi. From this letter it appears that Cossa had been placed on the same level as the other painters employed in the palace, which caused him great mortification, as he believed himself to have already won some repute as an artist. Towards the close of this year (1470) he must have left Ferrara for Bologna. In 1472 he painted the "Madonna del Baracano," which is now entirely ruined. This noble master then, and his colleague Ercole Roberti, were the true founders of the early school of Bologna, and not Marco Zoppo, the pupil of Squarcione, whom local writers represent as the disciple of Lippo Dalmasii, and the master of Francesco Francia. An estimate of the art of the Bolognese in the first half of the fifteenth century may be formed from the few works which have been preserved, such as those by Lippo Dalmasii at Bologna, a signed "Madonna" by the same artist in the English National Gallery (No. 752), and a signed panel picture by Jacopo de Avanzi in the Palazzo Colonna ai SS. Apostoli at Rome.

Vasari's account of the early Ferrarese painters and their works is most inaccurate, and has caused the greatest confusion in the history of that period of Italian art. As he confounded Cossa with Costa, and Ercole Roberti with Ercole di Giulio Cesare, and also with Cossa, it is not surprising that later writers—Italian and foreign—should have followed him without question.

The only representatives of the early school of Ferrara in the Dresden gallery are, Francesco Cossa and Ercole Roberti.[1] On the other hand, we meet with many works there by Dosso, Garofalo, Mazzolino, and Girolamo da Carpi, all Ferrarese painters of the first half of the sixteenth century.

FRANCESCO COSSA, or DEL COSSA.

The late Dr. Hübner doubtfully ascribed the picture representing the "Annunciation" (No. 43) to Antonio Pollaiuolo. He, however, observed at the same time that it more probably belonged to the early Florentine school, a further proof that the general impression is not always sufficient to enable even the director of a gallery to discern the local school to which some great and characteristic work belongs. Messrs. Crowe and Cavalcaselle (i. 527) rightly recognised in this picture the hand of a Ferrarese painter, though they were undecided whether to attribute it to Baldassare Estense[2] or to Ercole Grandi di Giulio

[1] The 'Hercules Ferrariensis Pictor,' who is mentioned in a document as standing godfather to the son of Bartolommeo Garganelli in 1483 was mistaken by Vasari's Florentine commentators (iv. note 1, ed. Milanesi, iii. 141) for Ercole Grandi di Giulio Cesare. It is evident, however, that he was Ercole Roberti, the same who, after the death of Cossa, executed frescoes in the Cappella Garganelli.

[2] This little-known master was not a painter by profession, but a soldier. He was said to have been an illegitimate member of the House of Este. His only existing works, as far as I know, are some profile

Cesare. The Madonna is of the same type as the Virgin
in Cossa's signed picture of 1474 in the gallery at Bologna,
though the latter is there more perfect in expression. The
brown flesh-tints in the portrait at Bologna recur in the
face of the angel here. The full flowing folds of the
Madonna's mantle and the closely-laid undulating plaits on
the hem of her robe also recall the picture at Bologna,
and the form of the hands with the broad fingers is similar
in both. These characteristics have induced me to regard
this most interesting painting as an early work by
Cossa.[1]

Messrs. Crowe and Cavalcaselle seem to have formed
no very clear conception of this master. On the authority
of the guide-books at Bologna they still ascribe the
magnificent figure of St. Jerome in S. Petronio (Capella
Castelli) to Lorenzo Costa, though it shows all the charac-

portraits. Two, signed with his
name, were formerly in the Costabili
gallery at Ferrara. One of them is
now in London, the other, greatly
damaged, was in the collection of
the picture dealer Signor Guggen-
heim at Venice. In 1472, Baldas-
sare was commissioned by the Duke
Borso to retouch the portraits in
Cossa's frescoes; this probably
meant to embellish them, as Bal-
dassare was principally a portrait-
painter ('Et per acconzare 36 teste
de Schifanoio del duca Borso et parte
de' busti, et per altre teste, de
comission del duca Borso—ducati
36;' 'and for repairing 36 heads in
the Schifanoia of Duke Borso and
parts of the figures, and for other
heads commissioned by the Duke
Borso—36 ducats'). Baldassare was
born apparently soon after 1440,
and studied painting at Ferrara.
His wife was a native of Pavia; in
1462 he was employed by the Duke

Galeazzo Sforza to decorate the
palace in that city with frescoes.
Towards the close of 1469 he
returned to Ferrara and entered the
service of Duke Borso, Galeazzo
Sforza having recommended him in
the warmest terms. Though he
was, like Cosimo Tura, regularly
engaged by the Duke, his salary was
extremely small, and he lived in
great poverty. In 1502 he painted
a large altar-piece for the Duke
Ercole, which appears to have
perished.

[1] Braun has published an admir-
able photograph of this picture,
which I advise all students to pro-
cure. My attribution, which was
long disputed, having now received
the sanction of Dr. Woermann, may
be considered as generally accepted.
Cossa probably painted this altar-
piece about 1471 for the Chiesa
dell' Osservanza at Bologna.

teristics of Cossa [1] (†). This splendid picture is unfortunately almost hidden by a modern production. Another very characteristic work by this important painter, who has hitherto received but scant attention, is the circular window in the Church of S. Giovanni in Monte at Bologna,

representing St. John in Patmos. It is signed (Francesco Cossa). Another smaller window representing the Madonna with the Child and the little St. John, with the arms of the donor, is also by Cossa, and not by Costa, as usually stated in the guide-books. In the same church, in the sixth chapel on the left, is a much repainted Madonna with two boy angels. It must originally have been by Cossa, or at all events must have been executed from a drawing by him.

The letter to which I have already referred, written by Cossa in 1470 to Duke Borso, proves that in the early part of that year the painter had completed the three principal frescoes in the ante-room of the large hall in the Schifanoia.[2] The face of Borso, and probably also the heads of some of the other principal figures, were retouched, as we have already seen, by Baldassare Estense at the Duke's

---

[1] Dr. Bode (ii. 621) also attributes this St. Jerome to Costa. To this painter he further ascribes the pictures in the Marsilii Chapel of the same church—the "Martyrdom of St. Sebastian," the "Annunciation," and the "Twelve Apostles." It is incredible that a critic of the standing of Dr. Bode should have considered all these very dissimilar pictures to be by the same hand. The "Martyrdom of St. Sebastian" seems to me to be by some unknown Ferrarese painter; the "Annunciation " by an assistant of Francesco Francia, from a cartoon by the master; while the "Apostles" recall Cossa in the types of the faces and in the forms. I think it probable that they were executed after his death, from his drawings or cartoons, and that they were the work of one of his pupils or assistants.

[2] Herr Fritz von Hark, a young and promising art-critic in Dresden, first recognised the hand of Francesco Cossa in these frescoes.

command, and Cossa's hand is hardly to be recognised in
them. The landscape, however, appears to me very cha-
racteristic of this master. It is identical with those in the
" Madonna del Baracano," and in the predella representing
the " Miracles of St. Hyacinth " in the Vatican. This last-
named picture by Cossa is attributed to Benozzo Gozzoli,
while at Ferrara two extremely characteristic " Tondi," by
Cosimo Tura, pass under the name of Cossa. In the
Staedel Institute at Frankfort there is a much damaged
figure of St. Mark by Cossa. It is wrongly ascribed to
Mantegna, and bears the signature of that master, which,
however, is a palpable forgery (†). Many years ago I saw
two canvases in the collection of Herr von Kestner at
Hanover, representing a kneeling donor and his wife, which
were ascribed to Cossa, but erroneously it appeared to me.

The English National Gallery has the good fortune to
number among its many treasures of Italian art a small
panel by Cossa. It represents St. Dominic, or, as some
think, St. Vincentius Ferrer. It was the central panel of
a triptych,[1] and Dr. Frizzoni considers it to be the one which
was formerly in the Church of S. Petronio at Bologna, and
which Vasari cites as a work of Costa.[2]

Cossa must have been born between 1430 and 1440.
He was already dead in 1481. I have never met with any
authentic drawings by him. We will now proceed to speak
of his younger fellow-countryman and colleague at Bologna,
Ercole de' Roberti.

ERCOLE ROBERTI.

According to Napoleone Cittadella,[3] this master was the
son of a painter named Antonio, whose death is recorded

---

[1] The two wings of this triptych
belong to Signora Barbi-Cinti at
Ferrara.

[2] iv. 248 (ed. Milanesi, iii. 142).

[3] *Notisie relative a Ferrara*, p.
583.

as early as 1479. Ercole must, I think, have been born about 1445; [1] he was already dead in 1496. We gather from a letter dated March 19, 1491,[2] that he had several children and was in bad circumstances. He had at that date been for several years in the service of Duke Ercole, having probably quitted Bologna for Ferrara in 1486. From this letter, addressed by Ercole Roberti to his patron, we should judge him to have been a man of a gentle and dignified character. Moreover, we know that at the Court of Ferrara he was treated as a friend rather than as a paid servant of the State,[3] more especially by Prince Alfonso and his gifted sister Isabella. On the marriage of this lady in 1490, Roberti accompanied her to Mantua, and for some time is said to have filled the post of keeper of the wardrobe at that Court, an office held by Velasquez under Philip IV. of Spain.

No well-authenticated works have come down to us under the name of Ercole Roberti, but two extremely interesting pictures came to the Dresden gallery from the Church of S. Giovanni in Monte, at Bologna,[4] under that of

[1] The Cavaliere Venturi considers that he was born between 1450 and 1460.

[2] Published by Cavaliere Venturi.

[3] See, on this subject, an interesting article by Signor Venturi in the *Archivio storico dell' Arte*, No. viii. 1889.

[4] According to Vasari, three small pictures, forming the predella to the principal altar-piece in that church, were painted by Ercole Grandi. By this altar-piece he could not possibly have meant—as recent writers consider—Costa's large picture now in the choir of that church. This picture could not have been painted before the first decade of the sixteenth century, while the two pictures in the Dresden gallery are probably some thirty years earlier in date. The Bolognese writer, Pietro Lami, observes in the *Graticola di Bologna*, which he wrote in 1560: 'E sopra l' altar maggiore sono dipinte doe istorie fate a olio [?] de ma [mano] d'ercole da Frara [Ferrara]: l' una è quando Cristo fù condotto alla croce trai due ladroni, l' altra quando Cristo fù tradito da Juda. E nel mezzo la Madonna con Cristo morto in braccio.' ('And over the high altar are two episodes painted in oil by the hand of Ercole of Ferrara. One is when Christ was led to the Cross between two thieves, the other when Christ was betrayed by Judas; and in the

Ercole Grandi. This church, as we have already seen, contains two works by Cossa and two by Costa, from which we may infer that, in the last half of the fifteenth century, its decoration was almost exclusively entrusted to the Ferrarese painters [1] living at Bologna. The characteristic and lifelike figures in the two pictures at Dresden (Nos. 45 and 46) clearly prove, I think, that Jacopo and Giovanni Bellini (about 1460) must have exercised a more powerful influence over the development of Ercole Roberti than even Mantegna.[2] Ercole Roberti, whom Vasari always confused with Ercole Grandi di Giulio Cesare, is so interesting and vigorous a master, that I shall take this opportunity of imparting what little I know with respect to him.

centre is the Madonna with the dead Christ in her arms.') In 1749, Luigi Crespi, 'Canonico' of the church, sold two compartments of a predella with these subjects to the Dresden gallery. There seems every reason to believe that these two pictures are those mentioned by Lami in 1560. The central panel —the "Pietà"—is said to be in the Institute of Fine Arts at Liverpool.

[1] A Ferrarese painter was working in one of the chapels of this church as early as 1455. His name was Galasso de Matheo Caligaro (*i.e.* 'the shoemaker'), and he is mentioned in the *Cronaca di Giovanni Borselli* (*Rerum Italicarum Scriptores*, v. xxiii.) as 'Galassus juvenis ingegnosus.'

[2] Students who would satisfy themselves on this point should study the small "Crucifixion" in the Correr Museum at Venice, which appears to me to be an indisputable work of Giovanni Bellini—produced between 1450 and 1460. It is there ascribed to Mantegna, while Messrs.

Crowe and Cavalcaselle give it to Ercole Roberti. In addition, I should advise them to examine Jacopo Bellini's sketch-books in the British Museum and in the Louvre, and to compare Giovanni Bellini's interesting early work, the "Agony in the Garden" (No. 726 in the English National Gallery), with the predella by Ercole Roberti. The figure of Christ in both is taken from a drawing by Jacopo Bellini. The undue length of the upper part of the body, both in Giovanni Bellini's "Ecce Homo" in the English National Gallery and in Ercole's "St. John the Baptist" in the Berlin Museum, points to the influence of Jacopo Bellini. Whether this was direct or indirect in the case of Ercole Roberti, I am unable to say. His true master was undoubtedly his fellow-countryman Cosimo Tura. Lami, in his *Graticola di Bologna*, speaks of Ercole as the pupil of Cossa. Had he called him the colleague or assistant of that master he would probably have come nearer the truth.

In Prince Mario Chigi's collection at Rome there is a
small picture of "Melchizedek blessing Abraham," which
vividly recalls Ercole Roberti. On the back of the panel
we read in old characters the name 'Ercole de Ferrara.' It
is, unfortunately, so much damaged that it is impossible to
say whether it be an original; but, should it prove to be
only an old copy, it must in any case have been taken from
a picture by Ercole. Among the early works of this master
I should now include the " St. John the Baptist " (No. 112c)
in the Berlin gallery. The picture formerly belonged to
the Dondi Orologio family at Padua, and at that time I
believed it to be by Cosimo Tura. On seeing it again at
Berlin, however, it at once struck me as the work of Ercole
Roberti. Messrs. Crowe and Cavalcaselle saw correctly,
therefore, when they ascribed it to the so-called ' Stefano da
Ferrara,' to whom Ercole's large altar-piece in the Brera
was formerly attributed. Signor Venturi discovered that
in the old guide-books of Ravenna, and in Barruffaldi's
'History of the Ferrarese Painters,' the picture now in
the Brera was mentioned as by Ercole Roberti. A closer
examination of this work, which has now been assigned a
better place in the gallery, proved that this attribution was
correct. The landscape background in it corresponds in
every particular with that in the picture at Berlin.

The two compositions in the Dresden gallery, together
with the " Pietà " at Liverpool, certainly formed the pre-
della of an altar-piece, and I think it is not too rash to
assume that the latter was by Francesco Cossa. It
appears that this painter was employed by a Bolognese
noble, Domenico Garganelli, to adorn his family chapel
in S. Pietro—the cathedral of Bologna—with paintings.
In 1480 Cossa, assisted by Ercole Roberti (?), commenced
the work. He began with the ceiling, which he decorated
with figures of evangelists, doctors of the Church, and

prophets. But scarcely had he completed this part than he died suddenly. Ercole Roberti was then appointed to carry on the work,[1] and he fulfilled his task so admirably that Garganelli, as a mark of his satisfaction, gave him a large present in addition to the remuneration agreed upon.[2] Vasari also gives high praise to these works.

The following pictures belong, I think, to the last years of Ercole Roberti's sojourn at Ferrara : The large altar-piece, formerly in a church near Ravenna, and now in the Brera ; the "Pietà," once in the collection of Count Zeloni at Rome, and now in that of Herr Blumenstihl[3] (it is much disfigured by repainting, and has also a forged inscription) (†) ; the "Death of Lucretia," a poor and un-attractive picture in the gallery at Modena; and the "Gathering of the Manna," in the English National Gallery (No. 1217), of which there is a feeble copy in the Dresden gallery (No. 47). Messrs. Crowe and Cavalcaselle, following Luigi Crespi of Bologna,[4] erroneously ascribe this copy to Ercole Grandi di Giulio Cesare.[5] In the collection

[1] See Lami's *Graticola di Bologna*, and also Vasari (iv. 248; ed. Milanesi, iii. 143) : 'Dopo la morte del quale [Cossa] fù messo Ercole da Domenico Garganelli a finire la cappella.' ('After the death of Cossa, Ercole was employed by Domenico Garganelli to finish the chapel.')

[2] When this Church of S. Pietro was restored in 1605, these frescoes, which Vasari described with such enthusiasm, were in part sawn out of the wall and placed in the Palazzo Tanari. In 1820 some fragments were removed from there to the gallery, where they eventually perished from neglect. An old copy of one of them—"The Crucifixion"—was bought in England not long ago by Dr. J. P. Richter. This is the sole surviving relic which has

come down to us of the great work upon which Ercole was engaged for so many years.

[3] The large "Descent from the Cross" belonging to Cavaliere Santini at Ferrara, which came from the Church of the Carthusians in that city, was begun by Ercole Roberti and finished by some later painter. The St. John and the Magdalen there represented resemble the same two saints in Herr Blumenstihl's picture.

[4] Bottari, *Lettere Pittoriche*, iv. 368, ed. Mil. 1822.

[5] Dr. Woermann agrees with me as to this copy. Dr. Bode considers that Ercole di Giulio Cesare might have been the son of Ercole Roberti. I should be inclined to agree if, instead of son, he had said pupil, and possibly godson.

of Sir Francis Cook at Richmond there is also a small picture by Ercole Roberti, representing a woman endeavouring to rescue two children from a conflagration.

In Ercole's last period I should be inclined to place the " Concert " belonging to Mr. Salting, in London, and possibly also the admirable " St. John the Evangelist " in the Morelli collection.[1] To my great satisfaction, Signor Venturi acknowledges this to be a work of Ercole Roberti, though many other critics have questioned it. In conclusion, I would mention a picture in the Louvre (No. 1529), which, strangely enough, is there considered to be of the school of Luca Signorelli. It is a fragment, representing four men standing in the courtyard of a palace. The bases of the columns have representations in *grisaille* of equestrian combats. It appears to be much repainted, and hangs very high, so that it is impossible to express any decided opinion about it. It is, however, an interesting work, which, I think, may safely be ascribed to the Ferrarese school. Each time I saw the picture it produced upon me the impression not only of a work of this school, but it seemed to indicate the hand of a master of the character of Cossa or Ercole Roberti.

What has been said may be sufficient to show that this latter master, though of great importance, and a most interesting and dramatic artist, is at present very imperfectly known. It would be a satisfactory task for some young historian of art to make a careful study of this painter, together with some of his Ferrarese contemporaries.[2]

[1] Now in the public gallery at Bergamo.

[2] Since these words were written in 1880, Signor Venturi has supplied the want to which I alluded by his articles on Ercole Roberti and other painters. Among the reproductions of Ercole's drawings which he appends to his notice of that painter I can only recognise three as genuine—the pen drawing of the " Massacre of the Innocents " in the Louvre, that of the " Crucifixion " for the fresco in the Capella Garganelli, an admirable example, in the Print-Room at Berlin, and the

ERCOLE GRANDI.

This painter, who, though of no great importance, is not without interest, was the son of Giulio Cesare. I believe him to have been a pupil of Ercole Roberti, and later an assistant of Lorenzo Costa. He is not represented, as far as I know, in German or Russian collections, but his works may be studied in his native land, at Ferrara, Venice, and Milan. His early works show him to have been a pupil of Ercole Roberti. This is seen especially in his landscape backgrounds [1] and in the types of his heads. I should consider as works of his early period the eight tempera pictures with scenes from the Old Testament, formerly in the Costabili gallery at Ferrara. Two are now in Sir Henry Layard's collection at Venice,[2] four are in that of the Marchese Visconti-Venosta at Milan, one is in the Morelli collection,[3] and the eighth is now in England. The admirable ceiling-decoration in the Palazzo Calcagnini-Estense at Ferrara is, in my opinion, by Ercole Grandi (†), and not by Garofalo, as the late Signor Cittadella affirmed in a pamphlet which he published on these works. A Madonna with Saints by this master, somewhat repainted, belongs to the Marchese Strozzi[4] at Ferrara. It came to the Casa

"Betrayal" in the Uffizi, a study for a portion of the picture in the Dresden gallery. The other two appear to me wholly unworthy of so vigorous master.

[1] A series of drawings in the collection at Lille (Braun, Nos. 101, 103, 104-14), ascribed to Giacomo Francia, appear to me to be by a pupil of Ercole Grandi di Giulio Cesare. Most of them were probably intended for ' bronze plaquettes.'

[2] One of these pictures represents " Moses leaving the Land of Egypt." Some of the women, who are dancing, recall the " Parnassus " by Mantegna in the Louvre (No. 1375). Ercole probably saw that picture during his sojourn at Mantua with Costa, and took his idea from it.

[3] Now in the public gallery at Bergamo.

[4] Since the above was written the picture has been sold, and is now in

Strozzi from the Convent of S. Cristoforo degli Esposti under the name of Lorenzo Costa. Messrs. Crowe and Cavalcaselle (i. 546, 4) also mention it as by him. Grandi certainly approaches his master, Costa, very closely in this picture. The Madonna and Child are, in point of fact, borrowed from Costa,[1] and it requires a very intimate knowledge of the Ferrarese school to recognise the hand and the spirit of the pupil in this work (†). In the public gallery at Ferrara he is represented by two examples of his late period—a " Pietà " (No. 56) and a " St. Sebastian " (No. 57).[2]

The Dresden gallery, unfortunately, contains no works by Cosimo Tura or by his pupil (?), the younger Galasso Galassi, or by Francesco Bianchi, Domenico Panetti, and Lorenzo Costa. Recently, however, the director has purchased a small picture (No. 123), by Lodovico Mazzolino, an artist whose variegated and brilliant colouring made him a favourite with Roman prelates. He is still most frequently met with in Roman galleries. Mazzolino was better fitted to be a painter of *genre* than of history, and is only attractive when treating small figures ; his pictures, indeed, almost produce the effect of Flemish works. We need not here discuss the generally adopted theory which makes him a pupil of Lorenzo Costa, a master who worked chiefly at Bologna.

Let us now turn to the principal representatives of the

the English National Gallery (No. 1119), where it is rightly ascribed to Ercole Grandi di Giulio Cesare.

[1] The Madonna in Costa's fine altar-piece of 1497, in the Capella Ghedini of the Church of S. Giovanni in Monte at Bologna, should be compared with this Madonna by E rcole Grandi.

[2] The drawing in the Uffizi (No. 280), of six young warriors, ascribed to Ercole Grandi, and a very similar subject, attributed to Pintoricchio, in the Louvre (No. 255), are both copies, in my opinion. On the other hand, No. 436 in the Louvre, representing Judith putting the head of Holofernes into a sack held by her attendant, appears to me to be a genuine drawing by Ercole Grandi.

Ferrarese school in its zenith—Dosso and Garofalo. They occupy nearly the same position in this school as did Luini and Gaudenzio Ferrari in the Lombardo-Milanese school.

In no gallery north of the Alps are Dosso and Garofalo so well represented as in Dresden. Our discussion of these two painters may also include Girolamo Carpi, as the catalogue ascribes to him a picture of Venus and Cupid in a shell drawn by swans. Vasari regarded this painter as a pupil of Garofalo, though it appears to me that he was more directly influenced by Dosso. My own studies have convinced me that many of the decorative pictures in this gallery, though composed and drawn by Dosso, and in one instance also by Garofalo, were for the most part executed by Girolamo Carpi, and perhaps also by Battista Dossi, the younger brother of Dosso. All these paintings (including No. 143) probably adorned one of the rooms in the Ducal Palace at Ferrara,[1] and were in 1599 transferred by Cesare, the last Duke of Ferrara, to Modena, where the most varied names were eventually bestowed upon them. We will now examine them in order :—

No. 126, " Justice with the Scales and Fasces."[2] Both the figure and the landscape are composed in the spirit of Dosso, but I am not prepared to affirm that the execution is entirely his, though it is probable that it was so. Dosso's peculiar and glowing colouring is certainly absent from this picture, but that may be due to the dirt which covers the surface.

[1] Such decorative pictures were very common in Italy in the first half of the sixteenth century. Vasari says, in the *Life of Perino del Vaga* (ed. Milanesi, v. 598): ' E sopra il cammino di pietra, fece Pierino una Pace la quale abbruccia armi e trofei ' (' and over the mantelpiece of stone Pierino represented " Peace " burning weapons and trophies '). This painting must have been an allegorical figure similar to the one in this gallery, No. 127.

[2] Nos. 126, 127 are very similar in size to Nos. 124 and 125. All four probably adorned one of the rooms of the palace at Ferrara.

No. 127 represents "Peace." What was said of the preceding applies equally to this picture. The same figure, with certain modifications, was formerly in the Costabili gallery at Ferrara under the name of Girolamo da Carpi; it is now in the collection of the late Duc de Montpensier.

Nos. 126 and 127, together with No. 128—the "Four Fathers of the Church"—came from Modena to Dresden as works of Dosso, and have retained the attribution. No. 128 is undoubtedly composed and wholly executed by the master.

No. 139 came to Dresden as the work of Garofalo, and was there assigned to Dosso. I believe the composition, and possibly also the cartoon, to have been by Garofalo, while the execution was entrusted to a pupil of that master (†).

No. 130, one of the Hours with the chariot of Apollo. The picture came to this gallery under the name of Garofalo, and was here assigned to its rightful author. The composition is, I think, by Dosso, and the execution by the same painter who produced No. 139. The "Dream" (No. 131), which also came from Modena under the name of Garofalo, has now been ascribed to its true author, Dosso. The execution may be by Battista Dosso.

No. 144, "Judith with the Head of Holofernes," shows the influence of Parmegianino over Dosso. The elegant manner of the former master found favour throughout North Italy during a certain period between 1535 and 1550. By means of his engravings he had probably become very generally known, and painters of the most diverse natures sought to imitate him, such as Andrea Schiavone, Giacomo Bassano, Domenico Alfani, Luca Longhi, Defendente Ferrari of Chivasso, and others. This "Judith" was, I think, painted by Girolamo Carpi from a composition by Dosso (†).

We will now examine those works by Dosso which have either retained the names wrongly bestowed upon them at Modena, or have been deprived of the right attributions they originally bore.

No. 145, the "Rape of Ganymede;" the picture came from Modena as the work of Parmegianino, and has preserved this erroneous attribution. What has been said of Dosso's other decorative pictures applies to this and to the following, No. 142, an allegorical figure known as "Die Gelegenheit" ("Opportunity"). It represents a youth standing upon a ball, and holding in his right hand a knife; a female figure stands behind him. The picture came from Modena as the work of Girolamo Bedolo, known as Girolamo Mazzola, a cousin of Parmegianino, and retained this attribution in Germany.[1] There is a copy of this picture in the public gallery at Modena by Andrea Donduzzi, known as 'il Mastelletta'; the subject is also there called "l'Occasione." The compiler of the catalogue of that collection, Signor Tarabini, says of it: 'Il pittore avrà forse inteso di rappresentare l'occasione, che nel mondo fugge veloce, avendo sempre per compagna Motanea, ossia il pentimento, che resta indietro.' ('The painter perhaps wished to represent opportunities which are rapidly passing in this world, and are always accompanied by Motanea, that is, Repentance, which stays behind.')

No. 125, "The Archangel Michael in the act of slaying the Dragon," came to Dresden under the name of Dosso. Later, it was doubtfully ascribed to Francesco Penni, known as 'il Fattore,' probably because the composition is in every way similar to Raphael's treatment of the same subject.

---

[1] See Vasari, xi. 237 (ed. Milanesi, vi. 476): 'Girolamo Carpi dipinse nel palazzo del duca di Ferrara un quadro grande con una figura quanto il vivo, finta per un occasione, con bella vivezza, grazia e buon rilievo.' In the present catalogue of the Dresden gallery these pictures are ascribed to Girolamo da Carpi.

I consider that the name borne by the picture while at Modena was correct. It is not only full of Dosso's feeling, but was certainly also executed by him, and probably from Raphael's cartoon, which was at that time in the palace at Ferrara [1] (†).

No. 124, "St. George." This is an early work by Dosso, executed about 1506, before Raphael's original was sent to London as a gift to Henry VII.; traces of gilding are still visible in the saint's armour. The picture came from Modena as a Garofalo, and in Dresden was, like the preceding, renamed Francesco Penni. Both these attributions appear to me to be incorrect, for it is an undoubted work by Dosso (†). The Duke Alfonso probably commissioned Dosso to make a large copy of Raphael's small and beautiful picture of St. George, which that master had painted in 1506 for the Duke Guidobaldo of Urbino.[2]

No. 129 [3] was ascribed, in Dr. Hübner's catalogue, to a pupil of Dosso, but it is decidedly by the master himself (†). It is a fine work, rich in colour, and belonging to his earlier and best epoch. The Madonna kneeling before the Almighty is a noble and attractive figure, the four Fathers are full of life and action, and the landscape is of great charm. So far, therefore. we have found eleven Dosso pictures in the Dresden gallery, of which four are undoubtedly by his own hand, two may possibly have been also painted by himself,

[1] In 1518, Raphael was employed by Leo X. to paint a large " St. Michael " for King Francis I. of France and a " Holy Family " for the Queen ; both pictures are now in the Louvre. From the letters which passed between Duke Alfonso of Ferrara and his ambassador Costabili in Rome, we gather that Raphael had sent the cartoon for this " St. Michael " as an offering to the Duke. The latter in reply announces the safe arrival of the cartoon, and commissions Costabili to give Raphael twenty-five scudi in his name, in order that ' he may keep the feast of St. Martin, and bear him in memory at the same time.'

[2] Raphael's little picture is now in the Hermitage at St. Petersburg.

[3] This picture represents in the lower part the four Fathers of the Church. Above is seen the Almighty in a glory, blessing the Madonna.

while the remainder were probably composed by him and executed with the aid of Girolamo Carpi and of Dosso's brother Battista. Later we shall have occasion to discuss a twelfth work by him.

Nowhere out of Italy can this gifted painter be studied so satisfactorily as in the Dresden gallery. In other public collections in Europe he is either not represented at all or only by inferior works; in the Berlin Museum by a genuine but much repainted altar-piece, and in the public gallery at Vienna by an unimportant St. Jerome. There is nothing by him, as far as I recollect, either at Munich or Madrid, or in the English National Gallery. At Hampton Court, however, there are three pictures by this great Ferrarese colourist, and one in the choice collection of Mr. Mond in London.

The Dresden gallery has also some fine examples of the art of Dosso's rival, Benvenuto Tisi da Garofalo; most of them having been brought from Modena. Nos. 132, 134, 135, and 138 [1] are of the master's good period (1515–1530). The decline of Garofalo's power is apparent in No. 134, which is signed ' Benvenù ' (the Ferrarese for Benvenuto) 'Garofalo, 1530, Dec.' (December).[2] According to Napoleone Cittadella, it was not painted for the Church of S. Spirito, but for the Certosa of Ferrara. No. 140, " Christ among the Doctors," was formerly ascribed to the school of Dosso. It appears to me to be by Garofalo, though much disfigured by dirt.

Girolamo da Carpi, or, as he signs himself, ' Hieronymus

---

[1] No. 136, the " Holy Family," and No. 137, a " Madonna with Saints," appear to me to be works of his school. One of Garofalo's finest pictures, a mythological subject, is in the collection of Mr. Mond in London. Nearly every European gallery, with the exception of that of Madrid, possesses one or two examples by this very prolific painter.

[2] It represents the Madonna and Child surrounded by angel musicians appearing to SS. Peter, Bruno, and George.

de Carpis,'[1] was born in 1501 and died in 1556. His father Tommaso was a painter, and was employed in the service of Lucrezia Borgia in 1507. In 1538 Girolamo married Catarina Amatori at Ferrara. Cittadella relates that he not only worked as Garofalo's assistant—for instance, in the Palace of Coppara in 1535—but that he was also employed with Dosso.[2] In company with the latter he decorated several rooms in the 'Belvedere,' a palace on a small island in the neighbourhood of Ferrara. He probably learnt the rudiments of his art from his father; later, according to Vasari, he studied with Garofalo. To judge by his authenticated picture in S. Martino at Bologna, of 1530, he must at that period have felt the influence of Raphael's art. Between 1540 and 1550 he copied several of Correggio's paintings. In 1550 he took a number of these copies or imitations to Rome and showed them to Vasari. We need not, however, devote further space to this somewhat insignificant painter.

Besides the Ferrarese pictures already mentioned, the Dresden gallery contains four works by Ippolito Scarsella, known as 'lo Scarsellino.' They are numbered 146, 147, 148, and 149, and appear to me to be genuine. Scarsellino's large altar-piece in the Brera (No. 478) proves that this master formed his style principally upon Paul Veronese in Venice. It is an admirable work, representing in the lower part the four Fathers, with the Madonna and Child above, and was painted for the Church of S. Bernardino at Ferrara.

There are two pictures rightly ascribed to Francesco Mazzola, known as Parmegianino: No. 160, representing the Madonna and Child appearing to SS. Stephen, John

---

[1] Carpi was therefore his family name. Some writers wrongly call him Sellari (see *Napoleone Citta-* *della, op. cit.* p. 592).

[2] *Ibid.* p. 351.

the Baptist, and an ecclesiastical donor, and No. 161, the Madonna with the Child, who holds a rose in his right hand, a picture which is known as the "Madonna della Rosa." A noble and finely conceived portrait of a young man (No. 162) might also be by him (†), though classed as 'unknown' in the catalogue. It is still a valuable work, notwithstanding the injury it has sustained from restoration.

No 166, "The Madonna and Child enthroned, with SS. Sebastian and Francis standing in front," is not by Parmegianino, but more probably by his cousin and imitator, Girolamo Bedolo (†). This painter is often called Girolamo Mazzola, because he married a daughter of Pierillario Mazzola, the uncle of Parmegianino. Two pictures are wrongly ascribed to him in this gallery. One, No. 159, appears to me to be a copy by some inferior painter of the school of Correggio. The other, No. 142, we have already dealt with in speaking of Dosso [1] (†).

The "Martyrdom of SS. Peter and Paul" (No. 165) is a good and genuine work by Niccolò dell' Abbate. This painter was a pupil of the Bolognese artists Bagnacavallo and Prospero Fontana, and later, when in France, he became the assistant of Primaticcio, Abbate di San Martino as he was called. From him Niccolò probably derived the name 'dell Abbate' by which he is known. The influence of Giulio Romano is also apparent in this picture in Dresden.

There is a good work by Bartolommeo Schedone in the gallery, a so-called "Riposo," an incident of the "Flight into Egypt" (No. 167). Schedone was, in his day, one of the most popular painters, and his pictures, painted with a view to effect, fetched high prices from the amateurs of his time.

[1] In Dr. Woermann's catalogue, No. 162 is assigned to Parmegianino and No. 166 to Bedolo. No. 159, "St. George kneeling before the Madonna, while the Infant Saviour hangs a gold chain round his neck," is placed in the 'School of Correggio.' No. 142 is assigned to Girolamo Carpi.

We will now pass to the consideration of the works of Antonio Allegri, known as 'il Correggio.' They are among the principal ornaments of the collection, and to them, indeed, the Dresden gallery owes much of its world-wide reputation.

Correggio's master is considered to have been Francesco Bianchi of Ferrara, a pupil of Cosimo Tura, who had settled at Modena, a theory which has much show of probability. Bianchi, it is said, was intimate with Francia and Costa, and worked with them in fresco in the Palazzo Bentivoglio at Bologna. It is very possible, therefore, that Correggio, having completed his training with Bianchi in 1508 or 1509, should have been sent to Mantua to finish his education in the workshop of his first master's friend, Lorenzo Costa.[1]

His celebrated picture in this gallery,[2] No. 150, which was painted between 1514 and 1515, shows so much connection with Francia—for example, in the head of St. Catherine—and also with Costa—as in the *grisaille* medallion on the base of the throne—that I think students of art, those at least who have learnt to discriminate, will not reject as baseless my theory that Correggio proceeded from the school of Ferrara-Bologna.[3] This fine early work is, however, by no means the earliest of Correggio's productions. Before obtaining so important a commission he must have given decisive proofs of his capacity; and in those golden days of art a painter had usually mastered the technical difficulties of his profession by his fifteenth or sixteenth year. What, then, were the works produced by Correggio prior to

[1] See my *Critical Studies in the Borghese and Doria Galleries*, pp. 223–6.

[2] The Madonna and Child blessing St. Francis, St. Anthony of Padua standing behind him; on the opposite side are SS. John the Baptist and Catherine.

[3] I see, to my satisfaction, that Dr. Jean Paul Richter, in his excellent article on Correggio (in Dohme's *Kunst und Künstler*, lxxiv.), has accepted my views as to the development of this painter.

L 2

1514—that is, before he painted the altar-piece now in the Dresden gallery? According to my studies, as matured since I first wrote on the subject, they are nearly as follows :—

1. A small panel, formerly in the Costabili gallery at Ferrara, and now in the collection of Dr. Gustavo Frizzoni at Milan.[1] It represents the Madonna and Child enthroned between SS. Francis and Dominic; St. Anna stands behind, and in front kneels St. Catherine, to whom the Infant Saviour gives a ring. The picture, though of small dimensions and not well-preserved, is most attractive. The figure of St. Catherine more especially is one of indescribable charm, which already reveals in bud all the fulness of Correggio's genius. The colouring is Ferrarese in character, and of such brilliancy as to recall Mazzolino. The hands, with the broad metacarpus, resemble those of Lorenzo Costa, but the expression and movement of St. Francis are wholly Correggiesque, and such as we find in his later works. The form and decoration of the throne bear much resemblance to the throne in the altar-piece with St. Francis in the Dresden gallery. I should consider it to be one of the earliest examples of Correggio's first period.

2. The Madonna and Child, with SS. Joseph, Elisabeth, and the little St. John, in the public gallery at Pavia (Malaspina collection), where it is assigned to Francesco Francia (†). It may be earlier in date than Signor Frizzoni's picture.[2] Excessive repainting has deprived it of much of its charm.

Two other small works, which may be even earlier than those just mentioned, are the Madonna in the Uffizi

[1] Marcozzi of Milan has published a good photograph of this picture.

[2] In the Royal Library at Turin there is a drawing by Correggio representing the "Marriage of St. Catherine," which appears to me to belong to this early period of the master's career.

MADONNA AND CHILD WITH ANGELS.   BY CORREGGIO.
(In the Uffizi, Florence.)

To face p. 148.

Correggio—in the treatment of the curly hair, in the long fold of the drapery on the right, in the exaggerated curve of the shinbone, and in other particulars.

The following pictures appear to me to be rather later in date than the four preceding, though still closely connected with them :—

5. A small picture representing the kneeling Christ taking leave of His Mother, belonging to Mr. Benson in London, which has unfortunately been much restored. It is thoroughly Correggiesque in every part. The sorrowful scene is treated with simplicity though with profound feeling. The sublime resignation of the Saviour, the anguish of the Mother who is bowed down with grief, and the warm, true-hearted sympathy of St. John and of the Magdalen, two youthful figures who complete the group, are admirably depicted. In the background the painter has introduced a brilliant landscape.[1] This picture is of the highest importance for the history of Correggio's artistic development. Immediately after he may have produced the following :—

6. A much larger panel, formerly in London, where it was ascribed to the school of Dosso, and now in the collection of Signor Benigno Crespi at Milan. In my opinion this early work of Correggio is the most brilliant manifestation of his peculiar genius. It represents the "Nativity"; on the right is the manger built against the ruins of a Roman temple; St. Joseph is asleep on the ground; in front is the Infant Saviour, lying on white drapery, while His Mother adores Him with folded hands. Opposite is St. Elisabeth, who draws the attention of the little St. John,

---

[1] Lanzi speaks of this picture as the work of Correggio: 'Un quadretto di N. Signore che prima della passione si congeda della Vergine Madre, era in Milano, veduto già e riconosciuto per legittimo dal signor abate Carlo Bianconi' (v. iii 887).

CHRIST TAKING LEAVE OF HIS MOTHER.   BY CORREGGIO.

(In the Collection of Mr. Benson, London.)

To face p. 150.

MADONNA AND CHILD. BY CORREGGIO.
(In the Museo Municipale at Milan.)

To face p. 151.

seated on her knee, to the Redeemer. In the background is a boy angel of surpassing charm, who announces to the shepherds the birth of the Holy Child. In the air are two exquisite little angels—one being the counterpart of an angel in the altar-piece with St. Francis in the Dresden gallery. But what seems to me to be the most admirable part of this attractive picture is the landscape, with a radiant and cloudless sky above—'quel cielo di Lombardia, così bello quand' è bello, così splendido, così in pace!' as Manzoni has fitly described the sky of Lombardy.

In the two pictures last discussed the scale of colouring is Venetian; in this "Nativity," on the other hand, it is altogether Ferrarese. The type of the Madonna is the same as in Mr. Benson's picture. The drapery in both lacks freedom, and falls in the same crumpled folds; the broad metacarpus of St. Elisabeth and of St. Joseph still recall Lorenzo Costa; the hair of the little St. John is treated like that of the Faun at Munich.

Between 1512 and 1514 Correggio must have painted several of his small "Madonnas." One of the best is now in the Museo Municipale at Milan. The Virgin is represented supporting the Child on her knee with her right arm, whilst the little St. John, with his cross in his left hand, approaches him tenderly. The type of the Madonna differs from that in the preceding pictures, and approaches that of the Virgin in the Dresden altar-piece. The form of the Madonna's hands, especially the left, recalls Costa; the drapery is still broken into crumpled folds, but the harmony of the colours is neither Venetian nor Ferrarese, but wholly Correggiesque.

8. In this period I should place the Madonna belonging to Prince Hohenzollern-Sigmaringen—a picture which, to judge from the photograph, has been much injured by restoration. It represents the Madonna and Child, to

whom the little St. John is making some offering ; on the
right is St. Elisabeth, whose type is similar to that of the
same saint in Signor Crespi's picture. It was evidently
taken from Mantegna.

Another, and more important, early work by Correggio
must find a place here. This is Lord Ashburton's picture
of Martha and Mary between SS. Leonard and Peter, which
I consider was painted before the Dresden altar-piece with
St. Francis, about 1513 or 1514. The form of the hands
still recalls Costa, but the drapery is treated with more
breadth and freedom than in any of the pictures which I
have enumerated.

Among those works which Correggio painted shortly
after the altar-piece with St. Francis, in Dresden, I
should name a Madonna at Hampton Court and another
in the gallery at Modena, bequeathed to that collection by
the late Marchese Camponi. The two pictures in the Tribune
of the Uffizi—the " Holy Family resting during their Flight
into Egypt," and the " Madonna adoring the Child " [1]—are
probably also of this period—1518–1520.

It has often been affirmed that Lotto was not only the
pupil of Leonardo da Vinci, but that he also took Correggio's
works as his models, and sought to imitate that master.
In treating of the Munich gallery, I endeavoured to show
that this view was incorrect, and springs from a superficial
interpretation of the history and progress of painting in
Italy. I take this occasion to return once more to the
subject.

When the culture of a nation has reached its highest
stage of development, we always find that *charm* is more

[1] This little picture again shows
a very remarkable connection with
Lotto both in colouring and in
feeling. The large altar-piece which
Correggio painted for the Church of
Albinea in 1517 has not been pre-
served, and only two copies of it
have come down to us. One of these
is in the Brera, the other is in the
gallery of the Capitol at Rome.

thought of than *character* in art and literature, as well as in every phase of daily life. And such was the case in Italy in the last decades of the fifteenth century and the opening ones of the sixteenth. This instinct was exemplified by none so strikingly as by the great Leonardo da Vinci, perhaps the most richly gifted by nature among all the sons of men. He it was who first sought to depict the smile of inward happiness, the charm of the soul. To attain this object, however, an intimate knowledge of the principles of pictorial modelling, that is, of chiaroscuro, was necessary, and Leonardo, during his sojourn at Milan from 1485 to 1500, devoted himself assiduously to this study.[1]

The historical development of art led Giorgione to tread almost contemporaneously in the same path as Leonardo, though wholly independent of him. It is in this respect particularly that Lotto, the fellow-countryman of Giorgione, must, I think, be regarded as his comrade and follower. Although Leonardo was for a short time in Venice, towards the close of 1499,[2] it is improbable that Giorgione and Lotto were personally acquainted with him, or ever saw any of his works.

The same may be said most emphatically of Correggio. It was the fortunate lot of this master to strike the fullest sound from the chord which had already been touched by Leonardo, Giorgione, and Lotto. The similarity of feeling which we observe in the works of these artists cannot be explained by mutual contact, for there was never, I

---

[1] See on this subject some of the precepts laid down by Leonardo in his well-known *Trattato della Pittura*.

[2] Leonardo must have left Milan in the early days of October 1499, a short time before the French entered the city; he proceeded to Mantua by way of Pizzighettone. At Mantua he made a drawing of Isabella Gonzaga in profile (now in the Louvre, Braun, 202). From that city he went to Venice, and thence to Florence.

believe, any direct intercourse between them. It was rather the natural consequence of the development of the human mind at the period when they lived and worked. Freedom was beginning to assert itself, and the spirit pervading art in the early part of the sixteenth century was the same as that which animated the Greeks. It is the undisguised expression of artless and triumphant joy in the contemplation of man as a living and independent being, in the full possession of all his faculties, freed at last from the bondage of medieval thought. This sense of freedom victoriously acquired is equally apparent in the art of Michelangelo as in that of Correggio, for, though in all other respects their characters may have been totally opposed, these two masters must be regarded as the principal representatives of this tendency.[1]

Michelangelo came of a patrician family in Florence. He was educated in a city which, though opulent and magnificent, was torn by political dissensions, and the moral tone of which was fast declining. His proud, magnanimous and independent nature was revolted by the characterlessness and sensuality of his contemporaries, and this mood was intensified as time went on, more especi-

---

[1] The time had come when art, having attained its full maturity, could no longer brook restraint, but panting, as it were, for light and air and freedom, wrenched itself from the thraldom of the Church. As a result, we find idyllic pictures and the so-called 'Sante Conversazioni' of the Venetians coming into favour, whilst portrait-painting also attained greater popularity. No artist has revelled in this newly-found freedom with such unrestrained delight as Correggio, excepting perhaps Michelangelo. Towards the middle of the sixteenth century art was again forcibly reinstated in its former place, beneath the jurisdiction of the Church, in consequence of the Spanish Catholic reaction. But under what changed circumstances! Look at the pictured saints of that epoch: is it thus that pious and reverent persons would really demean themselves in the house of God? These passionately ecstatic gestures, these exclamations of anguish, do not they lack the note of sincerity? In truth, they but painfully conceal the void within.

ally after the fall of the Florentine Republic. We find indications of it in his celebrated statue of David ; but it is most powerfully embodied in the well-known lines which he inscribed upon his statue of " Night " :—

> Grato m' è il sonno e più l' esser di sasso,
> Mentre che il danno e la vergogna dura,
> Non veder, non sentir m' è gran ventura,
> Però non mi destar, deh, parla basso.[1]

Disgusted with his surroundings, Michelangelo early withdrew from the world and lived only for his art. Like Correggio, his nature was essentially pure and simple.[2]

Correggio, in this respect unlike his great contemporary, was the son of a modest burgher, and led a plain and re-stricted life. Beyond the love which he bore to his art, it is improbable that he was ever deeply stirred by other emotions. Like Michelangelo, he lived as a recluse for art alone, though under different circumstances; for, while Michelangelo was exposed to the bustle, the turmoil, and the passions of a city like Rome, Correggio's life was passed uneventfully among the Benedictine monks of a small pro-vincial town. His natural instincts led him to depict the charm of the soul in every phase of joy and sorrow, in the excitement of sensuous pleasure, and in the raptures of divine love. Michelangelo, on the other hand, was im-pelled by his lofty and high-souled temperament to treat the solemn and dignified side of human nature, to represent energy and strength, the noble pride of an unfettered spirit, scorning all that was vain, base, and unprincipled ; in a

---

[1] See Vasari, xii. 208 (ed. Milanesi, vii. 197).

[2] We gather this from a letter written by Michelangelo to Vasari, in which he tells him of the death of his faithful servant Urbino; as also from another addressed to one of his brothers who had wished to pay him a visit at Bologna: ' Son qua,' he writes, ' in una cattiva stanza e ho comperato un letto solo nel quale stiamo quattro persone e non avrei il modo raccettarlo come si richiede.'

word, he sought to embody in art all the virile qualities and passions of the soul under their nobler aspects. In his Titanic creations we seem to see the spirit of humanity contemplating with truly Olympian pride the broken fetters by which it once was bound, strong in the consciousness of its heaven-sent power.[1] It is curious that Correggio and Michelangelo, the representatives of these different modes of thought, should have flourished contemporaneously. Although Michelangelo's temper of mind was more in accordance with that of the era of Dante, he nevertheless exercised a more direct and powerful influence over his contemporaries than did Correggio, both by reason of his personality and from the fact that he worked principally in the service of the Pope and in the two intellectual capitals of the Italy of that day—Rome and Florence. All who came in contact with him were either completely dominated by him, or were diverted from their own natural course. It was chiefly owing to him that the decay of art was more rapid and disastrous than it might otherwise have been. The influence of Correggio, on the other hand, was felt indirectly, and principally through the Carracci, and it was not until the seventeenth century that his feeble imitators began to multiply. Midway between Correggio and the strong individuality of Michelangelo stands Raphael, the most serene, restrained, and perfect of painters, who alone, by virtue of these qualities, is worthy to rank with the Greeks.[2]

I must apologise for this long and perhaps somewhat

[1] The contortions often met with in the figures of Michelangelo were probably meant as a kind of protest against the bonds of conventionality which governed the compositions of his contemporaries. It is the spirit of modern humanity struggling against the fetters of the Middle Age.

[2] As a rule, we only learn to appreciate Raphael fully after long study. Michelangelo and Correggio, on the other hand, either attract us powerfully at once, or repel us very decidedly.

pedantic interlude, and we will now resume our discussion of Correggio's works. In those pictures of his early period which I have already mentioned, his own nature—simple, refined, and artless, with its tendency to morbid excitability—is strikingly apparent. His later works, on the other hand, such as his large altar-pieces, are lacking in freshness of feeling, and are somewhat conventional. Yet, as a rule, it is from them that an estimate of his art has been formed.[1] In treating incidents from Greek mythology, however, Correggio was in his element, and no other painter has ever dealt with sensuous subjects in so pure, so natural, so elevated a spirit as he.

The most tolerably preserved of all the master's pictures in the Dresden gallery is, fortunately, the "Madonna with St. Francis." It is replete with thought and feeling, and in no early work of a great artist, the "David" of Michelangelo alone excepted, do we find such marked individuality. Correggio's other three altar-pieces (Nos. 151, 152, and 153) have been so disfigured by repainting, more especially the first and the last, that they can afford us little pleasure now. I cannot but admire those art-critics who are able to go into raptures over his chiaroscuro in them! They all date from the years 1525 to 1532.

Two other works are ascribed to Correggio in the catalogue, Nos. 155 and 154. The first named is a male portrait known as "Correggio's Doctor," an extraordinary appellation, which was probably not bestowed upon it before the eighteenth century. Raphael Mengs was reminded in this picture of Giorgione, which would be incomprehensible were it not for the fact that no painter has ever been, and

[1] No one can claim to have thoroughly grasped the character of a painter without having made a study of his development, consequently, of course, of his early works. The saying that 'results can only be understood by their processes,' is eminently true in the history of art.

still is, so entirely misunderstood as Giorgione. This
portrait is a mere wreck : the face was first rubbed down,
and then entirely repainted, hence the mouth has lost its
original expression and has become crooked. The form of
the hand resting upon the book is unlike that peculiar to
Correggio, and there is no trace of the richness of touch
characteristic of the master. It may have been originally
the work of Dosso, and, as the public has no opinion of a
picture without an attribution, it might be desirable to
substitute his name for that of Correggio.[1]

With much trepidation I must now turn to the " Mag-
dalen " (No. 154). According to Pungileoni, it was painted
by Correggio in 1533, a year, therefore, before his death. But
this is pure supposition. As a matter of fact the picture
only came to light after 1680. Of all the pictures ascribed
to Correggio, this recumbent Magdalen in the Dresden
gallery is probably the best known and the most popular,
and the one which has been most frequently copied. Yet,
for all this, I must confess that I have never been able
to feel the slightest enthusiasm for it, though I feel some
compunction in openly expressing my heretical opinions
with regard to it.

The last time I saw the picture, as I was about to note
down some critical remarks upon it, an elderly gentleman
and his daughter approached it, evidently in order to
express their admiration of this supposed gem.

' What exquisite feeling ! ' exclaimed the lady as she put
up her gold-rimmed eye-glasses ; ' no other picture can
compare with it. The oftener I see it, and the more I
absorb its beauty, the greater is the spell it exercises over

---

[1] Dr. Julius Meyer, in his able
and learned book on Correggio,
pronounced this work not genuine.
The hand in this portrait should be
compared with the hands of the
"Fathers of the Church" in
Dosso's fine and genuine picture,
No. 128, and it will be seen that they
are identical, even to the rounded
form of the nails.

me, and I must confess that I prefer Correggio's beautiful
sinner to all the Madonnas of Raphael and Holbein. How
well it would look in our drawing-room with its north
light ! '

Her father, a little man of a florid complexion, rubbed
his hands and observed that such a picture would probably
fetch some hundreds of thousand marks.

I stepped aside in order to give the worthy couple a
better chance of studying the object of their admiration
more closely.

'Pray don't move,' said the gentleman politely. ' I
would not disturb you on any account, especially as I see
that you know how to appreciate this gem of gems. I and
my daughter here—Elise von Blasewitz, of Plauen—have
known the picture for years; indeed, I may say that we are
intimately acquainted with it and know it by heart, for we
have an excellent engraving of it at home. But you, sir,
appear to be a foreigner. Perhaps it is your first visit to
this gallery ? '

Sorely against my will, I found myself drawn into con-
versation with them.

' No,' I replied; ' though I am a foreigner, I know this
gallery pretty well.'

The next question was as to my nationality.

' Am I right,' said the lady blandly, ' in thinking that
you are an art-critic ? '

' Scarcely,' I replied; ' at most a student of art.'

'Oh, surely,' she said deprecatingly, with an affected
smile, ' I can see by the way you look at pictures that you
must be a connoisseur. We, too, have many learned art-
critics in Germany.'

' Far too many, I consider,' remarked her father con-
temptuously. ' Too much learning impairs vision, and
destroys spontaneous and healthy enjoyment. But may I

ask what you think of this Magdalen by Correggio?' he said, turning to me. 'I suppose you consider it the most beautiful, if not the most valuable, picture in the Dresden gallery.'

'I am sorry to be forced to answer in the negative,' I replied; 'but, as you are good enough to ask for my opinion, I feel bound in courtesy to state it frankly.'

'What!—do you mean to tell me you do not like it?'

'The somewhat coquettish demeanour of this Magdalen, the over-smooth execution, suffice to convince me,' I replied, 'that it is not the work of an Italian at all, much less of Correggio, but in all probability a Flemish production of the end of the seventeenth century' (†).

My interrogator drew back a step and cast a significant glance at his daughter, whose face, as she listened to my words, had assumed an expression of sincere commiseration.

'Pray do not let my rash opinions trouble you,' I added.

'Rash, indeed!' said Fraulein von Blasewitz in a cutting tone.

'If you will just look at the picture itself,' I said, 'perhaps you may yet come to agree with me that it recalls Adrian van der Werff.'

'Impossible!' she exclaimed; 'why he, of all painters, is considered by all our authorities in æsthetics to be the quintessence of mannerism.'

'That may be,' I said indifferently. 'But it was certainly no mere accident that when, in 1788, two pictures were stolen from the gallery, those selected should have been this "Magdalen" and Van der Werff's "Judgment of Paris." The theft was committed by a Dresden connoisseur named Wogatz, and in his eyes the two pictures were of equal value.'

'Really!' exclaimed Fraulein von Blasewitz warmly,

'this is too bad. But, perhaps,' she added, 'you are only joking.'

'On the contrary, I am very much in earnest,' I returned, 'and once more let me beg you to look at the picture. See how coquettishly this Magdalen lies and reads, almost as though she hoped to be surprised by her lover in this attitude. One of the principal qualities of Correggio's art is his naïve feeling; yet in this figure there is not a trace of artlessness. Observe, moreover, the crude ultramarine blue in the mantle, the very colouring of Van der Werff; the fingers, which are affected in form, the long tapering nails sharply touched with light at the tips, a method never met with in Italian pictures; the laboured miniature-like treatment of the little stones in the foreground and of the vase of ointment, which is cold and over-smooth in tone. Compare the trees with those in Van der Werff's pictures Nos. 1817 and 1818 of this gallery. Compare even the surface cracks and splits in this picture with those in the works of this painter and of his contemporaries, and you will, I think, be forced to admit, however unwillingly, that if not by Van der Werff himself, it must at all events have been by some contemporary and fellow-countryman; in any case, that it could not possibly have been by an Italian, and least of all by an Italian of the early part of the sixteenth century.'

'You will never convert me,' said the indignant lady with a scornful laugh. She was determined not to examine the picture, and after a pause proceeded: 'You have evidently never read Raphael Mengs' writings. He was an art-critic of great repute and learning, who studied Correggio profoundly, and entered thoroughly into his mode of thought and feeling. In his eyes this picture was the finest of all the master's works, and, moreover, our great poet Schlegel wrote one of his most charming sonnets in praise of this Magdalen, which you profess to despise.'

'You might recite it, Elise,' said her father, who was evidently proud of his daughter's learning.

'Certainly not,' she replied sharply; 'to preach to deaf ears is useless.'

'Possibly,' I returned, in answer to this somewhat cutting observation. 'What you say of Mengs may be very true; his appreciation of art coincided with the taste of his day. But as to the connoisseurship of the writers of the romantic and neo-Catholic schools, allow me to observe that I consider it absolutely worthless. Æsthetic doctrine is a matter of fashion, and undergoes a change every fifty years. A picture is a long-suffering thing, and there is nothing to prevent your æsthetic teacher from reading into it any kind of matter he happens to have in his head. The public delights in fine writing, and as a rule the "Magdalen" of the sonnet proves so all-absorbing that the picture itself is entirely neglected. Most persons are roused to enthusiasm rather by some illusion of the mind than by actual facts, and this gift of imagination enables us to see only as much as we wish. It is impossible for me,' I continued, 'to regard this "Magdalen" as the work of Correggio. Moreover, it is painted on copper, and no Italian master ever employed this material before the close of the sixteenth century.'

'I beg your pardon; Vasari expressly says that Sebastiano del Piombo painted upon copper,' retorted this erudite lady with a self-satisfied smile.

'You are perfectly right,' I rejoined, 'and I am quite aware that Vasari, in his life of this painter, records that Sebastiano not only painted on stone, but proved that silver, copper, tin, and other metals could be used as a surface for painting. He, however, carefully avoids specifying any painting on copper by this master, and I do not, therefore, attach any weight to his casual statement. I am acquainted with several paintings on slate by Sebastiano, but so far I have failed to discover a single painting on copper by any Italian painter of importance of the first half of the sixteenth century.[1] The use of copper as a substitute for panel or canvas appears to have been first introduced in the school of Antwerp, and I could name many pictures on this material by Martin de Vos, Bartel Spranger, the' elder Pourbus, Rolandt Savery, Brill, Brueghel, and others; but I am unable to name any by Italian masters of the best epoch of art.'

'Criticism,' observed the lady drily, as she adjusted her shawl, ' is like fire destroying all it comes in contact with. A short time ago the critics attacked our beautiful " Madonna" by Holbein, and now they have the audacity to disparage Correggio's world-renowned "Magdalen," another of the gems of our gallery. Such proceedings may be tolerated in Russia, where Nihilism is rampant, but in Germany, fortunately, we have so many admirable connoisseurs and students of art, that such pernicious and revolutionary attempts will soon be stamped out. Let us go now,' she said, turning to her father.

I have still a few more remarks to make about this picture; and, first, as to the question whether Correggio ever painted a recumbent and reading Magdalen. We know

[1] We find, it is true, many paintings on copper in public collections which are ascribed by the catalogues to Italian masters of this period. In the Louvre, for example, a " Holy Family " (No. 1275) is attributed to Dosso Dossi, which on closer inspection proves to be a Flemish work; and in the Munich gallery the portrait of a man holding a carnation (No. 166) was formerly attributed to Garofalo, but it has now been rightly assigned to a painter of the Netherlands. I could cite other instances of paintings on copper which pass for Italian pictures, though in reality they are merely copies by Flemish or other Northern artists. For the present, however, these may suffice.

from a letter written by Veronica Gambara to Beatrice
d'Este on September 3, 1528,[1] that a "Repentant Mag-
dalen" was produced in the master's workshop, but it is
impossible to say what became of the picture. We also
know that Correggio painted a "Reading Magdalen." This
appears from a letter written by Carlo Malaspina,[2] who was
employed in the library at Parma. In it he remarks that
Ortensio Lando had informed the Marchesa di Novellara
that Correggio had recently (?) painted a splendid "Read-
ing Magdalen"[3] for the 'magnifico Signore di Mantova.' We
may therefore conclude that Correggio did treat a subject
similar to the one we meet with in the Dresden gallery,
but what may have become of the picture?

According to Baldinucci, a "Magdalen in the Desert"
by Correggio was in the collection of Niccolò Gaddi, a
Florentine patrician, in 1660. This is Baldinucci's state-
ment, and we may take it for what it is worth. On
his authority, however, the catalogue of the Uffizi ascribes
to Allori the recumbent and reading Magdalen in that
collection, though every impartial connoisseur will see
at once that it is a Flemish copy. The landscape back-
ground is wholly Northern in character. There are no
stones in the foreground as in the Dresden example; a skull
and a vase of ointment are introduced, and, in addition,
the Magdalen holds a crucifix in her left hand. The
Flemish copy at Florence is probably earlier in date than
that at Dresden (†).

In conclusion, let me briefly sum up my opinion with
regard to this coquettish recumbent Magdalen, whose charms
are designed to appeal to the senses. It does not belong to

---

[1] See the *Life of Correggio*, by
Dr. Julius Meyer, p. 219.

[2] Published by Signor Guglielmo
Bracchirolli of Mantua in the *Gior-*
nale di Erudizione artistica, vol. i.
Fascicolo xi. p. 332.

[3] He says nothing, however, about
its being a recumbent figure.

the first half of the sixteenth century, and therefore cannot possibly be by Correggio. In all probability it was produced towards the close of that century, and very likely in the school of the Carracci,˙ as may be inferred from the type of the head. As regards the celebrated example on copper in Dresden, I consider it to be a copy dating from the second half of the seventeenth century, and executed by some painter of the Netherlands who was closely connected with Adrian van der Werff.[1]

These numerous "Repentant Magdalens," so frequently met with between the close of the sixteenth century and the early part of the seventeenth, more especially in the school of Bologna, are simply a Jesuit rendering of the Venus of the Venetian painters. Between Giorgione's exquisite Venus, however, and Correggio's "Repentant Magdalen" lies the whole range of the Spanish-Catholic counter-Reformation.

Three pictures are attributed to Francesco Francia in this gallery, but only two are, I think, authentic—the beautiful little "Adoration of the Magi" (No. 49) and the much restored "Baptism of Christ" (No. 48).[2] The "Madonna" (No. 50) is only of the master's school.

As a work of the school of Ferrara-Bologna I would name the large altar-piece by Bartolommeo da Bagnacavallo (No. 113). The picture itself proves, better than any words of mine could do, that Bagnacavallo was not only a pupil but a plagiarist of Dosso. From a distance it might even be taken for a work by the latter painter. I maintain that Bagnacavallo belongs to the school of Ferrara-Bologna, and the fact that he was for some time in Rome, and there became an imitator of Raphael, does

[1] Replicas of this Magdalen ' by Correggio' are innumerable, and the ' Bolognese' original is, no doubt, among them.

[2] An old copy of this picture is at Hampton Court.

not affect this theory in the slightest degree. His best works, both frescoes and easel-pictures, are at Bologna. Among those in the public gallery, one, representing the marriage of St. Catherine in the presence of King David and SS. John the Evangelist, Anthony, and Dominic, is actually attributed to Gherardo Fiorentino (†). One of his finest works is in the Church of the Misericordia, over the second altar on the left. It is a panel picture, representing the Madonna with the Child enthroned on clouds, while two angels hold a crown over her head. Below, in a fantastic landscape, stand SS. Francis and Monica, while a man, a woman, and a girl kneel beside them in supplication.

I may close this chapter by directing the attention of students to some drawings by the principal representatives of the school of Ferrara-Bologna in the first half of the sixteenth century : Lorenzo Costa, Ercole Grandi di Giulio Cesare, Chiodarolo, Amico Aspertini, and Correggio. I have never met with any drawings which could with any certainty be ascribed to Dosso or Garofalo.

In the Uffizi we find pen drawings by Costa, Chiodarolo, and Amico Aspertini. A comparison between the technic in them and that in Ercole Roberti's sketch for the "Massacre of the Innocents," in the cabinet of engravings at Berlin, proves that all these four masters belonged to the same school.[1]

In the upper part of Lorenzo Costa's drawing in the Uffizi (Case 38, No. 178) is represented the "Coronation of the Virgin," in the lower stand six saints. It is the sketch for his large altar-piece in the choir of S. Giovanni in

[1] Amico Aspertini's frescoes at Lucca clearly show his connection with Ercole Roberti. A large altar-piece by Guido Aspertini is in the Church of S. Martino at Bologna, and another is in the public gallery in that city. This latter is, I think, erroneously ascribed to his brother Amico (†).

STUDY OF THREE CHILDREN.   DRAWING BY CORREGGIO.

(At Chatsworth.)

To face p. 167.

Monte at Bologna. Philpot has photographed it under the name of Filippino (†) (No. 763). The drawing by Chiodarolo (Case 36, No. 166) represents St. Cecilia before the proconsul, and is the sketch for his fresco in the oratory of St. Cecilia attached to the Church of S. Giacomo Maggiore at Bologna. This drawing was also photographed by Philpot (No. 2847) as by Filippino Lippi (†). In the drawing by Amico Aspertini are five nude figures in various attitudes (Philpot, No. 1237).[1] A sheet, containing a frieze by Aspertini, has been photographed by Braun (No. 558).

In the Louvre (Salle aux Boîtes, No. 436) we find a washed drawing which was attributed by Baldinucci to Mantegna, but which M. Reiset, with more discernment, assigned to Lorenzo Costa. It represents Judith with the head of Holofernes, and, if I am not much mistaken, is, as I have already had occasion to observe, by Ercole Grandi di Giulio Cesare (†) (Braun, 411).

The following are a few of Correggio's drawings : In the Uffizi, a slight sketch in charcoal of SS. Anthony, Stephen, Roch, and John the Baptist (Braun, 676). In the Louvre, a sketch for the frieze in the Church of S. Giovanni at Parma, representing two *putti*, one caressing a winged lion, the other an eagle (Braun, 450) ; three studies for a frieze (Braun, 452) ; and a red chalk drawing for his picture in the gallery at Parma—the martyrdom of two saints (Braun, 461). At Chatsworth there is a red chalk drawing by him of *putti* (Braun, 188).

Two drawings in the Uffizi by Bagnacavallo may be mentioned here, viz. four standing figures of saints, in wash (Braun, 559), and the "Annunciation" (Braun, 560).

[1] These drawings have also been photographed by Brogi of Florence.

THE VENETIANS.

We now come to the painters of the Venetian Republic, whose works glow upon the walls with the fascination peculiar to themselves. We meet with many brilliant examples in this gallery, though unfortunately few of the fifteenth century.

The portrait of the Doge Leonardo Loredano (No. 53) seems to be merely a copy of the school-picture in the gallery at Bergamo, and in the new catalogue is recognised as such. The "Madonna and Saints" (No. 54), formerly ascribed to Giovanni Bellini, is now rightly termed a feeble work of the school; I would go a step further, and call it a *pasticcio*. The Madonna is taken from Bellini, the St. Helena from Bissolo, and the St. Joseph from Catena. The body of the Child is incorrectly modelled, the folds on the sleeve of the Madonna are clumsy, the whole picture is a caricature, and I have my doubts as to its being of Italian origin at all. Ten years ago I made the mistake of connecting it with the name of Bartolommeo Veneto, and on that occasion gave some account of this Protean painter, who, though scarcely known, is not undeserving of consideration. I think it desirable to repeat what I then said about him, as it may encourage some young writer to make a closer study of this singular and variable artist, and to give a more complete notice of him than I have been able to do.

This eccentric painter does not always sign himself 'Bartolommeo Veneziano' or 'de Venecia,' for, on one of his pictures—in all probability his earliest work—we read, '*Bartolommeo mezzo veneziano e mezzo cremonese.*' We may consequently infer that he was a native of Cremona who had settled in Venice. This picture was once in the

FEMALE PORTRAIT. BY BARTOLOMMEO VENETO.

(In the possession of Duke Giovanni Melzi, Milan.)

To face p. 163.

possession of the late Senatore Leopardo Martinengo in
that city. Another early work by him is in the public
gallery at Bergamo (Lochis collection), and is inscribed:
'*Bartholomeus venetus faciebat* 1505.' The form and action
of the Madonna's hand are still wholly Bellinesque, the line
of the eyelid is very hard, the form of the ear recalls Gentile
Bellini rather than Giovanni, the arm of the Madonna,
which supports the foot of the Infant Saviour, is stiff and
awkward in movement, the folds of the drapery are coarse
and the clouds woolly, but the colouring is warm and of
great brilliancy. A portrait, dating from the same period,
belongs to Mr. Carew in London. It is signed: '*Bartolomeo
de Venecia* 1506.'

An attractive female portrait of a later period of the
master's career is in the collection of Duke Giovanni Melzi
at Milan. It is signed: '*Btōlamio de Venecia F.*' The
woman here represented holds a small hammer in one
hand, and in the other a ring. Her gold bracelet is
inscribed : ' Sfoza de la Ebra ; ' that is, ' Ebra's costume.' [1]
The colouring is brilliant; the shade of red in the woman's
hat recalls that used in the school of Quentin Massys. It is
not improbable that Bartolommeo, like other Venetian
artists before him, such as Jacometto, Jacopo de' Barbari,
and others, may have come in contact with painters of
the Netherlands at Venice. The hair falls in ringlets and
looks like twisted wire; the details are executed with
miniaturelike precision.

A most attractive female portrait in the Staedel Institute
at Frankfort (No. 11A), which is there ascribed to the
Florentine school, is in all probability by Bartolommeo, and
of the same period as the preceding. Like Duke Melzi's

---

[1] In the Venetian dialect, ' sfoza '
is used instead of ' foggia,' signi-
fying costume, or manner of array-
ing oneself. ' Ebra ' was probably
the name of the woman repre-
sented.

portrait, it represents an idealised Venetian courtesan. She is young and fantastically arrayed, and holds a nosegay of flowers in her right hand; a locket is suspended from her neck, and her head is encircled by a wreath of laurel. Her ringlets, as in the preceding picture, are like twisted wire.

There is another portrait of a woman (transformed into a saint) in the same room of the Frankfort gallery, which is also most probably by Bartolommeo, though it is attributed to a Lombard painter of far greater renown. I shall leave it to students to identify the picture. I would also direct their attention to two other works which, though neither bearing the master's signature nor a date, appear to me undoubtedly by him. One is in the Louvre (†), and represents a fantastically dressed woman holding a necklace in her left hand, the form of which is very characteristic for the master, and a pair of gloves in her right. It is described as by an unknown painter. The other, a Madonna, is in the collection of the Duc d'Aumale at Chantilly, but I do not recollect to whom it is there attributed.

A Madonna, with a varied landscape background, in the Ambrosiana (Sala Pecis) at Milan, attributed to Lotto, I believe to be by Bartolommeo and of his late period (†). To the same epoch I should also ascribe a " St. Catherine," assigned to Lotto, in the third room of the Borromeo gallery in the same city (†).

Dr. Woermann will perhaps be surprised and gratified to learn that the Dresden gallery also contains a work by this master. The discovery was made by Dr. Gustavo Frizzoni, the well-known connoisseur of Italian art, who is, I think, perfectly right in ascribing to Bartolommeo Veneto the " Daughter of Herodias " (No. 292 of this collection).[1]

[1] Now 201A, ascribed to Bartolommeo Veneto.

THE DAUGHTER OF HERODIAS.   BY BARTOLOMMEO VENETO.

(In the Dresden Gallery.)

To face p. 170.

According to Piacenza,[1] there was a Madonna in the Hercolani collection at Bologna bearing the following inscription : ' 1509, a di 7 Aprile, Bartolamio scholaro de ZE. . . . BE. . . .'

Both this writer and the Florentine commentators on Vasari[2] consider that 'ZE.' stands for Giovanni. I think, however, that this mutilated inscription can only be interpreted to mean ' Zentile Bellini,' for in the Venetian dialect Zuan, and not Zean, stands for Giovanni. As these writers had no knowledge of Bartolommeo Veneto, they unhesitatingly ascribed the picture to that great painter Bartolommeo Montagna—a mistake which one would suppose even a beginner in the study of art would scarcely have committed.

There are several works by this master in England. One, the portrait of "Lodovico Martinengo,"[3] is in the National Gallery, and is inscribed : ' Bartolom. Venetus faciebat M.D. XXX. XVI. ZVN. [June].' Another—the ' Giorgionesque' portrait of a woman signed and dated like the preceding 1530—belonged to the late Mr. Barker in London. Unsigned works by this painter are usually ascribed to more important masters. I could name several instances in which I believe this to have been the case, but for the present it may suffice to have directed attention to this little-known artist.

The Dresden gallery, as already observed, can boast of no work by Giovanni Bellini ; it possesses, however, a characteristic example of Andrea Mantegna,[4] his great

---

[1] See Baldinucci, iii. 210.
[2] vi. 127 (ed. Milanesi, iii. 649).
[3] The Martinengos appear to have been this artist's patrons. A work of his early period, as we have already noted, is an heirloom in the family of the Senatore Martinengo at Venice.

[4] Mantegna was born at Vicenza, and not at Padua. This may be inferred from a document in the State archives at Venice, which begins as follows : ' Pro Andrea Mantegna pictore, Pars posita in Consilio de XL.ª propter placitare Advocatorum Comunis quod istud compro-

contemporary, who was also his brother-in-law. The picture represents the "Holy Family," and is in Cabinet I. (No. 51). The master's earlier works are usually on panel. Those on canvas, such as the one in this gallery, are all of his last period, from about 1490 to 1506, in which latter year he died. Like all celebrated painters, Mantegna is often made responsible for the works of his imitators or of some of his contemporaries. I shall, therefore, enumerate in order those pictures, both on panel and canvas, which I think may with certainty be ascribed to him. We will begin with those of his panel-pictures which are still in Italy.

1. The large altar-piece in many compartments, with St. Luke in the centre, painted between 1453 and 1454 for the Church of S. Giustina at Padua, and now in the Brera. 2. The Madonna surrounded by a glory of singing angels, in the same gallery. 3. The large altar-piece in the Church of S. Zeno at Verona of 1460. 4. The "St. George" in the Venice Academy. 5. The Triptych in the Uffizi. 6. The "Presentation in the Temple" in the Querini-Stampalia collection at Venice.[1] 7. The Madonna with saints in the public gallery at Verona. 8. A similar subject in the gallery at Turin. 9. The small Madonna in the Uffizi (No. 1025).

The following are Mantegna's panel pictures out of Italy :—

10 and 11. Two compartments of a predella belonging to the altar-piece of S. Zeno at Verona, now in the collection at Tours. 12. The third compartment of the same predella, representing the "Crucifixion," now in the Louvre

missum rogatum de MCCCCXLVII. die XXVI Januarii per magistrum Franciscum Scarzono pictorem de Padua et Andream Blasij Mantegna de Vincentia pictorem, per quod se compromiserunt,' &c. (*Avog. di Comun.*—X, Fasc. 2, c. 57, 1455—2 *januarii*).

[1] Entirely ruined by modern restoration.

MADONNA. BY MANTEGNA.

(At Bergamo.)

To face p. 173.

(No. 1873). 13. The "Agony in the Garden," in the collection of Lord Northbrook in London. 14. The portrait of Cardinal Scarampi in the Berlin Museum. 15. The St. Sebastian in the public gallery at Vienna. 16. The "Ecce Homo" in the gallery at Copenhagen.

The following are the pictures on canvas which appear to me to be by the master himself:—

17. The series known as the "Triumphs of Cæsar," now at Hampton Court; they were begun in 1487 and completed in 1492. Unfortunately, in the reign of William III., these works were repainted and utterly disfigured by the artist Laguerre. 18. The Madonna enthroned with saints in the English National Gallery (No. 274). 19. Samson and Delilah in the same collection (No. 1145). 20. The Madonna in the public gallery at Bergamo [1] (No. 153), painted in tempera. 21. The

[1] This "Madonna" is of a totally different type to those of Raphael, Francia, Luini, and others. Mantegna's Madonnas are Old Testament types, and are allied in some degree with Michelangelo's sibyls; they will certainly afford no pleasure to those who delight in Sassoferrato or Carlo Dolci. The admirable little picture at Bergamo is executed with the most loving care. It may perhaps be one of the two mentioned by Mantegna in a letter which he addressed to Francesco Gonzaga on December 21, 1491, and which is as follows : ' Io perchè ho inteso che la Ex. V. ha donato el quadrettino a Milano ve ne mando un altro rimanendomi però lo stampo da farne degli altri per gracia de la gloriosa Vergine Maria, dalla quale sempre ho obtenuto molte più gratie che non ho meritato. Ma al presente in presentia de la Ex. V. la priego che la si metta in core di attendermi le promesse fate con quella liberalità che ha sempre fato et fa la Ex. V. ad ciò ch' el sia noto a tuto el mondo, che la mia lunga Servitù sia stata riconosciuta dalla Illma casa di Gonzaga, alla quale con tutte le force mie et virtù avute da Dio, mi o sempre sforzato di fare honore et al presente più che mai ne sono benissimo apto e disposto, non mi lasando mancare la Ex. V. el che parrà che quella faci conto delle cose mie.' This interesting letter may thus be translated : ' Having heard that your Excellency has given away the little picture to some one at Milan, I send you another, for by the grace of the Blessed Virgin Mary, who has bestowed upon me more blessings than I deserve, I still have the model which enables me to produce others. At present, however, in presence of your Excellency, I pray that you may be pleased to remember the promises which, with

Madonna in the Poldi-Pezzoli collection at Milan. 22. The
so-called "Madonna della Vittoria" in the Louvre (No.
1374).[1] 23 and 24. Two allegories in the same gallery—
"Parnassus" (No. 1375) and "Wisdom victorious over
the Vices" (No. 1376). 25. The Madonna in the Dresden
gallery. 26. The Madonna enthroned between saints and
angel musicians (of 1497), in the Trivulzio Palace at
Milan. 27. The "Baptism of Christ" in the sacristy of
S. Andrea at Mantua. 28. The Madonna with SS.
Joseph, Zachariah, Elisabeth, and the little St. John, in
the same church. These two last-named pictures are
regarded by Messrs. Crowe and Cavalcaselle (i. 416, 417),
and Dr. Bode (ii. 617), as works by Francesco Mantegna (†).
29. The "Triumph of Scipio" in the English National
Gallery (No. 902), painted in Venice about 1505 for
Francesco Cornaro. 30. The "St. Sebastian" of the
Scarpa collection at La Motta, near Treviso, a full-length
figure over life-size. 31. The "Pietà" in the Brera.
32. A representation of the Infant Saviour standing upon
a stone parapet, and holding a sphere, typical of the world,
in his left hand. On his right is the little St. John, point-

your accustomed generosity, you
made to me, in order that it may
be known throughout the world that
my long services have been recog-
nised by the illustrious House of
Gonzaga, whom I have ever sought
to honour with all my might and
with the gifts which I have received
from God. And now more than
ever do I feel myself able and dis-
posed so to do, in the hope that your
Excellency will let me want for
nothing, which would prove that
your Excellency knows how to value
my services.' If in these lines the
dignified self - confidence which
animated the great artist is dis-

closed, in another document he
shows himself as a highly irascible
personage, who will not let an in-
jury go unpunished, but insists
on prosecuting a neighbour who
had stolen some ripe figs from his
garden.

[1] Years ago I saw a copy of this
picture by some Northern painter in
the collection of Prince Lichtenstein
at Vienna, the feeble copyist having
added five angels. This miserable
production was of the class which in
Italy are known as *pasticci*. Sub-
sequently it was removed from the
collection and presented by the
prince to the Academy at Vienna.

MADONNA AND CHILD. BY MANTEGNA.

(In the Poldi-Pezzoli Collection, Milan.

To face p. 174.

ing to the Saviour with his right hand; behind him stands St. Joseph; in front is the Madonna, seen only to the waist. This admirable picture, treated with much originality, was formerly in the collection of Dr. J. P. Richter, the well-known connoisseur.[1] 33. A much damaged Madonna in the possession of the heirs of the late Vicomte Both de Tauzia, director of the Louvre.

In addition to these thirty-three pictures by Mantegna, there may possibly be others in private collections, though scarcely, I should say, more than half a dozen, for Mantegna, like Leonardo da Vinci, was not a rapid painter.

Having enumerated what I consider to be authentic works by Mantegna, I will now mention a few which, though always ascribed to the master in books, appear to me unworthy of him :—

1. The small panel of the " Death of the Madonna " in the Museo del Prado at Madrid (No. 295), by a feeble imitator of the master. 2. Two female figures representing Summer and Autumn, in the English National Gallery (No. 1125), by an able imitator of Mantegna. 3. A Madonna in the Berlin Museum (No. 27), by a painter of Murano who imitated Mantegna. 4. The so-called portrait of Elisabeth Gonzaga, wife of Guidobaldo da Montefeltro, in the Tribune of the Uffizi, by a Veronese master, probably Francesco Carotto. This picture is, however, so much disfigured by repainting that it is difficult to give any decided opinion about it. 5. A St. Mark in the Staedel Institute at Frankfort, probably by Francesco Cossa. 6. The " Transfiguration " in the Museo Civico (Correr collection) at Venice, an early work by Giovanni Bellini. 7. The figure of St. Euphemia in the Naples gallery, a picture entirely ruined by restoration ; the inscription upon it appears to me to be a forgery. 8. The Madonna with

---

[1] This picture is now in the collection of Mr. Ludwig Mond in London.

angels playing on musical instruments in the Palazzo Scotti at Milan, by some Paduan imitator of Mantegna. The inscription on it is a palpable forgery of recent date. 9. The portrait of Vespasiano Gonzaga in the public gallery at Bergamo (No. 154). This picture, together with a male portrait, bearing a forged signature, in the Sciarra-Colonna collection, is by Francesco Bonsignori (†). 10. The standing figures of SS. Jerome and Alexis in the gallery at Bergamo (Nos. 159 and 161), by Gregorio Schiavone.[1] 11. The "Resurrection" in the same gallery (No. 169), by an imitator of Mantegna. 12. The "Pietà" in the Vatican gallery. I have already expressed my opinion of this picture in a former volume.[2]

The following are the wall-paintings by Mantegna which have been preserved to us in a fairly good condition :[3]—

1. Two figures of SS. Anthony and Bernard over the principal door of the Church of S. Antonio at Padua, executed by Mantegna in 1452. 2. The history of St. James and the martyrdom of St. Christopher in the Eremi-

---

[1] This St. Jerome by Schiavone, who was a pupil of Squarcione, so vividly recalls Crivelli that it affords us a further proof that the latter master belonged to the school of Padua, and not to that of Murano.

[2] See *Critical Studies in the Borghese and Doria Galleries*, p. 272.

[3] By wall-paintings are usually understood frescoes, that is, paintings on *intonaco* or damp plaster. Mantegna's wall-paintings, like Leonardo's "Last Supper" in the refectory of S. Maria delle Grazie at Milan, are usually, but most inappropriately, termed frescoes, as they are executed in tempera upon dry mortar called 'stucco lucido.' Mantegna was engaged for six years upon his paintings on the walls of the Eremitani Chapel at Padua, and for the same space of time on those in the so-called 'Camera degli sposi' in the Palazzo Ducale at Mantua. It is well known how foolishly impatient the Prior of S. Maria delle Grazie was for the completion of Leonardo da Vinci's "Last Supper," and how frequently he complained to Lodovico il Moro of the painter's slow progress. The Prior had probably heard that fresco-painting did not require much time, and it was therefore incomprehensible to him that Leonardo should be so long about his work. The wall-paintings of both Mantegna and Leonardo were, however, executed with the care and finish of easel-pictures.

tani Chapel at Padua, executed between 1453 and 1459.
3. The paintings in the Palazzo Ducale at Mantua, repre-
senting scenes from the family life of Lodovico Gonzaga and
his wife Barbara of Brandenburg, their children and re-
lations, executed between 1474 and 1484. The frescoes
which Mantegna executed in the Vatican for Pope Innocent
VIII. between 1488 and 1490 have perished.

Finally, I may mention a few of Mantegna's drawings
as an aid to students in discriminating between those which
are genuine and those innumerable drawings which are
wrongly ascribed to him. They are as follows :—

1. The "Judgment of Solomon," a *grisaille* sketch on
canvas in the Louvre (No. 241, Braun, 408). 2. "Mucius
Scaevola," also in *grisaille*, in the Print-Room at Munich.
3. "Christ between SS. Andrew and Longinus" in the
same collection.

The following are in the British Museum in Vol. XX. :
4. A dying man lying on the ground ; a pen-and-ink draw-
ing (Braun, 56). 5. "Calumny," after Lucian's descrip-
tion ; a pen-and-ink drawing (Braun, 59). 6. A large sheet
representing "Mars between Diana and Venus ; " pen and
wash (Braun, 58), unfortunately retouched in colours by
some later hand. 7. The Madonna enthroned, with the
Infant Saviour standing on her knee ; below, on the right,
a boy angel is seated (Braun, 57).

8. "Judith with the Head of Holofernes," in the Uffizi;
pen and wash (Braun, 791). A copy of this drawing in
the Louvre (Braun, 410) is ascribed to Mantegna himself.
Another drawing in the latter gallery (His de la Salle col-
lection, No. 2240) is ascribed to Mantegna, but I believe it
to be by Francesco Bonsignori (†). It is the sketch for a
statue of Virgil. In the Brunswick gallery and in the royal
library at Turin, drawings, which I believe to be by Marco
Zoppo, are attributed to Mantegna (†).

The two pictures ascribed to Cima da Conegliano in the Dresden gallery (Nos. 61 and 63)[1] are authentic. The first of the two is much repainted ; the other was produced under the influence of Carpaccio. The head of Christ (No. 62), though greatly damaged, appears to me to be an original, and the director of the gallery is of the same opinion. Works by this noble and serious painter are not often met with out of Italy. The Madrid gallery and the Louvre have no examples of his art. One small picture by him is in the public gallery at Vienna, and another is in the Munich Pinacothek. Even in England he is represented only by a few pictures, which do not give the most favourable impression of his capacity ; a proof that only in the present century have Cima's merits been appreciated. His most important works are still in North Italy in churches and public collections.

The two pictures numbered respectively 55 and 56[2] are good specimens of the manner of Girolamo da Santa Croce, a painter who is sometimes confounded with Vincenzo Catena. This mistake, incredible as it may appear, occurs in the Venice Academy, where the " Scourging of Christ " (Room IX. No. 13)—a worthless production, undoubtedly by Girolamo da Santa Croce—is attributed to Catena (†) ; Dr. Bode also regards it as the work of the latter (ii. 658). How is it possible for young students, who are thus taught to regard this picture as a Catena, to form any true idea either of that master's art, or of the standard of taste of his contemporaries, who had a high opinion of Catena's merits as a painter ?

No. 66 was formerly described as by an unknown master. It is a charming picture, representing the Madonna and

[1] A figure of Christ in the act of blessing, and the " Presentation of the Madonna in the Temple."

[2] The Madonna and St. Joseph with angels adoring the new-born Saviour, and the " Martyrdom of St. Laurence," a subject which this painter often treated.

Child between two angels, and is, in my opinion, by the
Veronese master, Giovan Francesco Carotto (†). It is much
repainted, but to my satisfaction my attribution has been
accepted in the new catalogue.[1]

Some years ago an important work of the early Venetian
school was bought in Vienna for this gallery—the large "St.
Sebastian" (No. 52) by Antonello da Messina, which is un-
questionably thoroughly Venetian in character. The great
impression which Mantegna's paintings in the Eremitani
Chapel must have produced upon Antonello is discernible
in this picture. It has suffered much from repainting; all
the shadows have been daubed over, for instance, in the
architectural parts, on the broken column in the foreground,
and also on the body and about the eyes and brow of the
saint. The sky, too, must originally have been much lighter
and more transparent in tone. The picture is, nevertheless,
of great interest, though it has small claim to beauty. The
little figures in the middle distance and in the background
are cleverly painted and full of life, even to the sleeping
guard, though it must be admitted that the appearance of
the latter figure is almost ludicrous. Very attractive are the
couple looking down from a terrace. The execution of the
whole is minute and careful in every detail. It must have
been produced between 1480 and 1490. Antonello, as a
portrait painter, is worthy of the highest praise, but when
seeking to give expression to some deep emotion he appears

[1] The angel behind the Madonna recalls an angel in an altar-piece by Carotto in the public gallery at Verona, formerly in the Chapel of St. Euphemia in that city. The orange colour employed is also characteristic of the school of Liberale da Verona, to which Carotto belonged. The picture might well be cleaned, and should then be placed near the fine portrait (No. 201) by Cavazzola, the fellow-countryman of Carotto. I have only met with three works in Germany by this gifted Veronese artist—an early one signed with his name in the Staedel Institute at Frankfort (No. 22), a most attractive Madonna belonging to Baron Sternburg at Lützschena (†), and one of his last period, lately in the collection of Herr Edward Habich at Cassel.

empty and constrained. Compared with the inspired figure of St. Sebastian by Liberale da Verona in the Brera, or even with Dosso's treatment of the same subject, we feel at once how great was the gulf separating the artist of Messina from these two painters.

The representation of life-sized nude figures in painting was first attempted at Florence soon after 1470 by certain distinguished sculptors who also practised the art of painting, their object being to give proof of their knowledge of the human form and of their capacity in treating it.[1] One of the first examples of this kind was, if I mistake not, Antonio del Pollaiuolo's large "St. Sebastian," which he drew from life for Antonio Pucci.[2] All other life-sized representations of the human form by this master, such as the "Labours of Hercules," which he painted for Lorenzo il Magnifico, are said to have perished.

The large "Baptism of Christ" by his rival, Andrea Verrocchio, was probably produced about the same time. If we examine these works without prejudice, we shall be forced to admit that both are unsatisfactory. Verrocchio's, moreover, is in a deplorable state, having first been flayed and subsequently smeared over with oil colours, so that it is only in the heads that the great sculptor can still be re-

---

[1] Vasari relates that Antonio del Pollaiuolo, the best draughtsman of his day, was the first who attempted the anatomy of the human form: 'Egli s'intese degli ignudi più modernamente che fatto non avevano gli altri maestri inanzi a lui; e scorticò molti uomini per vedere la notomia lor sotto e fù il primo a mostrare il modo di cercare i muscoli, che avessero forma e ordine nelle figure' (v. 98; ed. Milanesi, iii. 295).

[2] This altar-piece by Antonio del Pollaiuolo was sold in 1856 to the English National Gallery (No. 292). The cartoon for this picture was certainly furnished by Antonio the sculptor; the execution, however, is unquestionably by his brother Pietro. A slightly washed pen sketch for the figure of St. Sebastian, by the hand of Antonio, is in the Morelli collection, and was reproduced in the work entitled *Quaranta disegni della Raccolta Morelli*, by Dr. Gustavo Frizzoni, Milano, Hoepli, 1886. [This drawing now belongs to Dr. Frizzoni.—TRANS.]

cognised. When treating the nude on a small scale, however, Verrocchio was unsurpassed, as, for instance, in his bronze " David " in the National Museum at Florence, or in the *putto* in the court of the Palazzo Vecchio in the same city. In the plastic character of his heads he is especially successful, and no other artist, with the exception of his great pupil Leonardo, was able to impart to them so speaking and lifelike an expression.

The example thus set by Pollaiuolo and Verrocchio induced many of their contemporaries, among them Sandro Botticelli, to attempt life-sized studies from the nude. St. Sebastian, the Apollo of Christian legend, was the subject almost exclusively represented, of which we have proof in nearly all the galleries of Europe. The most successful among the painters of the fifteenth century in the representation of the nude was undoubtedly Luca Signorelli. All who have seen his frescoes in the Cathedral of Orvieto will, I think, be disposed to share this opinion.

In the Venetian territories it was principally the pupils of Squarcione who attempted this study, and first among them was Andrea Mantegna. The representation of the martyrdom of St. Christopher in the Eremitani Chapel at Padua afforded him an opportunity of trying his powers in this direction, but it appears to me that he never fulfilled this difficult task in a manner worthy of himself. Even in his latest works—the "Pietà" in the Brera, and the large " St. Sebastian " in the Scarpa collection at La Motta—he showed himself, by sheer dint of too much learning, inferior to Botticelli and Liberale da Verona. The " St. Sebastian " is a positively repulsive picture.

Among those theories which in course of time have come to be regarded in the light of a dogma, and as beyond question, must be classed the belief that Antonello went to Flanders and there learnt the use of oil as a vehicle from Jan van Eyck. Some recent writers have substituted the name of Roger van der Weyden, or even of Hans Memling, for that of Van Eyck, who died in 1441. If I am not greatly mistaken, the whole story is a mere fabrication, due, in all probability, to the vanity and imaginative faculty of some Sicilian.

Let us examine the matter more closely, and without prejudice. That the painters of Europe were well acquainted with the use of 'oil medium,' to use a favourite expression of Messrs. Crowe and Cavalcaselle, long before the time of the Van Eycks, we gather both from the 'Trattato della Pittura,' by Cennino Cennini of 1437, and from a much earlier treatise, the 'Diversarum Artium Schedula,' by the monk Theophilus.[1]

In Jan van Eyck's epitaph there is no reference to his invention of oil painting:

Hic jacet eximia clarus virtute Joannes,
In quo picturæ gratia mira fuit, etc.[2]

No German writer of the fifteenth century refers to Van Eyck's 'discovery,' for though Martin Schongauer, Michael Wohlgemuth, Albert Dürer, Hans Holbein the elder, Burckmair, and other artists were well acquainted with the process of painting with oil as a vehicle, which had been perfected by the brothers Van Eyck, no great account was taken of it north of the Alps. Even in Italy the new Flemish method of painting does not seem to have produced any sensation before the appearance of Vasari's account of Antonello da Messina in 1550.

Bartolomeus Facius, in his book entitled 'De Viris Illustribus,' written in 1456, declares Johannes Gallicus—

[1] In Lorenzo Ghiberti's second commentary this passage occurs with reference to Giotto: 'Costui lavorò in muro, lavorò in tavola, lavorò a olio,' &c. (see Vasari, ed. Le Monnier, i. xviii.).

[2] See Zani, *Enciclopedia*, &c. ii. 305.

i.e. Van Eyck, whom as a practical painter he terms 'princeps pictorum'—'multa de colorum proprietatibus invenisse, quæ ab antiquis tradita, ex Plinii et ab aliorum auctorum lectione didicerat.'

A contemporary of Facius, the Florentine architect and sculptor Antonio Averulino, known as Filarete, says, in his 'Trattato della Architettura,' Book 24 [1]: 'With oil also these colours can all be employed on canvas or upon wood; for this, however, another system of painting must be adopted, which is very agreeable for those who are acquainted with it. In Germany (Lamagna) they work well in this manner, and more especially distinguished are Master Johan of Bruges and Master Roger (Van der Weyden), who both paint admirably with oil colours. Question: Tell me how this oil is employed, and of what kind it is? Answer: Linseed oil. Question: Is it not very dull? Answer: Yes, but the dulness can be removed, though in what way I am unable to state,' &c.[2]

In 1464, when the treatise of Filarete appeared, Antonello must have been fifty years of age, if, as art-historians affirm, he was born in 1414. Yet, as we have seen, Filarete makes no mention of him in connection with oil-painting, and both Ciriacus of Ancona and the Tuscan Albertini are equally silent with regard to him.

The only writer of the fifteenth century who names him is the Sicilian Matteo Collaccio, in a letter addressed to his fellow-countryman Antonio Siciliano, the Rector of the University at Padua, in which he alludes to some of the distinguished men of that day: 'Habet vero hæc ætas

[1] The original manuscript is in the Magliabecchiana (National) library at Florence, and a copy of it in the Trivulzio library at Milan.

[2] From this it is evident that, at the time of Filarete, the new system of the Van Eycks was theoretically known, but that among the Italian masters none had as yet seen reason to forsake their own method of tempera painting.

Antonellum Siculum, cujus pictura Venetiis in Divi Cassiani æde magnæ est admirationi.'

Albert Dürer, who visited Venice for the first time in 1494, very shortly, therefore, after the death of Antonello, never mentions him, either in his notes or later in his letters. This is a further proof, I think, that Antonello was not of such importance, nor did he enjoy so great a reputation in Venice, as Vasari's biography of him, written fifty years later, would lead us to suppose.

In 1524, Marcantonio Michiel, a Venetian patrician and a patron and connoisseur of art,[1] applied to the Neapolitan architect Summonzio for some information relating to Antonello da Messina. The following was the answer which he received: ' Since the time of King Ladislaus, we have never had anyone who showed such great aptitude for painting as our Neapolitan master Colantonio, and had he not died young he would truly have accomplished great things. If Colantonio did not reach the perfection in his art to which his pupil Antonello attained in your city of Venice, it was solely due to the times in which he lived. Colantonio, like all other artists of his day in Naples, sought to paint in the manner of the Flemings, and being passionately devoted to his art, he determined to go to Flanders in order there to perfect himself in painting. King Roger of Anjou,[2] however, dissuaded him from this resolve, and himself instructed him in the use of oils and in the mysteries of mixing colours. From Colantonio, who died young, his pupil, Antonello, learnt the method.'[3]

Modern criticism has clearly proved that this painter Colantonio, mentioned by Summonzio, was one of the many

---

[1] I am of opinion, with others, that this Marcantonio Michiel was the writer known to us as the ' Anonimo.'

[2] Roger reigned at Naples from 1435 to 1442.

[3] See Lanzi's *Storia Pittorica della Italia* (Milan, 1824, ii. 319).

inventions of ardent Neapolitan patriotism.[1] This has nothing to do with the case in point; but my object is to show that Summonzio, the first who gave any account of Antonello's artistic training, relates that he learnt the new Flemish system of oil painting, in Italy, and not, as related by Vasari, in Flanders.[2]

. The account of Antonello, furnished to Vasari five-and-twenty years later by one whom I have reason to suspect was a Sicilian scholar, is totally opposed to that of the Neapolitan Summonzio. According to him, Antonello first learnt drawing in Rome (from whom ?), and thence went to Palermo,[3] where he soon gained a great reputation. After some years he returned to his native city of Messina, where he continued to maintain the credit he had won at Palermo. It chanced, however, that he went to Naples, and there saw the fine picture by Jan van Eyck, which had been sent from Flanders to King René. The glow and brilliancy of the colouring so impressed him, that he immediately resolved to go to Bruges. There he was most kindly received by Jan van Eyck, who at once initiated him into the mysteries of painting in oil. On his return from Flanders (which must have taken place in 1440 or 1441, as Jan van Eyck died in the latter year), Antonello only remained a short time at Messina, and then went to Venice —probably, therefore, about 1442 or 1443.

According to a later Sicilian chronicler, Maurolicus (*Hist: Sican fol.* 186), Antonello: ' Ob mirum ingenium

[1] See Crowe and Cavalcaselle, and also Dr. Frizzoni, *Arte Italiana del Rinascimento.*

[2] No student of art who is acquainted with the writings of the Neapolitans De Dominici and Sanazzaro will feel any surprise at the ignorance displayed by Summonzio, or at the childish and absurd vanity of his patriotism. The human mind, especially in southern climes, is much addicted to boast most loudly of the very gifts which it least possesses.

[3] From this passage we may, I think, infer that the information was supplied by a native of Palermo.

Venetiis aliquot annos publice conductus vixit : Mediolani quoque fuit percelebris.' It is curious, however, that no contemporary Milanese writer should allude to the presence in the Lombard capital of this celebrated painter.

The account given þy Summonzio, as we have seen, showed little intelligence, but that furnished by the Sicilians Matteo Collaccio and Maurolicus, and by Vasari, in his biography of the painter, is even yet more absurd, proving the undisguised partiality of the local writers. Of all Vasari's ' Lives,' not one shows such glaring discrepancies, both with regard to chronology and history, as the biography of Antonello da Messina. To crown all, it concludes by giving the epitaph, which was supposed to have been inscribed on the tomb of this painter, who died in Venice in 1493. Up to the present time, however, notwithstanding the most diligent research, no vestige of this inscription has ever come to light. According to Vasari, it was as follows :—

D. O. M.

'Antonius pictor, præcipuum Messanæ suæ et Siciliæ [1] totius ornamentum, hac humo contegitur. Non solum suis picturis, in quibus singulare artificium et venustas fuit, sed et quod coloribus oleo miscendis splendorem et perpetuitatem (!) primus italicæ picturæ contulit, summo semper artificum studio celebratus.'

The whole narrative, together with the tale interwoven with it, respecting Domenico Veneziano and Andrea del Castagno, has not only little show of probability, but is positively ridiculous. It seems incredible that of all the Italian writers who, from the last century down to the present day, have sought to explain the biography of Antonello, not one should have been struck by the absurdity of

---

[1] A native of Central or Northern Italy would more probably have written 'Italiæ,' and not ' Siciliæ.'

Vasari's statements. In order to gain any knowledge of this master, we must pass over the biographer's account altogether and seek information elsewhere, letting Antonello's pictures speak for themselves.

His earliest signed and dated work is, I believe, the "Salvator Mundi" of the English National Gallery (No. 673). On the *cartellino*, which is of larger size than those on his later pictures, is the date 1465, and the name 'Antonellus Messaneus.' Both the colouring and the expression are very Flemish in character.

The same must be said of two small unsigned and much damaged pictures representing the "Ecce Homo"— one in the Casa Spinola delle Pelliccierie at Genoa, the other in the public gallery at Vicenza (Room III. No. 17). Both may perhaps have been produced before 1465. To the master's early Flemish period—1465 to 1470—I should also ascribe the "Ecce Homo" belonging to Signor Zir at Naples. These four pictures are poor in modelling, and very Flemish alike in conception and in the flesh-colouring, which is of the reddish tone peculiar to the school of the Van Eycks. Compared with the master's works of ten years later, they betray the hand of a very inexperienced artist.

In the early part of 1473 Antonello must have completed the Triptych for the Church of S. Gregorio at Messina.[1] It is not known whether he executed it at Messina or at Venice. He was certainly in the latter city during that year, and there would have been no difficulty in sending it thence by sea to Sicily.

Antonello's knowledge of the new method of finishing

---

[1] This picture, in a much damaged condition, is now in the university at Messina. It is signed, '*Año. Dm. m°. cccc° septuagesimo tertio. Antonellus Messañesis pinxit.*' It is very Flemish in appearance, and proves that the painter, though possessed of admirable technical qualities, had not mastered the difficulties of the human form. Messrs. Crowe and Cavalcaselle appear to be of the same opinion (ii. 86).

with glazes of oil, pictures grounded in tempera—a method
before unknown in Venice—no doubt gave him a greater
importance in the eyes of the Venetians than his artistic
endowments would have warranted, and he was com-
missioned in 1473 to paint an altar-piece for the Church
of S. Cassiano in Venice. Matteo Collaccio and Sabellico
both speak of this picture in terms of the highest praise;
but it has unfortunately long since disappeared. Over and
above his commissions from church patrons, he found
employment from members of the Venetian patriciate
eager to have their likenesses painted according to the
new method; and to judge from the number of his portraits.
of these years in existence, he must at that date have been
the most admired portrait-painter in Venice.

A male portrait of 1474, signed ' Antonellus Messaneus,'
much disfigured by repainting, was in the Hamilton collec-
tion,[1] and the celebrated and very fine portrait in the Salon
Carré of the Louvre, bearing a similar signature, is of 1475.
The signed " Crucifixion " in the Antwerp gallery is of
the same year, and shows slight, but to me unmistakable,
traces of the influence of Carpaccio. A similar picture by
Antonello is in the Corsini gallery at Florence, and another,
dated 1477, is in the English National Gallery (No. 1166).

Though to Antonello may belong the merit of having
introduced the new system of painting into Venice, yet as
an artist he must undoubtedly have felt himself inferior to
the Bellini, the Vivarini, and even to Carpaccio. His later
works seem to me to prove that his intercourse with the
great Venetian masters and his study of their works was
advantageous to his own art. He gradually attained to that
more perfect rendering of form and treatment of linear
perspective which we distinguish in his portraits of the
years 1475, 1476, and 1478, but which are conspicuously

[1] Now in the Berlin Gallery, No 18A.

MALE PORTRAIT. BY ANTONELLO DA MESSINA.

(In the Trivulzio Collection, Milan.)

To face p. 189.

absent in his earlier representations of the " Ecce Homo."
Up to the year 1478 he adheres to the reddish flesh-tints of
the Flemings ;[1] in that year, however, he adopts the lighter
tone which we see in Giovanni Bellini's portraits. This is
apparent in a portrait by him, dated 1478, in the Berlin
Museum, which I consider the finest of all his works of
this class. In his other portraits the linear perspective
of the eyes is so exaggerated as to impart to them an un-
naturally keen expression. We find this both in his earlier
portraits and in those of 1480 to 1490 ; for example, in the
admirable portrait of a man in the English National
Gallery (No. 1141), formerly belonging to Signor Molfino at
Genoa, and in another, representing a man crowned with
laurel, in the Museo Municipale at Milan. We meet with the
same defect in Dürer's portrait of one of the Holtzschuher
family, now in the Berlin gallery (No. 557B), which in all
other respects is a magnificent example of his art.

In addition to the " St. Sebastian " of the Dresden
gallery, I should assign the following pictures to Anto-
nello's later or Venetian period—1480 to 1485: Another
representation of the same saint in the gallery at Bergamo
(Lochis collection, No. 222)—a picture of much smaller
dimensions, but showing far more refined feeling than the
example at Dresden—a good portrait of a young man
wearing a Venetian dress in the Berlin gallery (No. 25),
and the much repainted " St. Sebastian " in the Staedel
Institute at Frankfort.[2] The admirable portrait of a man
in the Naples gallery, there attributed to Bellini, and the
figure of Christ in the collection of Sir Francis Cook at

---

[1] For example, in the male por-
trait of 1476 in the Trivulzio col-
lection at Milan, in one in the
Borghese gallery at Rome, and in
the Giovanelli collection at Venice.

[2] The saint in this picture is
represented only to the waist. There
are several old copies of it in exist-
ence: one is in the gallery of Berlin,
another in that of Bergamo (Lochis
collection) (†).

Richmond, both belong to this later period of the master's career. The two last-named pictures clearly show how Antonello must have developed and perfected his art by studying the works of Giovanni Bellini.

It is hardly probable that these few pictures, mostly of small dimensions, were all that Antonello produced from 1478 up to the time of his death in 1493. We may reasonably suppose that other and larger works by him are in existence, but I am unable at present to give any clue as to where they may be found. We have seen that no earlier date than 1463 or 1464 can be assigned to any of his pictures, and that those belonging to this period show the hand of a very inexperienced artist. If he were born in 1414, which, owing to Vasari's statement, has been generally assumed, what, it may be asked, have become of his early works? for it is hardly to be supposed that he only applied himself to painting in his fiftieth year. Yet, though his biographer affirms that he was born in 1414, he also tells us that he died in 1493 at the age of forty-nine.[1] If we accept the last statement, the year of Antonello's birth must have been 1444, which appears to me the most probable date in every respect. Gallus, in his 'Annals of Messina,'[2] places the birth of Antonello eleven years before the death of King Alfonso, who died in 1458, which would make it 1447. Let us, therefore, assume that the painter was born in the early part of 1445 and died in 1493. He would then have painted the "Salvator Mundi" in the English National Gallery in his twentieth year—a conjecture which agrees well with the character and execution of the picture. From this period up to the year 1471 we

[1] Contradictory statements of this description frequently occur in Vasari's writings. In the *Life of Masaccio*, for instance, he gives the correct date of his birth, 1402, but records that he died in 1443, aged six-and-twenty.

[2] See Hackert, *Memorie dei Pittori Messinesi.*

MALE PORTRAIT.   BY ANTONELLO DA MESSINA.

(In the Naples Museum, attributed to Giovanni Bellini.)

To face p. 190.

are able to follow his progress almost year by year. His Italian nature gradually breaks through the Flemish crust acquired from his first teacher, which had imprisoned his mode of expression and execution. His portraits of 1475 and 1476, respectively in the Louvre and in the Palazzo Trivulzio at Milan, are already quite southern in character, while the portrait of 1478 in the Berlin gallery (No. 18) shows us the fully Venetianised Sicilian. The change which Antonello's art underwent and its subsequent development were evidently due more to Giovanni Bellini than to any other painter in Venice, but the " St. Sebastian " in the Dresden gallery proves, as I have already had occasion to observe, that Mantegna's wall-paintings at Padua were not without influence on his progress.[1]

From all that precedes it may be assumed that the art of Antonello first reached its full development at Venice, which would hardly have been the case had he only come to that city at the age of fifty-eight or fifty-nine. I have still to add that Scardeone, in his ' Antiquitates Patavienses,' mentions that the Paduan sculptor Andrea Briosco, or Riccio,[2]

[1] Baron Rumohr, one of the more careful among art-historians, took a totally different view of Antonello's importance in the development of Italian art. In his book, entitled *Drei Reisen in Italien*, he observes : ' In addition to the fine Van Eycks, the Berlin Museum has three pictures by Antonello da Messina. This gallery, therefore, has one unique advantage. It affords us undeniable proof that the school which from Antonello transmitted its teaching to the Bellini, and so to others, and which it is usual to speak of simply as the Venetian school, had not only acquired the technical processes of oil-painting, but had also adopted its naturalistic tendencies,

from the early masters of the Netherlands.'

[2] Andrea Riccio of Padua, a pupil of Vellano, is well known as the author of the celebrated candelabra in the choir of the Church of the ' Santo ' at Padua. The bronze bas-reliefs in the hall of the Caryatides in the Louvre are also by him. They originally formed part of the ornamentation of the tomb of Girolamo della Torre in the Church of S. Fermo at Verona, but were carried off at the time of Napoleon I. It is probable, however, that Scardeone meant not the Paduan Andrea, but the Veronese sculptor, Antonio Riccio, who was born about 1440.

was greatly afflicted at the death of Antonello, who was one of his most intimate friends, a statement which seems scarcely credible if Antonello was eighty at that date, for Riccio, who was born in 1470, was then only twenty-three.

I cannot refrain from here putting the question, Why should it have been necessary for an Italian to go to Bruges in order to learn what was equally attainable in his own country? In the middle of the fifteenth century were there not Flemish painters of the school of the Van Eycks at Naples and in other parts of the peninsula? We know that Roger van der Weyden himself had then been in Italy for several years. No one, I think, will deny that Antonello could as easily have learnt the Van Eycks' method from a Flemish painter in Italy as in Flanders. If this be granted I ask no more, but will leave each intelligent student to draw his own inferences. Antonello's sojourn in Venice, extending over a period of more than twenty years, and the prominent position which he there held as a portrait-painter, could not be without effect upon the art of his fellow-countrymen in Sicily. In the churches of Messina and all along the east coast of the island as far as Syracuse we still find representations of the Madonna in painting and sculpture which not only recall Antonello, but also Giovanni Bellini, and in some instances even Cima da Conegliano. All who have seen these works will, I think, agree with me that the theory of a local school of Messina is as untenable as is that of a local school of Palermo. All the works of Antonio da Messina,[1] Pietro da Messina,[2]

[1] In the collection of Sir Francis Cook at Richmond there is a Madonna bearing the signature of this feeble Sicilian artist.

[2] Pietro becomes, in the Venetian dialect, Piero; Pino da Messina is probably a later corruption of the same name. There is a Madonna by this painter in the oratory of the Church of S. Maria Formosa at Venice, and another, in the possession of the Marchesa Arconati-Visconti, at Milan. Both are signed 'Petrus Messaneus.' This mediocre painter was an imitator of his master Antonello; at times, also,

Maso,[1] Antonello Saliba,[2] Salvo d' Antonio, of the so-called Francesco Cardillo and others, as also the marble statues of the Madonna and Child in churches at Messina, Taormina, Catania, Syracuse, &c., bear the impress of the

of Giovanni Bellini, and even of Cima da Conegliano. I have met with several pictures which, though bearing no signature, may, I think, be attributed to him; for example, a Madonna on a gold ground adoring the Infant Saviour, in the first room of the gallery of the university at Messina; a much repainted Madonna with the Holy Child asleep in her arms in the second room of the same collection; and some pictures in the collection of Signor Guggenheim at Venice, one of which was bought by Count Pourtalès, of Berlin. The Madonna behind the high altar of the Church of the Scalzi at Venice, which, though much disfigured by restoration, is still admired as a Bellini, is also by Pietro da Messina, if I am not greatly mistaken, and the same may be said of a small Madonna in the public gallery at Padua (No. 23), and of one ascribed to Cima in the Uffizi.

[1] A Madonna on a gold ground, with the portrait of the donor, dated 1516, and signed ' Maso,' is in the Church of S. Lucia at Messina. This painter appears to have been influenced more by Pietro da Messina than by Antonello.

[2] A panel picture, by Antonello Saliba of Messina, is in the Museum of Catania. It represents the Madonna enthroned offering a flower to the Child, who stands upon her right knee. On a cartellino is the inscription *Antonellus Missenius Saliba hoc ƥfecit opus 1497, die 20 Julii.* This painter

also belongs to the school of Antonello and of Pietro, and so too does Salvo d' Antonio, by whom there is a "Death of the Virgin" in the ' Sagrestia dei Canonici' in the Cathedral of Messina, signed with his name. Later, Salvo must have derived instruction from the Milanese school. I am unable to say if Francesco Cardillo of Messina, to whom is attributed a " Visitation," in the convent-church of Montalto at Messina, ever existed. The picture is certainly the work of a painter who was closely connected with Pietro da Messina. Other examples of this school may be seen at Messina: in the Churches of the ' Spirito Santo,' of the ' Annunziata dei Catalani,' and of the ' Cappucini;' at Taormina, in the Church of S. Agostino, and elsewhere. This Venetian school of Antonello was dominant on the east coast of Sicily throughout the last two decades of the fifteenth century and the first of the sixteenth, until the appearance of Girolamo Aliprandi, the so-called Raphael of Messina, about 1519. Though a degenerate imitator of the worst type, this painter nevertheless eclipsed all other artists of Sicily. His pictures are in the Cathedral of Messina (' Sagrestia delle Messe '), and in the Churches of S. Niccolò and of S. Dionizi. Later, Polidoro da Caravaggio founded a school in that city which dragged out a feeble existence and became extinct with his pupil Tonno, who, I may add, was also his murderer.

O

Venetian school. This leads us to infer that all these artists of Eastern Sicily were attracted to Venice by the presence of their renowned fellow-countryman Antonello, and subsequently were there trained as painters or sculptors.

Antonello's influence was felt not only by his Sicilian fellow-countrymen, but also by painters of North Italy, as is proved by the portraits of Jacopo de' Barbari, Filippo Mazzola, and Andrea Solario.[1]

Antonello[2] leads us to speak of his contemporary Jacopo de' Barbari,[3] who was closely connected with him and owed much to him. The Dresden collection has the good fortune to possess more works by Jacopo than any other gallery in

[1] See, for example, the portrait of a Venetian senator by this painter in the English National Gallery.

[2] The only drawing with which I am acquainted by Antonello is in the Malcolm collection in London (†). It is a washed drawing from life, on tinted paper, for the celebrated portrait (No. 1134) in the Salon Carré of the Louvre. In the catalogue of this collection it is numbered 342, and attributed to an unknown master of the early school of North Italy (Braun, *Beaux-Arts*, No. 189). I may here observe that the small picture of St. Jerome in his study in Lord Northbrook's collection, as to the author of which the 'Anonimo' could give no decisive information, is, in my opinion, neither by Jacopo de' Barbari, as M. Ephrussi conjectures, nor by Antonello da Messina, as Mr. Weale affirms. The painter might, perhaps, have been Jacometto (†), whose works are otherwise wholly unknown to us. (See *Notizia d' opere di disegno*, edited by Dr. Gustavo

Frizzoni, Bologna, Zanichelli, 1884, p. 188.)

[3] The 'Anonimo' calls him Jacopo de Barbarino, and adds to this 'Veneziano,' that is, Venetian by birth. Geldenhauer, in his *Vita Philippi Burgundi*, &c., also calls him 'Jacobus Barbarus, Venetus.' Notwithstanding this, however, some German critics, such as Harzen, in *Naumann's Archiv* (i. 210, 1855), and Passavant, in *Le Peintre-Graveur* (iii. 134), speak of Jacopo de' Barbari as a native of Nuremberg, while Zani makes him out to be of Dutch or even French origin. Thausing, in his *Life of Dürer*, first assigned to Barbari his proper place in the history of art, and restored to him his Venetian nationality. The greater part of his engravings and the few paintings by his hand which are known prove his Venetian descent. Many of his works have until now remained unrecognised, and have been ascribed, as will be seen, to Giovanni Bellini and Antonello da Messina, and even to the schools of Ferrara and Florence.

PORTRAIT. DRAWING BY ANTONELLO DA MESSINA.
(In the Malcolm Collection, London.)

To face p. 194.

the world. No collector of engravings is unacquainted
with the rare, delicate, and curious examples by the master
of the Caduceus; but, rare as are his engravings, his
paintings are still more so. Messrs. Crowe and Cavalcaselle,
the most assiduous of recent art-historians, can only name
four : the two Saints in the Dresden gallery (Nos. 58 and
59), a figure of Christ in the collection at Weimar, and a
still-life subject, of 1504, in the Augsburg gallery.

The late Professor Thausing, whose early death was a
severe loss to science, was the first who was able to show in
a clear and convincing manner how close were the relations
between Barbari and Albert Dürer. For further informa-
tion about this impressionable painter, whose style shows a
mixture of Italian and Northern art, I refer my readers to
this writer's admirable work on Dürer (chapter x.).

In the catalogue of the Dresden gallery of 1876, a third
picture is ascribed to Barbari, in addition to the two
already mentioned. It is a figure of Christ blessing (No.
57). We may now examine these three pictures more
closely. In the catalogue of 1867 the figure of Christ (then
No. 1804) was ascribed to Lucas van Leyden, while the
SS. Catherine and Barbara (then Nos. 1795 and 1796)
were mentioned as works by an unknown master, though
many years before that date M. Renouvier had rightly
ascribed these two wings of a triptych to Jacopo de'
Barbari. In the last catalogue issued by the late Dr.
Hübner, the three pictures are given to the latter master.
They all bear the impress of a Venetian-German character,
more particularly the two saints, and were probably painted
in Germany and not in Venice. The following are some of the
master's characteristics which we find in these pictures :—

(a) In each the mouth is half open, a peculiarity
which is more frequently to be observed in Northern than
in Italian paintings.

(*b*) The upper eyelid is very prominent, and forms a very deep furrow at its root or base.

(*c*) The skull is round in form, and the top of the thumb is remarkably round and clumsy. Moreover, his drapery is always characterised by long clinging and closely laid folds; the outer opening of the ear is high and narrow, and the limbs of his female figures are always of disproportionate length.

We meet with all these characteristics in another picture in this gallery (No. 274), which the late Dr. Hübner ascribed doubtfully to Sandro Botticelli, but which the present director, with more discernment, speaks of as the work of some North Italian painter.[1] It represents Galatea standing upon a dolphin, and it seemed to me at first the work of an Italianised Fleming. But, on studying the picture more closely, I recognised in it the manner of Jacopo de' Barbari, and a recent visit to Dresden has confirmed this impression. The mouth has been entirely daubed over, but were the repainting removed, Barbari's characteristic mouth would undoubtedly reappear[2] (†). The following works were all, most probably, executed out of Italy; they plainly show, I think, the influence which Northern art must have exercised over the Venetian painter: The figure of Christ at Weimar, which is still Venetian in expression; the same subject in the collection of Dr. Lippmann at Berlin; and the still-life in the Augsburg gallery.

Germany, as we have thus seen, possesses seven acknowledged works by this master, and to these I would now add an eighth—an admirable half-length male portrait

---

[1] Now 59A, ascribed to Barbari by Dr. Woermann.

[2] The picture has suffered severely, but other characteristics of Barbari may still be seen in it—the position of the lower limbs, the drawing of the eye, the clumsy treatment of the upper part of the thumb, &c.

PORTRAIT BY JACOPO DE' BARBARI.

(In the Gallery at Vienna.)

in the public gallery at Vienna.[1] The late Mr. Mündler, I believe, had already recognised this picture as being by Jacopo de' Barbari. Dr. Engerth, the director of the gallery, placed it in the early Florentine school, and, in order to particularise it still further, he pronounced it a later copy after a work by Masaccio da S. Giovanni. The young man represented is of an Italian type, and wears the Venetian costume of the second half of the fifteenth century—a black robe and a black cap. Above, on the left of the picture, the painter has introduced a small lamp, the colouring of which appears to me very northern in tone. The arabesque foliage on the white curtain forming the background recalls the manner of Giorgione and his imitators, such as Boccaccino, Marco Marziale, and others. The method employed in the painting is that which was introduced into Venice by Antonello da Messina, and which had been adopted by Giovanni Bellini in the last twenty years of the fifteenth century. The half-open mouth, the prominent eyelid, the deep indenture in the corner of the eye, and the treatment of the hair, are all characteristics in which Jacopo de' Barbari is more particularly to be recognised.

The best known engravings by this master of the Caduceus were, for the most part, I think, produced at Nuremberg or at Brussels, and date, therefore, from the last ten or twelve years of his life. Jacopo also furnished designs for other engravers on copper as well as for wood-engravers.[2] An engraving from such a design is in the Ambrosiana, and represents a girl asleep in the arms of a young man, signed ' Z. A.'—Zuan Andrea. The drawing shows the hand of Jacopo de' Barbari ; the engraving itself

[1] No. 27 of the present catalogue.

[2] For the benefit of students, I may mention two engravings in the Malaspina collection at Pavia, which were, I think, executed from drawings by Jacopo de' Barbari (†). They represent respectively a procession of satyrs and an allegorical subject.

appears to be an early work of Zuan Andrea (†). As an example of his designs for wood-engraving may be taken the large view of Venice executed at Venice in 1500 by a northern wood-engraver, who probably came to that city for the purpose at the instance of Jacopo de' Barbari. The treatment of the lines in this design is bold. In Barbari's later period, on the other hand, as for example in a drawing at Dresden, the strokes are fine and sharp, showing the influence of the northern method of drawing.[1]

It is not likely, however, that the master, while in Venice, was exclusively employed in making drawings for engravers on wood and metal. He must certainly have received orders for paintings from his fellow-countrymen, for, as Dürer observes in one of his letters to Pirckheimer, Barbari was considered by his friend, Anton Kolb—a Nuremberg merchant settled at Venice—to be the greatest painter in the world. We must, however, conclude that Jacopo de' Barbari was not held in such high repute at Venice, or he would scarcely have quitted that city; moreover, Vasari makes no mention of him.

The celebrated frescoes surrounding the tomb of the senator Agostino Onigo in the Church of S. Niccolò at

---

[1] I may here mention a few drawings which, I think, should be ascribed to Jacopo de' Barbari:—

1. In the Christ Church collection at Oxford: A sheet with Tritons and sea-nymphs executed in silver point on coloured paper, and heightened with white. It is there attributed to Mantegna (†).

2. In the British Museum: A nymph asleep in a grotto, pen and ink, the original study for one of the master's engravings, register mark: 1883-8-11-35.

3. In Herr Habich's fine collection at Cassel: A most interesting portrait, in black chalk, of a young man with long hair, seen in full face.

4. An admirable red chalk drawing, in the same collection, of a young man, also in full face. It has been reproduced in the publication already mentioned, edited by Dr. Eisenmann.

5. In the Malcolm collection in London: A sheet with various sketches in red chalk (†). In the catalogue it is numbered 347, and is attributed to an unknown North Italian master of the close of the fifteenth century.

PORTRAIT IN BLACK CHALK.   BY JACOPO DE' BARBARI.
(In the Habich Collection at Cassel.)
To face p. 198.

Treviso I should ascribe to this master (†). The commission for the tomb was given in 1490, and the paintings were probably executed in the last years of the fifteenth century. These beautiful frescoes represent two warriors or heralds standing on either side of the monument; one holds a long sword, the other an iron mace, of the form known as ' morning star.'[1] They are two fine and lifelike figures, so closely connected with the school of the Bellini that Vasari ascribed them to Giovanni Bellini himself, in which he was followed by Messrs. Crowe and Cavalcaselle (i. 171), while Carlo Ridolfi[2] attributed them to Antonello da Messina.[3] The only art-critics, as far as I know, who have accepted my attribution to Barbari of these figures are Dr. Frizzoni and Professor Karl von Lützow in his attractive volume on the ' Art-treasures of Italy.' The upper and lower parts of the monument are decorated with arabesques, the sides with trophies of war, all in *grisaille*. Between the arabesques on the lower part are two medallions with various representations—battle-scenes, sirens borne by centaurs and satyrs. These *grisaille* figures, with their characteristic rounded form of head, should dispel any doubt as to the correctness of my attribution.[4] We meet with the same feeling and technic in the figures introduced in the arabesque decoration on the façade of a house (No. 1548) in the Piazza

[1] Similar weapons are held by two heralds in some frescoes by Bramante in the Casa Prinetti at Milan (Via Lanzone, 4).

[2] *Le Meraviglie dell' Arte*, i. 86.

[3] The warrior with the sword has been much damaged, but the one with the mace, on the right side of the monument, is very well preserved, and it is in this figure that all Barbari's characteristics are apparent. The technical treatment of the hair vividly recalls the portrait in the gallery at Vienna and the head of Christ in the Dresden gallery (No. 57).

[4] These combats recall Barbari's two well-known engravings representing a struggle between satyrs and men. The pen-drawing of the " Rape of a Siren " in the Dresden collection is merely a modified repetition of the same idea which Barbari carried out in colour on the wall beneath the tomb of Onigo.

del Duomo at Treviso, and I am therefore inclined to ascribe these paintings also to Barbari (†).

Both the tomb of Onigo and that of the Admiral Melchiorre Trevisani in the Church of the Frari at Venice [1] were the work of the Lombardi; [2] the last-named monument was executed in 1500, and here also we find trophies of war in *grisaille* at the sides, and, above, decorative representations of Tritons. After a close study of these paintings, we cannot but accept the opinion of Dr. Gustavo Frizzoni,[3] that they too are by Jacopo de' Barbari. The frescoes just mentioned, which served to adorn the tombs of two distinguished men, lead us to infer that Barbari worked in conjunction with the sculptors known as the Lombardi, his fellow-countrymen ;[4] the artistic relations existing between the painter and the sculptors explain certain peculiarities in Barbari's engravings, both in the composition and in the characteristic treatment of the drapery, the long, hard, clinging folds of which recall those of the Lombardi, and more especially of Tullio.

In his early period, however, Barbari was undoubtedly strongly influenced by Giovanni Bellini, and still more by Antonello da Messina, and his works, as we have already observed, have been ascribed to both these masters by distinguished art-critics.

I am acquainted with several other works of Barbari's early Venetian period (1480–1490); for example, three small panels, all representing the " Salvator Mundi." One belongs to Signor Federigo Antonio Frizzoni at Bergamo,

---

[1] In the second chapel on the right of the choir.

[2] The good statue of Trevisani is in all probability by Antonio Lombardi, and I think that he must also have worked with his brother Tullio at the tomb of Onigo.

[3] *Archivio Veneto*, t. xv. and xvi. 1878.

[4] Antonio and Tullio Lombardi were Venetians by birth, but their father, Pietro, came from Carona, a place on the Lake of Lugano.

another is in the 'Giustinian alle Zattere' collection at Venice, and the third is in that of Signora Barbo-Cinti at Ferrara (†). They are all in a much injured condition.

Two portraits in the gallery at Bergamo I also believe to be by Jacopo de' Barbari (†), though they are unaccountably attributed to Holbein. One, which is somewhat rubbed, is the likeness of a young man with fair curly hair seen in full face; the other (No. 148), that of a young man with brown hair, is seen in three-quarter face. The hand of Jacopo de' Barbari is seen in the treatment of light on the hair and in the drawing of the eyes, which resembles the manner of Antonello. The name of Barbari may still, though with difficulty, be deciphered on the back of the last-named panel.

If, as I believe, I am right in ascribing to Barbari the pictures I have named—the "Galatea" at Dresden, the portraits at Vienna and Bergamo, the three representations of the "Salvator Mundi," at Venice, Bergamo, and Ferrara, the drawings at Oxford and in London, and the frescoes at Treviso and elsewhere—it follows that this master must have been hitherto undeservedly neglected. Though very unequal and susceptible to extraneous influences, he is a gifted painter deserving of attention. In Germany, and more especially in Belgium, there are doubtless many of his works which have either been ascribed to other painters or have remained altogether unknown. I should advise some young student of art to endeavour to trace them out and to make a special study of this master.

Jacopo de' Barbari must have been born at Venice between 1440 and 1450; it is not known from whom he learnt the elements of his art. There is no doubt that between 1460 and 1478 he was much influenced by Giovanni Bellini, and in a very marked degree by Antonello da Messina between 1480 and 1490; the portrait at

Bergamo must date from this latter period. About 1490 we may, I think, conjecture that he paid his first visit to Germany. I infer this from a passage in Dürer's writings, in which he says that he had 'never known any man able to describe how to draw the human form in proportion save one Jacob, a native of Venice, a good and attractive painter.'[1] Dürer would scarcely have spoken of Jacob as a 'native of Venice' had his first meeting with him taken place in Venice itself in the year 1494. Dürer then continues : 'He showed me a man and woman which he had drawn according to the laws of proportion, so that at that time his opinion was of more value to me than a kingdom, but,' he adds, 'I was young then, and had never before heard of such things.'[2] At that time (1490) Dürer would have been about nineteen. Hans von Kulmbach's apprenticeship to Barbari also serves to confirm my theory. He is always rightly regarded as a pupil of Jacopo, and in 1490 he would have been thirteen or fourteen.[3] Be this as it may, one thing is certain, I think, that Barbari must have been at Nuremberg for some time prior to 1500. Some of his engravings—for example, the "Mars and Venus "— have a decidedly northern character, and might be regarded as his first attempts in that art made north of the Alps. Most of his engravings date from the later years of his life, which were spent partly at Nuremberg and partly at Brussels.

[1] 'Er habe niemand gefunden, der da etwas beschrieben hätte von menschlicher Maass zu machen, als einen Mann, Jacobus genannt, von Venedig geboren, ein guter lieblicher Maler.' (See Thausing, op. cit. p. 222, and Zahn's Jahrbücher, i. p. 14.)

[2] 'Der wies mir Mann und Weib, die er aus der Maass gemacht hatte, so dass ich in dieser Zeit lieber sehen wollte, was seine Meinung gewesen wäre, denn ein neu Königreich . . . aber ich war zu derselben Zeit noch jung und hatte von solchen Dingen nie gehört.'

[3] Hans von Kulmbach kept so closely to the manner of Barbari, and imitated him so accurately, that he even adopted the peculiarities of his master ; for example, the half-open mouth, the form of hand, and other characteristics.

The desire to learn the art of engraving may, indeed, have prompted his first visit to Germany. I am unable to say if Barbari had adopted the Caduceus as his monogram prior to the publication, in 1500, of his large woodcut of the city of Venice, as I have not had the opportunity of examining any complete collection of his engravings. I must leave this question to be decided by others. For the present it may suffice to have directed attention to certain works which are in my opinion by Barbari, and which may serve to throw fresh light upon a far from uninteresting painter. To judge from his paintings and engravings, he must have been by nature an artist of a soft, wavering, and impressionable disposition.

About 1502 we find him domiciled at Nuremberg, and at that time he became more closely connected with Dürer, and exercised an influence over that great artist which is perceptible not only in Dürer's engravings of that date, but even in some of his paintings.[1]

At Brussels, in 1511, Barbari received a pension from the Archduchess Margaret, regent of the Netherlands, ' in consideration of his advanced age and infirmities.' He was already dead in 1516.

The chronological order which we have followed in examining the pictures in the Dresden gallery would now lead us to speak of the works ascribed by the catalogue to Giorgione. But I shall first speak of two pictures, one of which was in Dr. Hübner's catalogue, attributed to another painter of the March of Treviso—Vincenzo Catena. This, Dr. Woermann has now restored to its rightful author. It represents the Madonna and Child between SS. Helena, Catherine, Anthony, and Nicholas of Bari (No. 64), and was attributed to Catena by Messrs. Crowe and Cavalcaselle (i. 257), as well as by Dr. Hübner. It

[1] See, on this subject, Thausing's *Life of Dürer*, pp. 222–35.

appears to me to be the work of Francesco Bissolo,[1] an artist of Treviso, who, like Catena, proceeded from the school of Giovanni Bellini [2] (†). The "Holy Family" (No. 65) is, on the other hand, a genuine work by Catena, and I am glad to find that Messrs. Crowe and Cavalcaselle and Dr. Woermann are of the same opinion. Both the hands and the ears in this picture are identical in form with those in a signed picture by Catena in the gallery at Pesth. The peculiar treatment of light coincides with that in three pictures by this master in the English National Gallery. The first of these (No. 234) represents the Madonna seated, before whom kneels a knight in armour adoring the Child ; St. Joseph stands beside the Madonna. On the right an attendant holds the horse of the knight; in the distance is a hilly landscape. In my estimation, this is a splendid work of Catena (†), wholly Giorgionesque in feeling. The catalogue still continues to ascribe it to the school of Giovanni Bellini. The second—"St. Jerome in his Study" (No. 694)—formerly attributed to Giovanni Bellini himself, is in the last edition of the catalogue also given to his 'school.' In this work Catena shows himself an imitator of Lotto even more than of Giorgione. An old and good copy of this picture is in the Staedel Institute

[1] Even in the Brera these two painters are confused in three pictures (Nos. 237, St. Stephen, 285, St. Anthony of Padua, and 298, a bishop), which, though ascribed Catena, are undoubtedly by Bissolo (†).

[2] In the museum at Leipzig there is a much repainted but genuine Madonna by Bissolo or Bissuolo. In a document published by the late Signor Cecchetti, in the *Archivio Veneto* (v. 34, p. 205), this painter speaks of himself as, ' Io Francesco bissul de ser Vettor.' I may here observe that the Leipzig Museum also contains a Madonna by a Florentine contemporary of Bissolo, Giuliano Bugiardini, who usually signs his pictures 'IVL. FLOR.' (Julianus Florentinus). In the public gallery at Vienna there is also an example by this latter master (†) wrongly placed in Dr. von Engerth's catalogue in the school of Andrea del Sarto, to which Bugiardini did not belong. It represents the Madonna and Child with St. Joseph.

at Frankfort.   The third work by Catena in this gallery is
the "Adoration of the Magi" (No. 1160), ascribed this time
neither to Bellini nor to his school, but to that of Gior-
gione (†).   Messrs. Crowe and Cavalcaselle attribute it to
Giorgione himself.   There is a picture by Catena in the
Museo del Prado at Madrid (No. 108), representing Christ
delivering the keys to St. Peter, in which three female
figures—Faith, Hope, and Charity—are introduced.   It
was formerly assigned to Boccaccino.   An admirable signed
portrait of an ecclesiastic by Catena is in the public gallery
at Vienna; and the likeness of Count Raymond Fugger
—another fine work by him—is in the Berlin Museum
(No. 32).   These three pictures would seem to belong to
his latest period, 1520–1530.   Catena must, I think, be
regarded as one of those pupils of Giovanni Bellini who
attended the master's workshop in the two last decades of
the fifteenth century.   He, therefore, worked there in com-
pany with Cima, Rondinelli, Bissolo, Boccaccino, Lattanzio-
da Rimini, and others.   He must have been born between
1460 and 1470.   The earliest works by him with which I
am acquainted are, a Madonna and saints in the Palazzo
Balbo-Crotti at Venice, signed 'V. Caena,' and two single
figures of saints formerly in the choir of the Church of
S. Giovanni e Paolo in that city, also bearing the master's
signature.   The drawing and the colouring in these pictures
point to the hand of a very inexperienced painter.   The
Madonna with two Saints in the gallery at Padua, signed
'VINCENTIVS DE TARVIXIO,' appears to me to be a few years
later in date.   It is of a character recalling Bellini, though
somewhat dull and colourless.   It was only later, when
under the influence of his fellow-countryman Giorgione,
that Catena developed himself into a great colourist.   Two
of his pictures in the English National Gallery (Nos. 234
and 1160) are thoroughly Giorgionesque both in feeling and

colour, and, if I am not mistaken, were at one time attributed to Giorgione himself. The " St. Jerome " (No 694), on the other hand, as already observed, shows the influence of Lorenzo Lotto over Catena.

In his day Catena must have enjoyed a considerable reputation at Venice. We gather this from a letter written from Rome in 1520 by Marcantonio Michiel to a friend in Venice—Antonio Marsilio—in which the following passage occurs : [1] 'Il Venerdi Santo di notte a ore 3 morse il gentilissimo eccellentissimo pictore Raphaelo da Urbino con universal dolore. . . . Molto minor danno, al mio giudizio benchè altramente parà al volgo, ha sentito il mondo dalla morte de M. Agustino Gisi (Chigi) che questa notte passata è mancato. . . . Dicesi Michelangelo esser ammalato a Fiorenza. Dite adunque al nostro Catena, che se guardi, poichè el tocca alli excellenti pictori.' 'On Good Friday, at 3 at night, the most delightful and excellent painter Raphael of Urbino passed away, to the great sorrow of all. The world has suffered less, in my estimation, though the public may think otherwise, by the death of M. Agustino Chigi, who this night ceased to live. It is said that Michelangelo is ill at Florence. Therefore, bid our Catena beware, for the turn to die of the excellent painters has come.'

Giorgio Barbarelli, known as Giorgione, came, like Bissolo and Catena, from the March of Treviso. The old catalogue assigned no less than five works to this rare master. I am glad to see that the present director agrees with me with regard to them all. They are the following :—

No. 192, the " Meeting of Jacob and Rachel." Every part of this picture proves it to be by Palma Vecchio; the rosy flesh-tints characteristic of this master's third or so-called blonde manner (1520–1525), the type of Rachel which

---

[1] See the 'Anonimo,' second edition, pp. 210-12.

coincides with that of the Venus by Palma in this gallery, her robust and somewhat heavy figure, and the manner in which the shepherd-boy is drawn and painted, the form of whose ear would alone betray the hand of Palma. I know no other work of the master so full of pleasantness and charm, and so poetically conceived, as this delightful idyll.

Messrs. Crowe and Cavalcaselle have observed that many of the figures in this picture, more especially those of Jacob and Rachel, recall the shepherds in the mountainous districts of Bergamo, and that their movements and gestures have more connection with the school of Palma than with the manner of Giorgione. It is, however, to be regretted that they should have added that they were unable to ascribe it either to Giorgione or to Palma, though they thought it might be by Cariani. The initials on the wallet on the ground—' G. B. F.'—might, they considered, be interpreted ' Giovanni Busi fecit.' [1] I must, however, point out that Cariani never signs himself ' Busi,' but always ' Joanes Carianus,' [2] or ' J. Cariani.' His forms, too, are

[1] See Crowe and Cavalcaselle, ii. 555.

[2] For example, in the " Resurrection," in the Casa Marazzi at Crema, of 1520 ; in the " Madonna and Child between SS. Jerome and Francis," belonging to Signor Frizzoni-Salis at Bergamo ; in the fine portrait in the gallery in that city; and in the " Madonna " of 1521, belonging to Signor Francesco Baglioni, also at Bergamo. Had Cariani signed his name in Italian —a rare occurrence in those days— he would not have put ' Giovanni Busi,' but ' Zuan de Busi.' The initials 'G. B.,' which were evidently inscribed with intent to deceive, were certainly not meant to signify Giovanni Busi, who was little thought of then, but, without doubt, Giorgio Barbarelli. I have noticed that Messrs. Crowe and Cavalcaselle are apt to confuse Palma's two pupils, Cariani the Bergamasque and Bonifazio the Veronese. In their chapter on Cariani they are disposed to attribute to this master two large pictures in the public gallery at Vienna—the " Triumph of Cupid " and the " Victory of Chastity over Love," which are undoubtedly by Bonifazio ; as such, they were mentioned by Ridolfi in his *Vite dei Pittori*, i. 376. On another occasion these writers mistake Previtali for Cariani, as in th fresco lunette of one of the side doors of S. Maria Maggiore at Bergamo. In this case, however, the painters confounded were both Bergamasques.

coarser than those of Palma, his shadows blacker, and his landscapes totally dissimilar to those of the latter master. His works, moreover, are never so nobly conceived as those of the author of this most poetic painting. Both Cariani and Bonifazio were pupils of Palma, but each preserved his own character. Cariani never frees himself from a certain coarseness of fibre, natural to the mountain race from which he sprang, while Bonifazio, in the grace and sprightliness of his manner of conception and representation, is always true to his Veronese instincts. The second work, once ascribed to Giorgione in this gallery, is the " Adoration of the Shepherds " (No. 210). It came from the Palazzo Pisani at Venice, where it was assigned to Palma Vecchio, and only at Dresden was it dignified with the name of Giorgione. It appears to me an undoubted work of Bonifazio the younger. Messrs. Crowe and Cavalcaselle were also ' reminded of Bonifazio ' in it (ii. 163).

The third picture (No. 221) represents a man embracing a girl—a trivial composition, the general aspect of which recalls Michelangelo da Caravaggio in a measure. Messrs. Crowe and Cavalcaselle ascribe it to a painter of whom they make frequent mention—Domenico Mancini. I must confess that I am unable to specify the author of this picture, though it is probable that he belonged to the March of Treviso. An old copy of it is in the Scarpa collection at La Motta, near Treviso.

The fourth picture in this category is a male portrait (No. 219), said to represent Pietro Aretino—a designation as incorrect as is its attribution to Giorgione. Aretino, born in 1492, was only eighteen when Giorgione died, whereas the subject of this portrait is evidently more advanced in age. The picture has been so entirely disfigured by repainting that it is unworthy of a place in a public gallery.

The fifth and last picture, once attributed to Giorgione, is an allegorical subject (No. 186) representing, according to the late Dr. Hübner, an episode from Ariosto's 'Orlando Furioso.' In the former edition of these studies I had occasion to observe that the 'Orlando Furioso' first appeared in 1516, about six years after the death of Giorgione. Mons. Baschet, however, cites the picture as his work. Messrs. Crowe and Cavalcaselle, on the other hand (ii. 154), ascribe it to Girolamo Pennacchi. I think that it is probably an old copy of an original by Giorgione; but I am unable to say whether this original be still in existence.

Giorgione, who, together with Giovanni Bellini and Titian, is perhaps the noblest of the Venetian masters, has for centuries been little more than a myth to writers on art, who, as we have seen, have ascribed to him works by the most divers painters. In Munich, Titian, Palma, and Cariani were confounded with him. In Dresden works by Palma Vecchio or his pupils—painters who were at least direct or indirect imitators of Giorgione—were attributed to him. Elsewhere he was made responsible for paintings by Sebastiano del Piombo, Lotto or Dosso Dossi, while at times he has even been held responsible for the feeble and servile imitations of such painters as Domenico Caprioli or Pietro Vecchia.[1]

[1] In the Turin gallery one of the many copies of the so-called portrait of Giuliano de' Medici, by Raphael, is actually ascribed to Giorgione. Another copy of this portrait is in the Uffizi. The following are a few of the painters whose works have been ascribed to the master: Sebastiano del Piombo, the so-called "Fornarina" in the Uffizi; Vincenzo Catena, the two pictures in the English National Gallery; Palma Vecchio, the "Meet-ing of Jacob and Rachel" in the Dresden gallery, and an allegorical female figure in the collection of the Royal Academy at Burlington House (this is an old copy after Palma); Dosso Dossi, the "St. Sebastian" in the Brera; Girolamo da Santa Croce, No. 38 in the gallery at Bergamo; Bernardino Licinio, a female portrait in the same gallery; and pictures by the Bonifazios in many instances.

How are we to gain any true insight into the art of this most refined and imaginative of painters, or to acquire any knowledge of him in the midst of such bewildering confusion? That Giorgione was truly great in his art cannot be doubted. The high opinion entertained of him by all his contemporaries testifies to this, and the wide and far-reaching influence which he exercised over the most gifted of his fellow-pupils and contemporaries is a further confirmation of the fact. There seems to me, therefore, to be but one way out of this labyrinth of difficulties, and that is, to make a close and careful study of the few undoubtedly authentic works by the master which have come down to us. These are :—

1. The large altar-piece in the church at Castelfranco. This glorious picture was so terribly repainted some years ago by the Venetian Fabris, a 'restorer' so-called, that we can no longer see, but only guess at, the original harmony of the colours. I should recommend all students to procure the photograph of this picture, which has been published by Naya of Venice.

2. "The landscape on canvas with the storm, the gipsy, and the soldier" ("El paesetto in tela con la tempesta, con la zingana e soldato"). The picture is thus mentioned by the 'Anonimo,' who, in 1530, saw it in the house of Signor Gabriel Vendramin.[1] This exquisite and fanciful picture passed later into the Manfrin collection, from whence it was purchased some years ago by the late Prince Giovanelli of Venice. The picture is well preserved, and, like the preceding, was photographed by Naya.

3. "The oil-painting on canvas with the three philosophers in a landscape, two standing and one seated, contemplating the sun's rays" ("La tela a olio delli tre filosofi nel paese, due ritti e uno sentado che contempla i raggi

_____

[1] See the 'Anonimo,' p. 218.

solari," 'Anonimo,' p. 164). This picture, the 'Anonimo' adds, was begun by Zorzi da Castelfranco, and finished by Sebastiano Veneziano (Sebastiano del Piombo). In 1525 it was in the possession of Signor Taddeo Contarini at Venice. It is now in the public gallery at Vienna in an unsatisfactory state of preservation.

Of the pictures and frescoes seen by Vasari in Venice some thirty years later, the latter have long since fallen a prey to the ravages of sea-air to which they were exposed on the façades of Venetian houses; while the pictures are probably hidden away in some Italian palace or English country-house. I have never had the good fortune to meet with any of them.

The painter Carlo Ridolfi, a most uncritical writer of the last century, mentions first among works by Giorgione[1] the so-called "Concert" in the Pitti (No. 185), which in his day was in the possession of Paolo del Sera, a Florentine merchant settled at Venice. Though nominally an amateur, del Sera was not above making a good bargain out of his pictures when opportunity offered, and he not unfrequently sold some specimens from his collection to his patron, the Grand Duke of Tuscany.[2] Thus, many Venetian pictures came to Florence under the names bestowed upon them by del Sera or by del Teglia, another of the Duke's agents in Venice, and they have retained these attributions down to the present day. This has been the case with the celebrated picture in the Pitti known as the "Concert." It has unfortunately been so much damaged by a restorer

---

[1] Among other works ascribed by Ridolfi to Giorgione, which modern criticism no longer recognises as his, are the following: A picture in the public gallery at Vienna, known as the "Bravo," the "St. Sebastian" in the Brera by Dosso (No. 383), and the "David" by the same master in the Borghese gallery at Rome.

[2] See Michelangelo Gualandi: *Nuova raccolta di lettere sulla pittura, scoltura ed architettura*, iii. 167.

that little enough remains of the original, yet from the form of the hands and of the ear and from the gestures of the figures we are led to infer that it is not a work of Giorgione, but belongs to a somewhat later period. If the repaint covering the surface were removed we should, I think, find that it is an early work by Titian.[1]

In the seventeenth century, as we have seen, art-historians attributed to Giorgione works by Sebastiano del Piombo, Catena, Palma Vecchio, Dosso Dossi, and paintings of Titian's early period. In the last century, however, it was the two elder Bonifazios who usually had the honour of being confounded with him. It was then that the "Adoration of the Shepherds" at Dresden, which came to that city as a Palma Vecchio; the beautiful "Finding of Moses" in the Brera; the "Madonna with Tobias and the Angel" in the Ambrosiana, and the small "Finding of Moses" in the Pitti; to say nothing of many works of the school of the Bonifazios—were all attributed to the great master of Castelfranco.

Vasari's statement that Giorgione learnt the new method of painting from Leonardo da Vinci's pictures is again one of the many fables devised by municipal vanity. Where, we may well ask, should Giorgione at that date have seen pictures by Leonardo at Venice?

Other writers again maintain that Giovanni Bellini, in the picture which he executed in 1505 for the Church of S. Zaccaria at Venice, modified his former manner of painting according to the new system of Giorgione. The picture which Bellini painted for the Church of S. Giobbe at Venice[2] in the last decade of the fifteenth century, is,

[1] Mr. Claude Phillips, one of the most discerning and gifted of English critics, has rightly observed that the expression of the Augustinian monk in this picture vividly recalls that of the young man in a portrait by Titian in the Louvre.

[2] This altar-piece, which, notwithstanding the injuries it has sustained, is still a magnificent work,

however, a direct contradiction of this theory; it was the pupil probably who learnt the method from his master, and not the reverse. Dürer was, I think, right when, in writing to his friend Pirckheimer from Venice in 1506, he observed that Giovanni Bellini was still the greatest painter in that city, for it was only in the last six years of his short life (from about 1505-1511) that Giorgione's power and greatness became fully developed. His frescoes, as we have already seen, have all perished, but the few works by him which have been preserved are so fully imbued with his original and intense poetic feeling—his own personality, simple, unconventional, and refined, appeals to us in them with such irresistible fascination—that the impression they produce can never be forgotten by those who have once been enabled to understand him. No other artist ever succeeds in enthralling our imagination so powerfully yet with such simple means, though often enough we are unable to explain the signification of the scenes he depicted. Even Vasari observes that it was difficult to give any explanation of Giorgione's representations.[1] His nature was that of a true poet, profoundly thoughtful, yet at the same time taking an innocent pleasure in life. He was a lyric poet in contradistinction to Titian, who was essentially a dramatist. The art of Titian is unquestionably more powerful and energetic, but Giorgione is, in my estimation at least, a painter of more refined and subtle feeling. In his landscape backgrounds, in the charm of his lines and of his colouring, few have equalled Giorgione, and none, excepting perhaps Titian, have ever surpassed him. The principal objects of his devotion were music, fair women, and above all his own lofty art. His independent spirit rendered him totally indifferent to the favours of the great. He would certainly never, like

is now in the Venice Academy (Room XIII. No. 1).

[1] See Vasari's *Life of Giorgione,* vii. 84 (ed. Milanesi, iv. 96).

Titian, have sacrificed to them his liberty, and still less his dignity. Such, in the main, is what we gather from Vasari's narrative touching the character of Giorgione, and the account is probably correct. His works are unfortunately extremely rare, and are all cabinet pictures so-called. He appears only to have painted altar-pieces as an exception. The ' Anonimo' does not cite more than a dozen pictures by Giorgione as being in Venice in his day, that is, between 1512 and 1540. Vasari mentions about the same number, and I am not able to name many more. I should advise my readers to study these pictures, or at least to procure photographs of them, for Giorgione is an artist with whom every student should hold daily intercourse, in order by degrees to gain a more intimate knowledge of the forms and of the feeling of this most refined of all Venetian painters.

I shall now enumerate in chronological order those works which I believe to be by Giorgione, and which are easy of access :—

1. and 2. The so-called " Trial by Fire " and the " Judgment of Solomon," probably the earliest works by the master which have come down to us. These most interesting pictures are in the Uffizi (Nos. 621 and 630). In character they belong to the fifteenth century, and may have been painted by Giorgione in his sixteenth or eighteenth year. We find in them all his characteristics—the long oval of the female faces, the eyes placed somewhat near together, the hand often with the first finger extended, the fantastic costumes, the poetically conceived landscape background with the tall trees, &c.[1] Near these two pictures in the Uffizi is placed Giovanni Bellini's " Sacred Allegory " (No. 631), a work which, at the suggestion of Herr von

[1] Dr. Bode (ii. 733) will not allow that these two pictures are by Giorgione, but regards them as works of the school.

Liphart, has been unaccountably attributed to Basaiti. This beautiful work of the master, which is full of interest for the history of Venetian painting, should be compared with the "Trial by Fire" and the "Judgment of Solomon," and it will be evident that Giorgione must have drawn the inspiration for his own work from that of his master Bellini. This picture was, indeed, formerly attributed to Giorgione. We may, therefore, assume that the new tendency in Venetian art which Giorgione and Titian subsequently followed, and to which we owe some of their most splendid works, emanated from Giovanni Bellini (†).

3. A much-damaged half-length figure of "Christ bearing the Cross," belonging to the heirs of the late Countess Loschi at Vicenza. The glance of the eyes is remarkably keen. Like the two preceding pictures, it recalls his master Giovanni Bellini. A later copy of this picture, ascribed to Leonardo da Vinci (!) is in the gallery at Rovigo (No. 25).

4. The Madonna enthroned between SS. Liberale and Francis in the Church of Castelfranco. This masterpiece was painted by Giorgione between 1504 and 1505, prior to the execution of his frescoes on the Fondaco de' Tedeschi at Venice; the type of the Madonna is similar to that in the picture in the Museo del Prado at Madrid.[1] We might, therefore, conclude that the model for both was the woman beloved by Giorgione. The effect of the early morning light upon the sea in the background of the Castelfranco picture is of indescribable charm. The serenity and peace pervading the whole painting has a hallowing effect and awakens devotional feeling. We are struck by the simple and natural demeanour of the two saints who stand on either side of the throne. How different are they to the saints in the altar-pieces, even of the middle of the sixteenth

[1] The Madonna between SS. Anthony and Roch.

century, who are saints only in name, and who, but a few years later, become positively repulsive ! Giorgione's saints are no fanatical impostors, but Christian heroes, animated by a true and living faith.

5. The stormy landscape with the gipsy and the soldier, in the Palazzo Giovanelli at Venice.

6. The Madonna and Child enthroned between St. Anthony on the right and St. Roch on the left with a landscape background. This charming picture, which is well preserved, is in the Madrid gallery, where it passes for a work by Pordenone, while Messrs. Crowe and Cavalcaselle[1] attribute it to Francesco Vecellio—the painter to whom they would also ascribe No. 1117 in the Munich gallery. I must confess that it was no small satisfaction to me to have at once recognised in this masterpiece of Venetian art the hand and the feeling of Giorgione (†).

7. The "Knight of Malta" in the Uffizi (No. 622), which, though much damaged, is undoubtedly genuine. Messrs. Crowe and Cavalcaselle are of the same opinion. To have connected this nobly conceived head with Pietro della Vecchia, as some have done, is positive heresy.

8. "Daphne and Apollo," in the Seminario at Venice. It is probably a so-called *cassone*[2] picture, of which Giorgione is said to have painted a great number. The picture has been restored in oil and is much disfigured[3] (†).

9. The so-called "Three Ages of Man," in the Pitti

---

[1] ii. 292.

[2] The *cassoni* of those days answered the purpose of our modern wardrobes, and were a kind of large chest. Vasari observes (iii. 47 ; ed. Milanesi, ii. 148) : ' Niuno era che i detti cassoni non facesse dipingere ; ed oltre alle storie che si facevano nel corpo dinanzi e nelle teste, in su i cantoni, e talora altrove, si facevano fare le arme ovvero insegne delle casate [coat of arms]. E le storie, che nel corpo dinanzi si facevano, erano per lo più di favole tolte da Ovidio e da altri poeti.'

. [3] Messrs. Crowe and Cavalcasell attribute this picture to Andrea Schiavone (ii. 165).

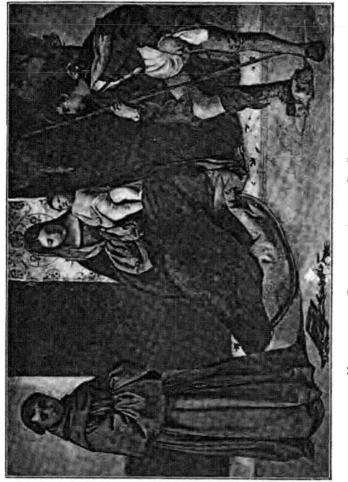

MADONNA AND CHILD WITH SAINTS.   BY GIORGIONE.

(In the Madrid Gallery.)

To face p. 216.

PORTRAIT OF A KNIGHT OF MALTA. BY GIORGIONE.

(In the Uffizi Gallery at Florence.)

To face p. 216

Palace at Florence, there attributed to Lotto. This finely conceived picture has unfortunately been damaged by restoration. The head—half in shade—of the boy, who holds a sheet of music, is, however, still so splendid and so thoroughly Giorgionesque, that I have no need of further proof of the authorship of the picture, and venture to ascribe it without hesitation to Giorgione.[1]

10. The so-called " Concert " in the Louvre (No. 1136). A most poetic idyll, which has been much disfigured by restoration. The figure of the youth with long hair seated in the foreground, the ' zazzera ' (head of hair), as the Italians term it, was copied by Giorgione's pupil, Titian, for his fresco in the ' Scuola del Santo ' at Padua.

11. The Esterhazy gallery at Buda-Pesth, which contains so many fine Italian pictures, possesses, I think, a work by Giorgione, though only a fragment (No. 95). It represents two young men, carelessly attired in the Venetian costume of the fifteenth century, and barefooted, standing on rising ground ; behind them, on a hill, is a house, and in the distance is seen the sea, illuminated by the first rays of the rising sun. One of these two fine and vigorous figures rests his left arm on the shoulder of the other, and seems pointing out some occurrence not far off in a significant manner. The other looks in the same direction, and appears astonished and almost alarmed. If I am not mistaken, this is a fragment of a picture mentioned by the ' Anonimo ' (p. 167) in the following passage : ' 1525, in casa de M. Taddeo Contarino : La tela del paese con el

---

[1] Dr. Bode, on the other hand (ii. 769), regards the picture as a work of Lotto. The same critic also ascribes to this refined and gifted painter the uncouth St. Roch in the Giovanelli collection at Venice, while he attributes to Giorgione (ii. 753) a male portrait in the gallery at Rovigo, which is merely a copy after Palma Vecchio. I am, therefore, once more forced to point out that our views regarding these two masters are totally opposed.

nascimento de Paris, con li dui pastori ritti in piede, fù de mano de Zorzo de Castelfranco, e fù delle sue prime opere.' [1] In this picture, then, we have the two shepherds of Mount Ida, under whose care Paris grew up. The other part, representing his birth, is unfortunately missing. The landscape vividly recalls that in the background of the "Venus" in the Dresden gallery (No. 185) (†). My view has been confirmed by Professor Wickhoff of Vienna, to my great satisfaction.

Another picture in the gallery at Pesth bears the stamp of Giorgione. This is the refined and noble portrait of a young man (No. 94). His black velvet doublet is open in front, and shows the white shirt. His long brown hair with the straight parting is confined in a net. He rests his right arm upon a parapet, his left hand is on his breast. We linger over this melancholy figure, fascinated by the expression which seems so full of meaning, as though this young man were about to confide to us the secret of his life. The picture has suffered much, and the master is not to be recognised in the technical qualities of the painting, but the whole feeling of the picture and the conception seem to point to Giorgione. The impression which it made upon me ten years ago was that of a thoroughly Giorgionesque work, but one executed by a later hand rather than by the master himself. Competent critics who have examined the picture in the meantime insist, however, that it is a true original by Giorgione. I must leave the final decision of the point to others.

My own studies now enable me to add a few more to the twelve pictures by Giorgione already mentioned; and,

---

[1] Giorgione appears to have treated this subject twice. We infer this from some most interesting documents published in the *Archivio Storico dell' Arte* (Fascicolo i. 1888, p. 48) by Signor Alessandro Luzio. From these records also we gather that Giorgione died early in October 1510. If, therefore, as Vasari stated, he died in his thirty-fourth year, he must have been born in 1477.

PORTRAIT OF A YOUNG MAN.   BY GIORGIONE.
(In the Esterhazy Gallery, Buda-Pesth.)

To face p. 218.

FEMALE PORTRAIT.   BY GIORGIONE.

(In the Borghese Gallery.)

To face p. 218.

PORTRAIT OF A YOUNG MAN.   BY GIORGIONE.

(In the Berlin Gallery.)

To face p. 219.

first, let me name a mysterious female portrait in the Borghese gallery (see illustration), which I have already dealt with at some length in my ' Critical Studies in the Borghese and Doria Galleries ' (pp. 248, 249). A picture in the Pitti, representing a nymph and a faun (No. 147), I also believe to be by the master. Though much damaged, it shows, I think, all the characteristics of an early work of Giorgione—the type of the nymph with the low forehead, the charming arrangement of the hair upon the temples, the eyes placed near together, and the hand with tapering fingers.[1]

A brilliant half-length portrait by the master of a young man with a keen expression was recently acquired by Dr. J. P. Richter.[2] In it we have one of those rare portraits, such as only Giorgione, and occasionally Titian, were capable of producing, highly suggestive, and exercising over the spectator an irresistible fascination.

In the second room of the gallery at Hampton Court we find a picture of a young man with a shepherd's pipe in his hand, attributed, and I think not without reason, to Giorgione. As, however, I only saw the picture in a bad light, I am unable to vouch for the correctness of the attribution.

The late Herr Daniel Penther, a Viennese connoisseur, recognised the hand of Giorgione in a figure of " Judith " in the Hermitage at St. Petersburg, there attributed to Moretto da Brescia. To judge from the photograph, I should say that he was right, but it remains to be seen whether the picture be an original or merely an old copy after Giorgione.

The " Three Philosophers "[3] in the gallery at Vienna, of

[1] Messrs. Crowe and Cavalcaselle ascribe this picture only to some unknown pupil of Giorgione and Titian (ii. 162).

[2] This picture has now passed into the Berlin gallery.

[3] This picture was at one time in the collection of the Archduke

which I have already spoken, and which the ' Anonimo ' saw in 1525 in the house of Taddeo Contarini, belongs to Giorgione's latest period.

In the same year we find an entry in the work of this anonymous writer to the effect that he saw in the house of ' Jeronimo Marcello a San Tommade, la tela della Venere nuda, che dorme in un paese con Cupidine; fù de mano de Zorzo da Castelfranco, ma lo paese e Cupidine furono finiti da Tiziano.' ('The canvas with the nude figure of Venus sleeping, in a landscape, with Cupid, was by the hand of Giorgio of Castelfranco; the landscape and the Cupid were, however, finished by Titian.'[1]) I shall return to this remarkable picture, but first I would note that the ' Anonimo ' mentions another work by Giorgione which he saw in 1530 in the house of Gabriel Vendramin: ' El Cristo morto sopra el sepolcro, con l'anzolo che el sostenta, fù de man de Zorzi da Castelfranco, reconzato da Tiziano.' ('The dead Christ on the tomb, with the angel supporting Him, is a work by Giorgio of Castelfranco restored by Titian.') From this we gather that Giorgione painted a "Pietà," but whether the picture has been preserved, and where it may now be, I am unable to say. The ' Anonimo ' certainly could not have meant the ' world-renowned dead Christ ' in the Monte di Pietà at Treviso, as some affirm, for in that picture the Saviour is supported not by one angel but by three or four. With the exception of Messrs. Crowe and Cavalcaselle, and of a few other writers, most art-historians state that this picture at Treviso is one of Giorgione's finest works—a further proof of what I have already pointed out, that the principal authorities on art still know and understand little of this great master.

Leopold William, Stadholder of the Netherlands, and was copied on a small scale by Teniers. This copy is now also in the gallery at Vienna.

[1] See the ' Anonimo,' p. 169.

Let us now return to the picture mentioned by the
' Anonimo ' as being in 1525 in the house of Jeronimo
Marcello at Venice. His description, ' A sleeping Venus
with Cupid in a landscape,' though slight, is fairly correct.
This exquisite picture is generally supposed to be no longer
in existence. Whether this be really the case is another
question, and one which I think I may answer in the
negative, for I believe the student has but to seek for it in
the Dresden gallery. It has been no small satisfaction to
me to have been able to discern the genius and the hand
of Giorgione in this marvellous picture before I discovered
that it had been mentioned by the ' Anonimo ' as his
work.

It is incomprehensible that such a work, the quint-
essence of Venetian art, should not have been recognised
by critics. Long experience, however, has taught me that
the most incredible things are possible where art is con-
cerned. The so-called " Madonna di Caitone," in the next
room of this gallery, was extolled as an original by Moretto,
and that by critics of the learning and authority of Von
Quandt and Rio, while very few appear to have been the
least aware of the value of this "Venus"—the most perfect
of all representations of the kind, whose beauty, though
dimmed by restoration, still shines forth with marvellous
power. Such a state of things is indeed deplorable and
disheartening, for of what avail is the culture we hear so
much of in these days, and of what use our annual exhibi-
tions of pictures, or the lectures and countless publications
on art, if we are wholly unmoved by one of the most
sublime works of art ever produced, unless it be specially
brought to our notice ? The greatness of Giorgione has
been little understood in the present day, and even shortly
after his death how few among his own countrymen were
capable of comprehending him ! How many pictures have

been recognised as specimens of his brilliant genius which
are in reality but caricatures. Those who are incapable
of seeing the beauty of this "Venus" by him can have
no true appreciation of the art of Raphael, Leonardo,
Correggio, or Titian. What other artist, even among the
Greeks, ever displayed a more refined feeling for line than
Giorgione has shown in this picture? How coarse and
unrefined, by comparison, is the nude female figure by
Palma Vecchio in the same room of this gallery; and how
commonplace and devoid of all inward grace is Titian's
celebrated "Venus with Cupid" in the Tribune of the
Uffizi![1] The landscape background in Giorgione's work is
also of the highest charm. If the dirt and the repaints at
present disfiguring this picture were carefully removed, it
would, I think, prove to be one of the greatest art-treasures
in existence.

This "Venus" became the prototype, among painters
of the Venetian school, for all other pictures of the class,
but Giorgione far surpassed all his imitators in refinement
of feeling and nobility of conception. A comparison with
Titian's celebrated representations of Venus and of Danae
strikingly proves this. His treatment of the latter subject,
indeed, is so realistic, nay, even so degraded in feeling,
that the old hag introduced beside "Danae" involuntarily
suggests to us a woman of the lowest class. On the other
hand, when compared with Botticelli's "Venus" in the
Uffizi, and with Correggio's "Danae" in the Borghese
gallery at Rome, this "Venus" of Giorgione shows a ten-
dency to realism, although in the highest and noblest sense
of the word.

Giorgione was by nature more vigorous, healthy, and

[1] About twelve years ago this pic-
ture, which in many respects is an
admirable work, was irreparably in-
jured by restoration. In its present
condition it is comparatively value-
less.

SLEEPING VENUS. BY GIORGIONE.

(In the Dresden Gallery.)

To face p. 222.

joyous than Correggio. The aim of the latter in representing
the "Danae" was totally different to that of the Venetian
master in dealing with the sleeping Venus. Sensuous delight
has probably never been represented in so highly spiritualised
a form as by Correggio. We see this in his "Leda" in the
Berlin gallery, as well as in the "Danae" at Rome. Titian's
representations of the latter subject and of Venus appear
coarse in conception beside Correggio's work. Yet I admit
that Titian was unsurpassed in all technical qualities of his
art—in the manipulation of the brush and in the skilful
disposition of light and shade.[1]

In 1646 Ridolfi published his 'Meraviglie dell' Arte.'
In all probability he did not know of the existence of the
manuscript of the 'Anonimo,' but he, too, speaks of this
sleeping Venus as the work of Giorgione, and in his day
it was still in the Casa Marcella: 'Una deliziosa Venere
ignuda dormiente è in Casa Marcella, ed a' piedi è Cupido
con augellino in mano che fù terminato da Tiziano.'
('An exquisite nude figure of Venus sleeping is in the Casa
Marcella, and at her feet is Cupid holding a little bird,
which (that is, Cupid) was finished by Titian.'[2]) This, there-
fore, was the traditional appellation in the Casa Marcella,
but the picture came to Dresden, as Dr. Hübner stated in
his catalogue, as the work of Titian: 'At the feet of Venus
was a Cupid, but the latter was in so damaged a condition
that it was removed, and the picture was then restored by
Schirmer.' Subsequent to this process it was described

[1] The recumbent "Venus" by
Titian in the Tribune of the Uffizi
(No. 1117) is probably nothing but
a copy of Giorgione's picture. In
this case, however, the figure is no
longer represented sleeping, and the
head is the portrait of Eleonora
Gonzaga, Duchess of Urbino. The
picture was probably executed be-
tween 1510 and 1520, by order of
her husband, Francesco Maria della
Rovere, Duke of Urbino. Titian
had before that painted the portrait
of Eleonora on her marriage, which
picture is now in the public gallery
at Vienna.

[2] See *Meraviglie dell' Arte*, i.
180.

as 'in all probability a copy' (!), and was, moreover, attributed to Sassoferrato (!).[1]

After the lapse of ten years I may be permitted to express my satisfaction at seeing this glorious work of Giorgione now accepted as an undoubted original, not only by Dr. Woermann but by the majority of art-critics in Europe. This one fortunate discovery, which in a propitious moment I was enabled to make, will perhaps atone in some degree for my many other shortcomings and mistakes.

If I am right in attributing the pictures I have named to Giorgione, Italy may then lay claim to possessing ten of his works, or rather eleven, counting the portrait in Dr. Richter's collection.[2]   The remainder, which are no longer in Italy, are :—

1. The " Madonna with Saints," in the Museo del Prado at Madrid, ascribed to Pordenone (†).

2. The " Concert," in the Salon Carré of the Louvre.[3]

3. A young man with a shepherd's pipe, at Hampton Court, attributed, and probably rightly, to Giorgione.

4. The " Sleeping Venus," in the Dresden gallery (†).

5. The " Judith " (?), in the Hermitage at St. Petersburg, attributed to Moretto.

6 and 7. The pictures in the Esterhazy gallery at Buda-Pesth, rightly ascribed to Giorgione.

8. The " Three Philosophers," in the public gallery at Vienna.

---

[1] I am greatly surprised to find that Messrs. Crowe and Cavalcaselle accept this view of the picture (see *Life of Titian*, i. 275).   On the other hand, they claim to have discovered the original of this Dresden Venus in a picture in the Darmstadt gallery, which is there ascribed to Titian.   The latter work, however, appears to me to be a free and most inferior copy of Giorgione's " Venus " in Dresden, executed by some feeble German painter of the eighteenth century.

[2] This portrait is now in the Berlin gallery.

[3] The " Holy Family " (No. 1185) attributed to him in the same collection, is clearly the work of some pupil or imitator of Giorgione.

THE MARTYRDOM OF A SAINT.   DRAWING BY GIORGIONE.
(At Chatsworth.)

To face p. 225.

The sum total of his works is, therefore, barely nineteen.

Of the numerous sketches and drawings so gratuitously ascribed to him, scarcely three or four can be regarded as genuine. They are : A drawing in the collection at Chatsworth, representing the Martyrdom of a Saint (see illustration, Braun, No. 172) ; a pen and wash drawing in the Louvre (Room X. exhibited on the stand), representing two men seated in the foreground of a landscape ; a pen sketch of a landscape in the His de la Salle collection, and possibly another drawing of a landscape, also in pen and wash, in the Albertina at Vienna. It is placed among Raphael's drawings in a portfolio lettered ' V. C.' I am, however, inclined to think that it is by Domenico Campagnola rather than by Giorgione. This master imitated the latter, and also Titian in his Giorgionesque period, so closely that it is not surprising to find his fine and spirited drawings attributed to both these painters. Nearly all the pen drawings ascribed to Giorgione in the Uffizi are, in my opinion, by Campagnola.[1] The same misnomer occurs in three drawings at Chatsworth. One of them represents a woman with a cap on her head looking upwards. On the same sheet is the head of a man with curly hair (Braun, 171). The second drawing represents an old man and a boy, both recumbent, behind them two other figures ; in the third are two nude children with a dog. I shall have occasion to return to the subject of Campagnola's drawings, and shall then point out some of the characteristics which may enable us to distinguish his drawings from those of Giorgione, and more especially of Titian, with whom he is most frequently confounded.

[1] For the benefit of students I may name a few of these drawings : No. 692, a man seated beneath a tree with a sheep (Philpot, No. 2813 ; Braun, 758); the head of a man, and a child lying on the ground (Braun, 753) ; a " St. Sebastian " (Braun, 752); a "Lucretia" (Braun, 751) ; and three heads.

In the adjoining room of the Dresden gallery hangs the picture which both Rio and Passavant[1] speak of with enthusiasm as the work of Moretto da Brescia. Dr. Hübner mentions it as follows : ‘The Madonna as she appeared at the time of the plague, in the year 1523, to a shepherd-boy, Filippo Viotti, of Monte Caitone, in the province of Brescia ; an altered replica of the altar-piece at Paitone ; above, on the dark background, is the inscription : “ *Imago Beatæ Mariæ Virg. quæ Mens. August.* 1533 [not therefore 1523] *Caitoni* [sic] *Agri Brixani Pago apparuit miraculor. operatione concursi. pop. celeberrim.*” ’

Mons. Rio, the amiable neo-Catholic writer, observes in his book, entitled ‘Léonard de Vinci et son Ecole,’ p. 312 : ‘C’est la Madone miraculeuse qu’il (Moretto) peignit en 1533 pour satisfaire la dévotion de ses compatriotes et la sienne. Pour comble de bonheur, c’était sur une bannière que devait être peinte l’image vénérée, avec le double caractère de reine des anges et de mère de miséricorde. C’était un problème analogue à celui que Rafael avait à résoudre en peignant la Madone de S. Sixte ; et les âmes pieuses, qui ont aussi leur compétence (?) bien différente de celle des connaisseurs ’ (which is very evident), ‘peuvent comparer, au point de vue de l’inspiration, ces deux chefs-d’œuvre que le hasard a réunis dans la même ville. La Vierge de Moretto est à Dresde, et fait partie de la collection de M. Quandt, excellent appréciateur des trésors d’art qu’il possède.’ The ‘ chef-d’œuvre ’ subsequently passed from this collection to the Dresden gallery.[2] Messrs. Crowe and Cavalcaselle include this “ Madonna di Caitone ” in their list of Moretto’s works, and even quote the inscription.[3] Considering that nearly all the most celebrated

[1] See Passavant’s *Raphael*, French translation, ii. 316.

[2] Passavant also regards this unpleasing copy as one of the five

pictures by Moretto which are in Germany (see *Raphael d’Urbin*, ii. 316).

[3] ii. 416 and 417.

writers on art are agreed as to the value of this supposed work by Moretto, it would show a want of intelligence on my part were I to refuse to admit that the 'Vierge miraculeuse' of M. Rio, 'celeberrima operatione miraculorum,' as the inscription has it, still continues to work miracles. I am, indeed, quite ready to acknowledge that a good copy may deceive even the most acute and experienced connoisseur; but that such a miserably feeble and clumsy production as this picture should have duped men who have made the study of art the business of their lives, and who have passed judgment on innumerable works by the old masters, is altogether incredible. The question naturally suggests itself, What idea can visitors to the Dresden gallery have formed of the art of Moretto from this "Madonna di Caitone"[1] if Moretto, who in all his works is remarkable for the charming and delicate harmony of his silvery colouring, and for nobility of form and elegance of movement, which exercise a powerful fascination over the spectator, is in this gallery—the rendezvous of art-critics of all nations—made responsible for the mere signboard figure of a vapid and hysterical nun?[2] In the name of this noble Brescian master

[1] In the Turin gallery a feeble copy of a Madonna by Moretto is exhibited as an original. It is numbered 116.

[2] It is scarcely necessary to draw the attention of more discerning critics to the many defects in this wretched copy of the last century—the flat, nerveless hands, the heavy and stupid expression of the Madonna, the crude brick-red of the ground, &c. The figure in the original cannot be regarded as one of the most successful of Moretto's female forms, which are usually so attractive. Nevertheless, there is something highly poetic in the effect of the silvery hue of her long white draperies. We seek in vain for these tints in the Dresden Madonna "di Caitone," and can only suppose that they have remained behind at Paitone, on the barren hill with its little chapel, situated at least a quarter of an hour from the village below. The representation of the Madonna, clad as a nun and standing on the earth, is significant in the original. There she is depicted speaking to the boy who stands before her, and who has been gathering blackberries on the

Q 2

I must indignantly protest against the wrong thus done to him. Dr. Woermann has now made reparation for the errors of his predecessors, and has described this wretched picture as a feeble copy of the original at Paitone, for which he is entitled to the gratitude of all who admire Moretto's art.

Titian, Moretto's great contemporary, is better represented in the Dresden gallery than the Brescian master. In Dr. Hübner's catalogue nine pictures were ascribed to him which we will now examine more closely.

The earliest among them is undoubtedly the celebrated picture known as the "Tribute Money" (No. 169), which is signed '*Ticianus*'—a form of signature which we meet with in nearly all the master's early works up to about 1528. Messrs. Crowe and Cavalcaselle assign it to the year 1508 ; Vasari, on the other hand, to 1514. I am disposed to accept the view of the first-named writers.[1] I know no work of Titian which is executed with so much care and love as this noble and thoughtfully treated head of Christ. The technical method is that derived from the Van Eycks, as may be seen in a spot where the glaze has disappeared —on the neck of the principal figure. It has been affirmed

hillside. She bids him return to the village and enjoin the inhabitants to raise a chapel in her honour on the hill if they would be delivered from the pestilence. In the copy in Dresden, however, it is impossible to guess at the meaning of this morbid, unhealthy-looking woman. For no one would ever dream of supposing that it was intended to represent the Blessed Virgin. In the parish church of Auro, a small village in the Val Sabbia among the Brescian hills, there is an old copy of the Madonna di Paitone, and it is scarcely neces-

sary to observe that the boy with his basket of blackberries has not there been omitted.

[1] Other writers affirm that the "Tribute Money" must have been painted between 1516 and 1522, as Titian was not at Ferrara prior to 1516. In that case it would have been painted several years after the "Assumption," a theory which I am unable to accept, as the type of the Saviour is identical with that of the "Christ bearing the Cross" by Titian in the Church of S. Rocco at Venice, undoubtedly one of the master's earliest works.

MADONNA. BY MORETTO.

(Paitone, near Brescia.)

To face p. 228.

that the "Tribute Money" was painted for Duke Alfonso of Ferrara, a question which we need not discuss here. One thing, however, seems clear, that the picture was bought by Alfonso IV. or by Francis I. of Este; and that it came to the gallery at Modena in this manner, thus forming one of the 'hundred pictures' which passed thence to the Dresden gallery.

Another splendid early work by the master is the "Madonna and Child between SS. John the Baptist, Jerome, Paul, and the Magdalen." Notwithstanding the injury it has sustained, it is still a miracle of glowing colour. I should place this fresh and brilliant early work in the period when Titian painted his celebrated "Assumption," for the Church of the Frari at Venice—that is, between 1514 and 1520.[1]

[1] It appears that Messrs. Crowe and Cavalcaselle (if I have rightly understood them, *Life of Titian*, i. 447, 448) do not acknowledge this picture as a work of Titian, but ascribe it to Andrea Schiavone. Æsthetic or technical proofs are of little avail in determining works of art. In support of my own views, I may direct the attention of students to a material, but most characteristic, peculiarity which I have observed in over fifty works by Titian—the ball of the thumb, which is too strongly developed in all of them, especially in the hands of the male figures. We may observe this characteristic in the hand of St. John the Baptist in this picture; in that of an apostle in a red mantle in the "Assumption"; in that of the Pharisee of the "Tribute Money"; in the hand of the figure representing "Sacred Love" in the Borghese gallery; in the Louvre in Nos. 1577, 1579, 1584, 1587, 1589, and elsewhere. A pupil or a copyist would certainly have avoided reproducing this defect. The picture in Dresden has suffered much, the figure of the Baptist is entirely repainted, the right arm of the Infant Saviour is disfigured, the glazes about the mouth of the Madonna have disappeared in part, so that the grey preparation with tempera is visible; St. Paul, too, has been repainted. Fortunately, however, the lovely figure of the Magdalen is fairly well preserved. It seems as though her extreme beauty had shielded her from the barbaric attacks of the restorer, and her left hand alone would prove to all who know Titian that she is a genuine creation of the master. The reds in this picture are similar to those in the "Assumption." The sky has also suffered, but notwithstanding its many injuries, the picture will have an irresistible charm for all who have any true feeling for art.

The third picture ascribed to the master in the Dresden gallery is the "Holy Family" (No. 175), with the donor and his family adoring the Infant Saviour. It is of Titian's mature period, and is genuine, though much restored.

The recumbent Venus (No. 177) crowned by Cupid, with a young man at her feet playing the lute, was already pronounced by Guarienti to be a copy, and Messrs. Crowe and Cavalcaselle are of the same opinion. The original is at Madrid, and this copy is merely by some Venetian Mieris, Metsu, or Terborch of the sixteenth century. Thus the conception of art in Europe passed through successive stages, from the Venus of Botticelli and of Giorgione to those of Titian, and so downwards to those of Mieris and Metsu, descending finally to the idylls of Adrian van der Werff. This Venus was long supposed to be the portrait of a princess of Eboli, and the lute-player was taken to be Philip II. of Spain. In all probability, however, the picture represents some young Venetian noble with a ' Cortigiana.'

The portrait of a young woman in a dress of a reddish hue holding a vase (No. 173) is so rubbed down and disfigured that it can afford no pleasure in its present condition. That of a lady in mourning (No. 174), on the other hand, is fairly well preserved and noble in conception. A male portrait (No. 172) is of Titian's later period, 1561. On the window-ledge, behind the figure, the painter has introduced a colour-box. Titian must have been about eighty-four when he painted this portrait.

We will now turn to the interesting likeness of a young and fair-haired lady clad in white and holding a fan (No. 170). Rubens has given us a masterly Flemish version of this portrait, now in the public gallery at Vienna. In the same collection we meet with this figure again, in Titian's celebrated picture of the " Ecce Homo " (No. 166), which was executed by him in 1543 for his patron d'Anna or Van Haanen, a rich Flemish merchant settled at Venice. In these three pictures the girl represented is Titian's daughter Lavinia. In the " Ecce Homo " at Vienna she appears as a girl of fourteen, dressed in white, and leading a boy by the hand ; in the Dresden portrait she seems to be eleven or twelve years older, and holds a little flag-fan, which was only carried by the newly married.[1] In 1555 she married Cornelio Sarcinelli of Serravalle,[2] and this fine

[1] Some writers affirm that the portrait represents a woman beloved by Titian. They do not, however, appear to consider that in 1555, when this portrait was painted, Titian was seventy-eight, an age at which it does not appear to me probable that he would have captivated the heart of a woman. The late Marchese Campori of Modena thought Titian presented the portrait to his patron Alfonso II. of Ferrara.

[2] Messrs. Crowe and Cavalcaselle, in their *Life of Titian* (ii. 510), have published the marriage contract, which, according to them, is still in the possession of the heirs of the late Dottore Pietro Carnieluti at Serravalle. The document, as reproduced by them, will most likely be unintelligible to many, and I have, therefore, thought it desirable to give the contract from the manuscript in the Trivulzio library at Milan, which in all probability is the original :—

1555. A di 20 marzo in Serravalle.

Al nome sia di lo Eterno Iddio et de la Gloriosa Vergine Maria et di tutta la Corte celestial et in buona ventura.

El se dichiara come in questo giorno si ha trattato [and not ' si fa

fratello,' which would have no sense] et concluso matrimonio fra il spscripto Cornelio, fiolo del qdam [and not ' ge '] Messer Marco Sarcinello, cittadino cinitense [of Ceneda] habitante in Serravalle, da una parte et la discreta [and not discritta] Madonna Lavinia, fiola del spscripto M. Titiano Vicellio pittore de Cadore, habitante in Venetia, dall' altra, si come comanda Iddio et la S. Madre Giesia [Chiesa].

Per parolle di presente fatte [and not ' et ptti '] et conto di dotte il spettabile Messer Titiano sopraditto li promette et si obbliga a dare al prefato M. Cornelio duc. [ducati] 1,400, a lire 6 e soldi 4 per ducato [and not ' due 7 mille e quattrocento al 604 et due 7,' which would be sheer nonsense] in questa forma, videlicet al dare della man [that is ' all' atto dello impalmare '] ducati 600 [and not ' 23 al dar della man due 7 seicento al 604 p̄. due 7 '] a Lire 6, e soldi 4 per duc. [ducato] et il restante, detratto il valore et lo ammontar de li beni mobili p̄. uso de la ditta sposa, li promette a dar in tanti contanti per tutto l' anno 1556, quali siano in tutto per lo ammontar et summa de li predetti ducati 1400

portrait was evidently produced in that year, and not in 1546, as Messrs. Crowe and Cavalcaselle suppose. In No. 171 of this gallery we see the same Lavinia fifteen or eighteen years older. Titian painted his daughter again in his ninety-fourth year, about 1570 or 1572. She must then have been nearly forty, and had entirely lost her good looks. The feather fan which she carries here was only borne by noble ladies in Venice, but, as the daughter of the artist whom Charles V. had raised—or, shall we say lowered ?—to the rank of count, she would, of course, have had a right to a title of nobility. Let it not be supposed

ut supra [Messrs. Crowe and Cavalcaselle again here read ' due ' instead of ' duc.' (ducati), and consequently give the dowry as 2,400 ducats, which is 1,000 ducats more than the sum given in the Trivulzio MS.]. La qual dotte il p̄fatto M. Cornelio con Madonna Calliopia sua madre simul et in solidum togliono et accettano sopra tutti li beni p̄ti et futī [presenti e futuri], li quali obbligano in ogni caso et evento di restituir et assicurar la ditta dotte. Et cosi il p̄fato M. Titiano, a manutention de la sopraditta dotte promette et obbliga tutti li suoi beni p̄ti et futī usque ad integram satisfationem [sic] et cosi l'una et l'altra parte di sua mano si sottoscrivono [and not ' sottoscriveranno '] p̄ caution delle soprascripte cosse così promettendo esse parti p̄. se et suoi eredi mantenir et osservar ut sopra continetur.

Et Io Juanne Alessandrino de Cadore pregado dalle parti testo.

Io Titian Vecellio sono [and not ' sarò '] contento et affermo et approbo quanto se contiene nell' oltrascripto contratto.

Io Cornelio Sarcinello son contento et affermo et approbo quanto se

contien nell' oltrascrito contrato.

1555 a dì 19 Zugno in Venetia. Io Cornelio Sarcinello soprascrito dal S⁰ʳ Titiano soprascrito, mio socero, schudi 500 et 55 d' oro, a L. 6 et 4 soldi l' uno [and not ' a L. 604 l' uno '), e questi ho riceputo per parte et a bonconto de dote promessami ut supra.

1556 a dì 13 Settembris in Venetia.

R. Io Cornelio Sarcinello soprascritto dal S⁰ʳ Titiano soprascritto, mio suocero, duc. 322, et questo per robe stimade fra nui da M. Francesco Sartor et d' accordo da una parte et l' altra.

Item per cadene, ori et fatura scudi Nr. 88 come appare per la polizza-de Balini zojelier.

a dì 23 Lujo 1557. Noto faccio io Cornelio Sarcinello qualmente mi chiamo satisfato de tuta la summa de la dotta promessa a mi Cornelio per il S⁰ʳ Titiano Vecellio, mio suocer, parte per danari et parte per perle et altre robe haute et zoje et così come appar p̄. li nostri conti, et in fede di ciò iò ho scrito di mia man propria. [This concluding receipt is not given by Messrs. Crowe and Cavalcaselle.]

that I wish to undervalue such distinctions. On the contrary, I have a regard for those who bear them, knowing that we are more likely to meet with men of refinement and culture among this class than in the ranks of the democracy. I merely wished to observe that it was certainly derogatory to the dignity of a great artist like Titian to be treated by the Emperor simply as one of the herd of title-hunters who surrounded him. In political and official circles, princes, counts, and barons, all have their appointed grades of precedence, but in the world of art Vecellio the count was a mere nonentity compared with Titian the artist.

Germany, it thus appears, may claim to possess four portraits by Titian of his daughter Lavinia : one introduced in the picture of the "Ecce Homo" at Vienna, in which she is represented as a girl of fourteen or fifteen ; two in the Dresden gallery ; and, finally, the idealised portrait at Berlin, which the master probably painted in 1549 for his friend Argentina Pallavicino of Reggio.[1] Among Titian's works in the Dresden gallery there yet remains to be mentioned a portrait of a young Venetian lady holding a marten boa. The picture is much injured and the glazes have almost entirely disappeared, but it seems to me to have been originally by Titian ; the director of the gallery is of the same opinion.

The Dresden collection, therefore, contains eight works by this most powerful and renowned of Venetian masters. Compared with the English National Gallery, which can only boast of five, the Dresden collection may be considered rich in this respect, though it falls far short of the Louvre and of the galleries at Vienna and Madrid. The Museo del Prado in the latter city has no less than forty-two genuine works by the master ; and the Louvre contains about fifteen, those numbered 1578, 1579, 1581, 1583,

[1] See Gaye, *Carteggio storico d'artisti*, ii. 375.

1584, 1587, 1589, 1590, 1591, 1592, being among his finest works. The public gallery at Vienna contains more works by the master than all the collections of Germany put together. In the present catalogue thirty-seven are connected with the name of Titian, though some of them are admitted to be works of the school. The number of genuine works is, in any case, considerable,[1] though several have been irreparably injured by restoration. Among the portraits formerly attributed to Titian, one (No. 430) has now been restored to its true author, Moroni. A Madonna and Child with Saints (No. 292) is merely a copy or a production of the school; the original, a splendid work, being in the Louvre. The male portrait in three different positions on the same canvas is, I feel sure, by a German painter (†). I notice that this was also the opinion of Michel. The person represented is very German in appearance. It is impossible that the picture should be by Lotto, as Messrs. Crowe and Cavalcaselle conjecture. Another male portrait (No. 268) also looks to me like the work of a northern painter. Messrs. Crowe and Cavalcaselle would ascribe it to Girolamo da Treviso, but their attribution cannot be sustained if the picture be compared with the fine male portrait by this master in the Palazzo Colonna ai SS. Apostoli at Rome.

Among Titian's imitators, Polidoro Veneziano is better represented at Dresden than in any other gallery. The two pictures ascribed to him in the catalogue are genuine and very characteristic specimens of the art of this master, whose works are usually attributed to other painters.

No. 214 represents a Venetian patrician presenting his child to St. Joseph to be dedicated to the Virgin. On the

---

[1] Among them may be named the following : Nos. 166, 175, 274, 276, 290, 291, 293, 298, 307, 473 (Eleonora Gonzaga), and 476 (Isabella Gonzaga).

right stands the Magdalen, to whom the Infant Saviour
gives a wreath ; in the background is the guardian angel.
In No. 215 is represented the "Marriage of St. Catherine"
in the presence of St. Andrew.

Another of Titian's imitators was Bonifazio III. (Vene-
ziano). This master in his later period—that is, after
1570—abandoned the manner of his relatives and in-
structors, Bonifazio I. and II., and took Titian as his
model. No. 213, a feeble and damaged picture, is probably
by him, and of his last epoch (?). It represents the Madonna
with the Child, who turns to St. Catherine, SS. Anthony
and Peter standing by.

The Dresden gallery contains a work (No. 847A) by the
celebrated Bergamasque portrait-painter, Giovanni Battista
Moroni—not Morone, as he is sometimes erroneously called,
even in Italian catalogues. It is the portrait of a man
resting his right hand on his hip. It dates from 1557, the
master's best period. Though skilfully painted, it is ex-
tremely stiff and uninteresting in treatment, and Moroni's
art does not show to advantage in it. Such was the hasty
judgment I formed of this picture ten years ago. On
seeing it recently in company with Dr. Woermann, I
could scarcely believe my eyes. 'Es irrt der Mensch so
lang er strebt,' I observed to him with some chagrin. It is
incomprehensible and unpardonable that, knowing the
Bergamasque school, as I thought, as well as most people,
and having had the opportunity of seeing scores of
Moroni's pictures, I should yet have taken this portrait
for his work, though its Flemish origin is conspicuous even
at a distance. Truly my mistake was wholly inexcusable,
et ergo humiliter me subjicio.

Andrea Previtali, another Bergamasque, is better repre-
sented in this gallery by a picture recently acquired (No. 60).
It represents the Madonna and Child with the little

St. John, and is inscribed ' A . . . eas [Bergo]mensis, 1510.`
Previtali must, therefore, have painted it in Venice ; he
probably only left that city to return to Bergamo towards
the close of that year.   All his works from 1511 [1] to 1525

[1] Messrs. Crowe and Cavalcaselle
consider, but I think erroneously,
that Previtali only settled at Ber-
gamo in 1515. A Madonna which
I once saw in the Casa Terzi in
that city was signed ' Andreas
Previtalus, 1511,' a proof that he
was in that year at Bergamo. Had
he painted it in Venice he would
have adopted the signature ' Bergo-
mensis.' On a picture in the 'Chiesa
del Conventino,' near Bergamo, there
is a *cartellino* beneath the figure of
St. Constantine inscribed, ' Andreas
Privitalus, 1512,' and the " Cristo
trasfigurato," which passed from
the Church of S. Maria delle Grazie
at Bergamo into the Brera at Milan,
is signed, ' Andreas Previtalus, 1513.'
This picture was never, as stated by
Messrs. Crowe and Cavalcaselle, in
the Church of San Benedetto, but
was already at the time of the
' Anonimo ' (see p. 138) in the
Chiesa delle Grazie. The small
" Crucifixion " in S. Alessandro della
Croce at Bergamo is also signed
' Andreas Previtalus ' and dated 1514.
The same writers affirm that Pre-
vitali's pictures occasionally have a
' Lombard look ' (i. 279). It is im-
possible, however, to say wherein
this ' look ' consists. They further
inform us that Previtali, in some of
his works, adopted the manner of
Basaiti and of Catena. Coming
from them, such a theory is natural
enough, as it is their wont to ascribe
Catena's pictures to Previtali. Thus
they attribute an attractive picture
by Catena in the Giovanelli collec-
tion to Previtali, and they fall into

the same mistake when speaking of
the " Circumcision " in the Manfrin
gallery at Venice. The first-named
picture represents the Madonna be-
tween saints, and bears the forged
signature, ' Joannes Bellinus.' The
Madonna is copied from one by
Bellini of 1507, in the Church of
S. Francesco della Vigna at Venice.
Neither of these pictures has any
connection with Previtali ; they are
both by Catena, and probably of the
same period as his altar-piece in the
Church of S. Maria Mater Domini
at Venice. Again, Previtali has been
confounded by Messrs. Crowe and
Cavalcaselle with Cariani, as, for
example, in the lunette over the
side door of S. Maria Maggiore at
Bergamo, while on another occasion
they attribute works by him to
Pellegrino da San Daniele ; for in-
stance, the " Descent into Limbus "
in the Palazzo Ducale at Venice
there ascribed to Giorgione (! !). In
short, Previtali, who, in point of
fact, is a dry, homely, and somewhat
monotonous Bergamasque painter,
becomes to these historians a veritable
chameleon, who appears alternately
as Cariani, Catena, Lotto, or Pelle-
grino da San Daniele. Their con-
jecture that Andrea Previtali is
identical with Andrea Cordegliaghi
seems to me equally untenable.
Both were fellow-scholars in the
workshop of Giovanni Bellini, an
it is undeniable that in some of their
works they closely resemble each
other ; but this may be explained
by the fact that the one probably
copied the cartoon or even the picture

are signed 'Andreas Previtalus,' proving that during these years he remained at Bergamo. Count Tassi [1] maintains, though without giving any reason for so doing, that Previtali died about 1528. The master's last dated work is of 1525. It is over the fifth altar to the right in the Church of S. Spirito at Bergamo, being a large poliptych with two main divisions, upper and lower. In the lower are the Madonna with the Infant Saviour between SS. Monica, Lucy, Catherine, and Ursula. Before the latter kneel three virgins in supplication; below the Madonna is the inscription, ' Andreas Previtalus, 1525.' In the centre of the upper part is the Saviour holding a red banner between SS. John the Baptist, Bartholomew, Peter, and James. This upper part was not executed by Previtali, but by Agostino da Caversegno, a grotesque Bergamasque painter, who was a pupil and imitator of Lotto (†).

of the other. The few signed works which I have met with by Cordegliaghi appear to me, however, to be more refined and lifelike in expression, and his landscapes are warmer and less vividly green in tone than those of Previtali. The name Cordegliaghi (that is, cordelle e aghi—i.e. tapes and needles), which he must have inherited from his forefathers, is Venetian, and not Bergamasque. In the latter district the pedlars cry their wares as ' nistole e guggì,' and not as in the Venetian district, as ' cordelle e agi ' (aghi). In the Bergamasque dialect ' nistola ' is the equivalent of ' cordella,' and ' guggì ' of ' aghi,' which in the Venetian dialect becomes ' agi.' In the Bergamasque ' agguglia, guglia ' is a needle; ' guggia, guggino, guggì,' a small needle, and ' guggiare ' is to knit (see Notizia d'opere di disegno, p. 161, second edition, by Dr. Gustavo Frizzoni,

where the subject is discussed).

Finally, I may add that the inscription on the Madonna belonging to Countess Porto at Vicenza is as follows : ' ANDREAS C. A. DI. [sic] IOANNIS BELLINI P.'; that on the back of the male portrait in the Poldi-Pezzoli collection at Milan, ' ANDREAS C. A. DI. [sic] IO [sic] B.' (discipulus Joannis Bellini). I cannot, unfortunately, recall the inscription on Cordegliaghi's picture belonging to Lady Eastlake. [The inscription on Lady Eastlake's picture is as follows : ' × 1504 Andreas Cordelle Agy, discipulus johannis bellini pinxit 24.'—TRANS.] On Previtali's pictures, on the other hand, the inscription is always, ' ANDREAS BERGOMENSIS D.I.B.' (discipulus Joannis Bellini), and not DI. IO. as on Cordegliaghi's works.

[1] Vite dei pittori, scultori, &c., bergamaschi.

Bergamo was ravaged by the plague in the years 1524 and 1525. I think it not unlikely that Previtali was among its victims, and that the lower part of this altar-piece was therefore his last work. It is very probable that Tassi, who gives 1528 as the year of his death, may have misread 'five' for 'eight' in some document. The altar-piece thus left unfinished by Previtali's sudden death was, I conjecture, completed later by Agostino da Caversegno.

Messrs. Crowe and Cavalcaselle mention a monogram which is to be seen on some of Previtali's pictures. I have never succeeded in discovering it, nor have I ever met with a work by this master showing the influence of Palma Vecchio. In his works from 1502 to 1515 [1] we see Previtali as a diligent, conscientious, and faithful imitator of Giovanni Bellini, somewhat uninteresting and inanimate in conception and treatment, but admirable as a colourist and attractive in his landscapes. In 1515 Lotto established himself at Bergamo in order to execute the large altar-piece for the Church of the Dominicans now in S. Bartolommeo, and we find Previtali at that period seeking to imitate him. So successful was he, indeed, that even Messrs. Crowe and Cavalcaselle ascribe several of his works to Lotto,[2] though the artistic nature of the gifted and sensitive Venetian differs entirely from that of the coarser-grained Bergamasque.

The 'Anonimo' does not mention a single work by Previtali in private collections at Venice, though he notices several by Palma Vecchio and Cariani, a proof that the

[1] For example, a work formerly in the possession of Count Cavalli at Padua, and the large altar-piece in the Church of S. Spirito at Bergamo, representing St. John the Baptist between four saints.

[2] For example, three small pictures in the sacristy of the cathedral at Bergamo, once forming the predella to Previtali's altar-piece of 1524, over the first altar on the right in the same church (ii. 524, note 1); and two in the second sacristy of the Church of the Redentore at Venice (†), the "Crucifixion" and the "Nativity" (ii. 531).

merits of the first-named master only obtained recognition at a later date. On the other hand, Previtali is greatly overrated by Lanzi, who ranks him nearly as high as Palma Vecchio. This was probably due to Count Tassi, who, in his ' Lives of the Bergamasque Painters,' bestows upon Previtali exaggerated praise. His technical merits are undoubtedly great. In brilliancy of colouring he is second to no other pupil of Giovanni Bellini, and his landscape backgrounds are usually pleasing and carefully executed ; but he lacks those special gifts which are the distinguishing marks of a great artist—power of imagination and originality of representation. His influence was not felt in the slightest degree in the development of Venetian painting, and but to a very limited extent even in the local school of Bergamo. In the galleries of Central and Southern Italy, Previtali is not represented, and he is rarely met with in English, German, or Russian collections. The English National Gallery has but one inferior specimen of his art; in the public gallery at Vienna there is a characteristic picture by him—a " Madonna " (No. 297)—which Dr. von Engerth only described as the work of a pupil of Bellini, 'showing some connection with Previtali, or even with Girolamo da Santa Croce.' In point of fact, however, these two painters are but distantly related. Previtali's portraits from life are as uninteresting as are his figures of saints. The donors portrayed in his Madonna pictures are, however, the only specimens which have come down to us from which we can form any opinion of this branch of his art.[1] I have never met with any drawings which might be attributed to Previtali.

The most justly celebrated of all the Bergamasque artists is Jacopo Palma, known as Palma Vecchio, to

[1] For instance, the portraits of the Casotti family in Previtali's picture in the public gallery at Bergamo (No. 188, Carrara collection).

distinguish him from his great-nephew, Palma Giovine. In dealing with the Munich gallery, I have already expressed my views with regard to the position which should be assigned to this admirable painter in the history of Venetian art. We have, therefore, now only to consider his works in the Dresden gallery; we shall find in it no examples of his first, but several excellent specimens of his second and third or 'blonde' manner.

The so-called "Three Sisters" (?) (No. 189) is a world-renowned picture, though greatly injured by the restorer. The figure on the right has suffered most, the features having been so distorted as to render the expression positively disagreeable. In 1525 this picture was in the collection of M. Taddeo Contarini at Venice, and is thus described by the 'Anonimo' : [1] 'El quadro delle tre donne, retratte dal naturale insino al cinto, fù de man del Palma.' ('The picture of the three women to the waist, painted from life, was the work of Palma.') A most beautiful picture of the same period of Palma's career is No. 188, the Madonna and Child with St. John the Baptist, who presents to the former a scroll; between them stands St. Catherine.

In the "Venus" (No. 190) we see the master on the verge of his third or 'blonde' manner. The same model appears to have sat for the so-called 'Bella di Tiziano' in the Sciarra-Colonna collection. The 'goddess' is no more than a well-painted nude figure.

No. 191, the "Infant Saviour on His Mother's knee caressing the little St. John in the presence of SS. Joseph and Catherine," is of Palma's third and 'blonde' manner —from about 1520 to 1525.

There is no doubt that these four pictures are genuine. With the beautiful idyll of "Jacob and Rachel" (No. 192) there are, therefore, five works by this able and vigorous

[1] See p. 65.

painter in the Dresden gallery, which is richer in this respect than any public collection, with the exception of that at Vienna.

Two other works were formerly ascribed to Palma, Nos. 194 and 211. The first, an unimportant picture, represents a woman resting her right hand on a mirror, with a man standing behind her. It can only be by an imitator of Palma, and such is the opinion of the director of the gallery. In No. 211 we have the Madonna with St. Elisabeth and the little St. John, who holds a scroll inscribed, 'Ecce Agnus Dei.' In the foreground are SS. Catherine and Joseph. This picture I believe to be by the second Bonifazio, the painter to whom I have ascribed the "Adoration of the Magi" (No. 210), formerly attributed to Giorgione. In the new catalogue my appellation has been adopted.

I shall take this opportunity of saying a few words about the different artists of the same family who bore the name of Bonifazio. The earliest mention of a painter of this name occurs in the 'Anonimo' (p. 160) : '1532, in casa di M. Andrea di Odoni' (at Venice) he writes, ' la Trasfigurazione de S. Paulo fù de man de Bonifacio Veronese.' In 1556, Francesco Sansovino's book appeared, entitled ' Dialogo di tutte le cose notabili che sono in Venezia,' &c., and in this work mention is made of ' Bonifazio da Verona,' a painter. In the same year a book with a similar title was published by Anselmo Guisconi, in which the writer names, among the best painters of the century, ' Bonifazio da Verona, Giambellino, Giorgione, Pordenone, Tiziano, Paris, Tintoretto, and Paolo Caliari.' Even Lomazzo, the Milanese author, only mentions a Bonifazio Veronese; [1]

---

[1] *Trattato dell' arte della Pittura et Architettura*, 1584, p. 684.

Vasari,[1] on the other hand, speaks only of a Bonifazio
Veneziano, and in this he was followed by Ridolfi, Boschini,
and Zanetti.

According to all these writers, then, there was but one
painter of this name, whose birthplace was variously given
by them as Verona and Venice. In 1815, Moschini, in his
' Guida di Venezia,' rightly observed that there must have
been two painters of the name, for in the ' Necrologia ' of
the Church of S. Ermagora at Venice the death of one
Bonifazio, a painter, was recorded as having occurred on
October 19, 1553 ; while works signed with this name are
dated 1558 and even 1579.

More recently the late Dr. Cesare Bernasconi discovered
in the archives of the Church of SS. Siro e Libera at Verona
that a painter named Bonifazio, who in 1523 had been
admitted to the guild known as ' il Collegio,' died in 1540.
Thus we have three painters of this name—one, who died
in 1540, a second in 1553, while a third was still working
in 1579.

There is a family likeness between the numerous works
of these three artists, as there is between those of the Da
Ponte family, better known as the Bassani, and it is not so
easy to distinguish them one from another. The elder Boni-
fazio may not only be regarded as one of the best painters
of the Venetian school, but also as its most brilliant colourist.
Though, as an artist, he ever preserved his Veronese
character, which shows itself in the gaiety of his com-
positions and in the easy grace of his figures, yet in all
technical qualities he is thoroughly Venetian. In this
respect he shows no connection with the school of Verona.
The harmony of his colouring is neither so refined and
striking as that of Giorgione, nor so spirited as that of
Lotto, nor has it the strength, depth, and intensity of that

[1] xiii. 109 (ed. Milanesi, vii. 531).

of Palma or Titian, but the sparkling brilliancy of his well-blended tones has a peculiar charm which arrests attention.

The second Bonifazio may have been a brother or certainly some relation of this painter. He followed him so closely and faithfully, both in his mode of conception and in his method of painting, that it is almost impossible to distinguish between them, especially in those works which, as I have reason to believe, they executed conjointly. There are, I think, several pictures of this description in existence.

The two elder painters of the name were probably born at Verona in the last decade of the fifteenth century, and must at an early age have entered the workshop of Palma Vecchio at Venice. They were certainly related, and may even have been brothers. One was an artist of great talent, the other a mere imitator. The youngest Bonifazio, the third of the name, was probably the son of one of them. It may be conjectured that he was born at Venice, and was therefore rightly called Bonifazio Veneziano. In 1568, the year in which the second edition of Vasari's 'Lives' appeared, he was the only one of the three still living. The biographer's Venetian informant was right in speaking of him as Veneziano, though it was a grave omission on his part not to have mentioned the other far more important painters of the name. We can only conclude that he knew nothing of them.

It appears to me, therefore, that there were two painters of the name of Bonifazio, natives of Verona, and one, or perhaps even two, who were born at Venice, and were thus entitled to be called 'Veneziano.' All art-historians have, however, until recently, recognised but one, and have ascribed to him all those works which, though showing a certain family likeness, are extremely unequal in merit. To add to the confusion, the compilers of

R 2

gallery catalogues, especially in Italy, have confounded this so-called Bonifazio Veneziano with Bonifazio or Facio Bembo, who was Court painter to Francesco Sforza, and flourished in the second half of the fifteenth century. He is always called by such writers Bonifacio Bembi.[1]

Facio Bembo, known also as Facio di Valdarno, has certainly no connection, artistic or otherwise, with the Veronese painters Bonifazio. He worked in the service of the Sforzas at Cremona[2] (in the Church of S. Agostino) at Milan, in the castle of Pavia, and elsewhere. There was also a Benedetto Bembo, who proceeded from the school of Squarcione, and by whom there is a signed work in the castle of Torchiara, in the province of Parma.

The late Signor Cecchetti discovered that the Bonifazios also bore the name of de Pittatis.[3] They laboured almost exclusively in Venice, and dated works by all three are extant ranging over the period between 1530 and 1579. Among their pupils I should include not only Antonio Palma, the father of Palma Giovine, but also Polidoro Lanzani, known as Polidoro Veneziano. In order to distinguish between these three painters we may designate the elder and more important of them Bonifazio Veronese, senior; the second, Bonifazio Veronese, junior; and the third, Bonifazio Veneziano.

'Bonifazio Veronese, senior, was called a pupil of Palma

[1] In the Turin gallery the feeble copy of some picture of the school of Rubens (No. 136, the "Three Graces") is attributed to this so-called Bonifazio Bembo.

[2] The only works which have come down to us by this once celebrated artist are the life-sized portraits of Francesco Sforza and his wife Bianca Maria Visconti, painted in fresco on the walls of the Church of S. Agostino at Cremona.

About thirty years ago they were still intact, but an unintelligent restorer has now destroyed even these last remnants of Bembo's art.

[3] *Archivio Veneto*, I. xxxiv. 207: 'De Pittatis Bonifacio, abitante nella contrà di San Marcuola, in la casa delle monache di S. Alvise: Io Bonifacio di Pitati da Verona pitor fo [fù] di ser Marzio, 1553, 26 luglio.'

by Ridolfi,[1] and I think rightly. His pictures prove this more convincingly than any written document could do. His early works are, indeed, usually attributed to Palma ; for example, the lovely picture of glowing colour in the English National Gallery (No. 1202). It represents the Madonna and Child and the little St. John in a landscape, between SS. Jerome, James, and Catherine. It was formerly in the Casa Terzi at Bergamo, where it passed for the work of Palma Vecchio, and Messrs. Crowe and Caval-caselle describe it as one of his masterpieces (ii. 473). A feeble copy in the Venice Academy is ascribed to Andrea Schiavone or Meldola.[2] Another work of the master's early period is in the Ambrosiana at Milan under the name of Giorgione (†). It represents the Madonna seated in a landscape offering some fruit to the Infant Saviour, who is in the arms of St. Joseph. The little St. John is also introduced, and on the left of the Madonna the Archangel Raphael with Tobias. Certain parts of this charming picture recall Palma, the master of Bonifazio, such as the figure of St. Joseph, the profile of the angel, and the landscape, but the type of the Madonna is identical with that in Bonifazio's picture in the English National Gallery, and the form of both hand and ear is characteristic of this painter. In this picture we also meet with those velvet stuffs of a deep-red tone which he introduces in nearly all his pictures, and which are quite peculiar to him. A picture in the possession of Dr. J. P. Richter appears to me to be a still earlier work. It represents the "Holy Family" in a landscape with St. Elisabeth and the little St. John. The drawing is

[1] See *Vite dei Pittori*, i. 369.
[2] I have already mentioned that Dr. Bode regards the copy in the Venice Academy as the original, and the picture in London as a copy (ii. 782)—a verdict not likely to meet with the approval of Sir Frederick Burton, who rightly considers that he has acquired in this picture an admirable early work by Bonifazio Veronese.

extremely awkward and defective, but the feeling, especially in the children's heads, is most refined. Messrs. Crowe and Cavalcaselle [1] have formed a totally different opinion of the picture in the Ambrosiana: 'This picture,' they observe, 'is by a modern who studied many of his predecessors. The St. Joseph is in the fashion of Pordenone, the Madonna has the round fulness of Palma Vecchio; but the painter, probably Calderara, is a coarse imitator.' [2]

Another early work by Bonifazio is in the Palazzo Colonna ai SS. Apostòli at Rome, where it is ascribed to Titian. It represents the Madonna and Child in a landscape, between SS. Joseph, Jerome, Lucy, and an angel. In the royal palace at Venice, in the room known as the ' Sala di Napoleone I.,' there is also a good picture by this master: the Madonna enthroned, with the Infant Saviour standing on her knee, between SS. John the Baptist, Barbara, and Omobono ; the latter saint is giving alms to a beggar ; in the background is a landscape with buildings. It is inscribed :

'1533—9 noembre.'

In the Pitti there is also a Madonna and Child, with St. Elisabeth, the little St. John and a donor by Bonifazio (†). It is there attributed to Palma Vecchio, while Messrs. Crowe and Cavalcaselle (ii. 489) speak of it as the work of some painter of Treviso or of the Friuli. Another of his works, nearly approaching Palma, is in the public gallery at Vienna (No. 261), and the same may be said of No. 1171 in

[1] ii. 160.

[2] Few of my readers will know anything of this painter—Giovan Maria Zaffoni, called Calderara—beyond his name. He is frequently mentioned by these writers, but is unworthy of attention. He is a feeble imitator of his fellow-pupil Bernardino Licinio da Pordenone. Those who wish to become acquainted with his works should go to Pordenone, where there are several of his paintings in the cathedral, and some frescoes in the little church of the S. Trinità near the town, representing "Adam and Eve," the "Expulsion from Paradise," and other subjects.

the Louvre. In the Dresden gallery the "Finding of Moses" (No. 208) appears to me to be his work. The subject was frequently treated by the two elder Bonifazi.[1] The colouring in this picture is still rich and brilliant, but it has been overcleaned, and the surface glazes have, in consequence, disappeared.[2] It is difficult, at times even impossible, to distinguish between the elder and the younger Bonifazio in their later works, more especially in those which I have reason to think they executed together. Among such works I would include the celebrated "Finding of Moses" in the Brera at Milan, the "Judgment of Solomon" of 1533, and the "Woman taken in Adultery," both in the Venice Academy, and "St. Anthony of Padua preaching" in the small Franciscan church of Camposampiero in the Paduan district. These pictures which I have just named are all distinguished by the strength and brilliancy of the colouring, and the same types of head, both male and female, recur in all, so that we should scarcely be led to infer that they are the work of two painters. But on comparing the drawings by these two masters, several of which are in my possession, we cannot fail to see that one artist far surpassed the other. Bonifazio junior shows a tendency to elongate his forms, while his outlines lack decision. The forms of the elder painter, on the other hand, are rounder and fuller, and stand out in a clear and lifelike manner; the light and shade is sharply and well defined.

The following pictures are, I think, executed entirely by Bonifazio junior. In the Brera, the "Supper at Emmaus "

[1] For example, in a picture belonging to Prince Mario Chigi at Rome; in another in the Pitti, under the name of Giorgione; and in others in the Brera and elsewhere.

[2] Of the other pictures formerly ascribed to Bonifazio in this gallery, No. 213—the Holy Family with SS. Catherine and Anthony—is apparently a work of the school, while the "Raising of Lazarus" (No. 212) is wholly disfigured by restoration, but was, perhaps, originally by Bonifazio Veneziano.

(No. 211); in the Venice Academy, Christ enthroned between David, SS. Mark, Louis, Dominic, and Anna, with an angel playing the cithara below, dated 1530; in the Uffizi, the " Supper at Emmaus " (No. 1037); [1] in the Borghese gallery, the " Return of the Prodigal Son " (No. 186).

In the Dresden gallery there are several works by this master. For instance, the " Adoration of the Shepherds," already mentioned, which formerly bore the name of Giorgione, and the Madonna and Child, with SS. Elisabeth, John the Baptist, Catherine, and Joseph (No. 211), formerly ascribed to Palma. I have several times had occasion to warn students against trusting exclusively to general impressions in determining the authorship of a work of art, and against allowing themselves to be guided by what they consider to be the technic of the painting; I endeavoured to show how easily even experienced connoisseurs may fall into the mistake of confounding the works of the master with those of his best pupils, or *vice versâ*, when their judgment is not based upon a systematic and practical method of study. In speaking of the fine picture representing the " Meeting of Jacob and Rachel " in this gallery (No. 192), we saw that Messrs. Crowe and Cavalcaselle confounded Palma with his pupil Cariani, and I must now point out that the same writers not unfrequently take the works of Bonifazio Veronese for those of his master. In the Stuttgart gallery, for instance, Nos. 14 and 329 are ascribed to Palma both by the historians of Italian art and by the director of the gallery. No. 14 represents the Madonna and Child in a landscape, with SS. Joseph, Elisabeth, Catherine, and the little St. John. It is much

---

[1] This much-damaged picture in the Uffizi is ascribed to Palma Vecchio, while Messrs. Crowe and Cavalcaselle (ii. 489) assign it to Andrea Schiavone. The well-known picture of the " Last Supper " in S. Maria Mater Domini at Venice, which is always attributed to Palma, I believe to be by Bonifazio junior.

repainted, but the touch and the manner of Bonifazio senior are discernible in it. No. 329, the Madonna and Child between SS. Peter and John the Baptist, with a landscape background, shows the hand of Bonifazio junior, notwithstanding the injuries which it has sustained.

The form of the hand in the works of these two painters differs, like that of the ear, from the hand characteristic of their master Palma Vecchio, which is more bony, more allied to the *quattrocento*—if such a mode of expression be permissible—than those of his pupils. The hand characteristic of the two elder Bonifazi is fuller in shape and softer than that of Palma, and the fingers are more tapering. Cariani's form of hand resembles that of the Bonifazi, but is coarser and more clumsy. Like Catena, who often introduces a little long-haired white dog of Bolognese breed into his pictures, Bonifazio has often as an accessory a white and liver-coloured lap-dog.

Cariani's Madonnas, though of a rustic type, are always serious, vigorous, and less worldly than those of Bonifazio. The sweet and tender expression which the latter imparts to his female figures, and their soft and gentle grace, often verge on sentimentality. We see this in his fine picture in the Venice Academy (No. 35, Room VII.), in which the younger of the two women seated beside the wealthy voluptuary, touched by the strains of the music, appears to be thinking remorsefully of the days of her innocence.

Cariani and Bonifazio differ also in the harmony of their colouring. That of the former is powerful and effective though often heavy and dark, while that of the Veronese is light, brilliant, and pleasing. Bonifazio's landscapes are among the brightest of Venetian representations of such subjects ; those of Cariani are of a yellowish-brown tone, and unpleasing in their lines. Among the works of

Bonifazio Veneziano, I may name numerous pictures containing two figures of saints. We find them in several churches in Venice and in the Venice Academy; for instance, in the latter collection, Room IX. No. 9, SS. Jerome and Margaret; No. 7, SS. Bruno and Catherine; No. 40, SS. Barnabas and Silvester;[1] No. 29, SS. Anthony and Mark; No. 24, SS. Andrew, John, and Anthony; and in Room VII. No. 39, SS. John the Baptist, James, and Peter.

All these pictures date from the year 1562, and are therefore of the master's early period; he must have been born between 1525 and 1530. I am acquainted with signed works by him of 1558[2] and 1563, which show a connection with Bonifazio senior in colouring and in manner. There are other works by this painter: at Venice in the Church of S. Alvise; at Milan in the Museo Civico—a " Supper at Emmaus " and an " Annunciation," and in the Brera a " Madonna " and a " St. Louis distributing Alms " (No. 322). In his later works we see that he endeavoured to imitate his great contemporary Titian. This is very apparent in his large picture in the Venice Academy—the " Madonna appearing to SS. Francis, Andrew, Clara, Peter, and James."

The workshop of these painters in the sixteenth century was as productive as that of the Bassano family, and we meet with numbers of works in Venetian churches and in most of the public and private collections in Italy which show their connection with the Bonifazi. Many of them are ascribed to Andrea Schiavone.

[1] This picture is dated 1562. The form of ear in these figures should be studied; it is broader and more rounded than that of Bonifazio junior, and therefore more nearly approaches Bonifazio senior.

[2] In the possession of Signor Guggenheim, at Venice, I once saw a picture by this master, which showed a close connection with Bonifazio senior. It represented the Madonna and Child between St. Louis of Toulouse and St. Peter—the latter being evidently the portrait of the donor—and was dated 1558.

The Dresden gallery possesses some good and characteristic works by Jacopo Robusti, known as Tintoretto, who was a younger contemporary of the Bonifazi,[1] and was at one time a rival of Titian. He was a grand and vigorous painter, but sometimes wanting in balance. Professor Justi, in his admirable work on ' Velasquez and his Times,'[2] has given us a more just criticism of Tintoretto than any art-historian before him has done. There are finer examples by this master in the Dresden gallery than in any other north of the Alps, with the exception of the public collection at Vienna.

Palma Giovine is also fairly well represented at Dresden, though not by works of his early period, which showed more promise than the event justified. The Stuttgart gallery, as already observed, is the only collection in which the father of this painter, who was also the nephew of Palma Vecchio, is represented. His picture there is the " Resurrection," with a landscape background, and is inscribed ' ANTONIVS PALMA, P.' It recalls the school of Bonifazio, and we see that the friendly intercourse which subsisted between the two painters of Verona and their master, Palma Vecchio, was continued in the case of the nephew of the latter—Antonio Palma. Another signed work by this master is in the sacristy of the parish church of Serinalta, Palma's birthplace, in the Bergamasque highlands. It is a processional banner representing the " Pietà," and is inscribed, ' M. D. LXV. ANTONIVS PALMA FECIT.' It is, therefore, of his later period. In it he comes near to his elder contemporary and fellow-countryman Girolamo da Santa Croce.

There are four works in this gallery by Paris Bordone of Treviso, a brilliant and at times most refined and excellent

---

[1] Tintoretto was born in 1518.   [2] English edition, p. 153.

painter.[1] They are Nos. 203, 204, 205, and 206, the last being only doubtfully attributed to the master. No. 204 is the only one which worthily represents his art.

In No. 203 we see Apollo and Marsyas; and in No. 204 Diana with two hounds holding a spear in her hand, while a nymph presents to her the head of a stag. No. 216, the Madonna adoring the Infant Saviour, recalls the manner of Polidoro Lanzani rather than of Bordone,[2] to whom it was doubtfully ascribed in the former catalogue.

According to documents recently discovered by Signor Michele Caffi, Paris Bordone was born as far back as 1495. From another document, published by the late Signor Cecchetti,[3] it appears that 'Paride di Giovanni pittore' had four children in 1563—Angelica, Zuanne, Cassandra, and Ottavia. On August 30 of that year he signs himself as follows: 'Io. Paris Bordon pictor fiol [son] del q^m Zuanne cittadin de Treviso, habitante in Venetia in contrà [street] di S. Marcilian.'

An admirable work—perhaps the best by this master in Germany—is in the gallery at Cologne, and represents Bathsheba bathing, attended by her maidens, while David is seen in the distance. The picture is mentioned by Vasari,[4] and was formerly in the possession of Count Charles Borromeo at Milan.

Drawings by this brilliant artist are extremely rare. I am only acquainted with one small sheet,[5] on both sides of which are various sketches in red chalk of the Madonna with the Infant Saviour and St. John. The technical treatment recalls that of his master Titian.

---

[1] As he shows himself in his picture in the Venice Academy, "The Fisherman presenting St. Mark's ring to the Doge."

[2] Now ascribed to Polidoro by Dr. Woermann.

[3] *Archivio Veneto*, I. xxxiv. p. 205.

[4] See Vasari, xiii. 50 (ed. Milanesi, vii. 465).

[5] This drawing, formerly in the Morelli collection, is now in that of Dr. Frizzoni.

In the former catalogue the " Christ bearing the Cross " (No. 222) was attributed to another Trevisan artist, Rocco Marconi, a pupil of Palma Vecchio,[1] and later an imitator of Paris Bordone. I believe this picture to be by Francesco Prato da Caravaggio, a little-known painter and a pupil of Girolamo Romanino of Brescia.[2] He is a very inferior artist, whose best works are at Brescia, in the churches of S. Francesco, of S. Rocco (under the name of Calisto da Lodi), and of S. Agata, and in private collections. They are usually ascribed to masters of greater note.

A decorative picture in *grisaille* in the Dresden gallery, known as " Liberality " (No. 217), was formerly attributed to Domenico Campagnola, but is more probably a work of the school of Bonifazio.

Four of the best existing works of Paul Veronese are in the Dresden gallery, two of them being in an excellent state of preservation, so that even in the Louvre and the Venice Academy this painter is not better represented than in this collection. Paul Veronese is always pleasing and dignified, though never grand and impressive in his art—a dramatist never ignoble, but occasionally showing a taste for Spanish magnificence and display.

In Dr. Hübner's catalogue the " Holy Family " (No. 241) was ascribed to Carletto Caliari, the son of Paolo. I think Guarienti was right in regarding it as the work of Carletto's brother Gabriel. Dr. Woermann is also of this opinion. It is almost impossible to distinguish the hands of the different painters employed in the workshop of Paul

---

[1] That this painter was a pupil of Palma Vecchio is proved by his early work in the royal palace at Venice—the "Woman taken in Adultery." It is signed ' Rocchus Marchonus,' and vividly recalls the manner of Palma.

[2] Dr. Woermann, I regret to say, is not of this opinion. He also regards this picture as of the school of Romanino, though not as the work of Francesco Prato. In time, however, I hope that he may come to see that the attribution is correct. ' Col tempo,' the Italians say, ' maturano le nespole.'

Veronese. Benedetto Caliari, writing to his patron Giacomo Contarini, says : ' Dunque come da me disegnato, da Carlo abatiato, e da Gabriel finito, prego lo accetti, e lo vegga come genio suo, concetto nelle nostre menti.' [1]

In speaking of the female portrait (No. 249), the late Dr. Hübner fell into a mistake which Dr. Woermann has now put right. This much-rubbed portrait was formerly attributed to Fasolo, an early painter of Pavia,[2] but has now been restored to Giovan Antonio Fasolo of Vicenza, a contemporary and colleague of Paul Veronese. This painter is buried in the Church of S. Lorenzo at Vicenza, and his epitaph is as follows :—

JOANNIS . ANTONII . FASOLII .
PICTORIS . EXIMII . HAEREDVM .
Q. SVORVM . VIXIT . ANN . XLII.
OBIIT . X . CALEN . SEPT . MDLXXII.

A " Pietà with Angels " (No. 86) is by Giuseppe Porta of Garfagnana, known as Salviati. Lanzi states, but I think on insufficient grounds, that this work was one of those which came to Dresden from Modena.

No. 352, " St. Francis Praying," is not by Girolamo Muziano, but more probably by some Bolognese painter. As such it is now described in the catalogue.

Mention must here be made of a good female portrait on which formerly no name was bestowed. Those who have been in Venice will remember the quaint representations of Venetian life in the last century, as seen in pictures on the walls of the Correr Museum and of the Academy (Contarini collection), and the name of Pietro Longhi, who may be termed the Goldoni of painters, will not be unfamiliar to them. I believe this portrait to be by him, and my attribution has been accepted by the present director.

[1] Gaye, *Carteggio*, ii. 551.
[2] A signed work by Bernardino

Fasolo dated 1518 (?) is in the Palace at Fontainebleau.

With Pietro Longhi, Venetian art, having run its brilliant course, practically ceased to exist, and with it the true Venetian also became extinct. Venice has fallen into utter decrepitude. Her palaces, indeed, are standing, but they are mournful and forsaken, like a nautilus shell within whose pearly walls many alien creatures have made themselves a home. The race beneath whose auspices this city of enchantment sprang into being, who alone were worthy to dwell within her borders, have passed away, and the glorious art of Venice and the political wisdom which combined to make her what she was have vanished also.

Before bringing our examination of the Venetian schools in the Dresden gallery to a close, I would draw attention to certain pictures which I consider unworthy to be classed among them. On the other hand, I should like to mention one eminently deserving of such an attribution, though the catalogue does not assign to it its proper place. The following are the pictures which are not to be regarded as the work of Venetian masters :—

1. " Christ bearing the Cross " (No. 102), attributed to Sebastiano del Piombo. Instead of being a ' replica of the picture in the Madrid gallery,' as stated in the catalogue, this work appears to me to be a Flemish copy. Dr. Eisenmann, if I have not misunderstood his meaning, is of the same opinion.

2. The " Woman taken in Adultery" (No. 197) is again a Flemish copy. The original, as the catalogue rightly states, is in the Louvre. Another copy of the same picture is in the Palazzo Spada at Rome.

3. The " Calling of St. Matthew" (No. 199) is another copy or imitation by a Fleming. Dr. Woermann also casts doubts on the authenticity of this picture.

4. I am equally unable to regard the coarse and uncouth figure of St. Sebastian (No. 194 B) as the work of so refined

a painter as Lotto. It is certainly not of his late period, as the catalogue conjectures, nor is it in his early manner ; more probably it is by some inferior Bolognese artist of the seventeenth century. Dr. Woermann is himself sceptical as to this attribution to Lotto, which was suggested to him by an 'English connoisseur,' and he wisely leaves the decision of the question for further consideration. On the other hand, I cannot but express my surprise that, on the advice of the same connoisseur, he should have purchased the following picture for the Dresden gallery as an original by Lotto.

5. This work (No. 195) was bought at Florence, and on being placed in the gallery was at once recognised as a counterfeit of Lotto's original in the Bridgewater gallery, coarsely executed by some Flemish painter. Dr. Woermann relied too much on what was said in praise of the picture by others, and made the acquisition in all good faith. I regret it the more, as I consider myself partly to blame for this unfortunate purchase, having in the first edition of these studies deplored the absence of works by Lotto in the Dresden gallery. It was natural, therefore, that Dr. Woermann should have been desirous of supplying this deficiency as speedily as possible. In point of fact, however, this collection has long possessed a work by this artist—a small but admirable "Madonna" of his Bergamasque period, 1520 to 1524. Ten years ago I was deceived as to this picture by the modern character of the colouring, in the same way that, misled by the colouring of the "Faun" in the Munich gallery, I took it for a work by Lotto, instead of recognising in it an early work by Correggio. Such is the consequence of not making the forms in an old picture the primary study. To Dr. Frizzoni is again due the merit of having first discerned the manner of Lotto in the Dresden "Madonna" (No. 194A). Without telling me of his discovery,

MADONNA AND CHILD.   BY LOTTO.

(In the Dresden Gallery.)

To face p. 256.

he one day showed me a good photograph of it by Braun,
and asked me to whom I would ascribe the picture. The
type of face of both the Madonna and the children, and
particularly the form of the Madonna's hand, at once con-
vinced me that it was a work by Lotto of his Bergamasque
period. Should Dr. Woermann visit Bergamo again, I
should recommend him to compare this Madonna with a
picture belonging to Signor Antonio Piccinelli, and I have
no doubt that he will then share our opinion.[1]

THE LOMBARDS.

The Lombard school proper can scarcely be said to be
represented in the Dresden gallery, for the few pictures it
contains of that school are hardly worthy of mention.

The earliest example of the Milanese school in this
collection is the tempera picture on canvas which was
formerly ascribed to Ambrogio Borgognone. It represents
the Madonna clad in white adoring the Infant Saviour;
above is the Almighty in a glory of angels. Messrs. Crowe
and Cavalcaselle [2] tentatively, but erroneously, assign this
feeble production to Ambrogio da Fossano, known as Bor-
gognone. It is the work of Ambrogio Bevilacqua, who was
a contemporary, and probably even a fellow-pupil, of
Borgognone in the school of Foppa, though far inferior to
him. We find signed works by this master in the Brera
and in the parish church of Landriano, near Milan. The
following pictures, though not signed, are in all probability

[1] In the autumn of 1891 a young
American critic, Mr. Charles Loeser,
discovered on this picture the sig-
nature 'Laurentius Lotus, 15 . 8,'

and all controversy respecting its
authorship is therefore now at an
end.
[2] ii. 50.

also by Bevilacqua: A small Madonna in the Palazzo Bagatti-
Valsecchi at Milan, a very early work, recalling Vincenzo
Foppa; a triptych in a small church near Soma, ascribed
to Borgognone; a large triptych in the little church of
Casareto, near Milan ; a picture belonging to Signor Reale,
the custodian of the Malaspina gallery at Pavia, representing
the " Adoration of the Infant Saviour " ; a small Madonna
in the public gallery at Bergamo (Lochis collection, No. 5),
and another in the collection of Signor Antonio Piccinelli,
in the same city, a work which shows a close connection
with this example in Dresden.   Dr. Woermann has not yet
been able to satisfy himself of the truth of my attribution.
In course of time I hope that he may do so.

    We have already discussed the " Daughter of Herodias "
(No. 201A), on p. 170.

    In Dr. Hübner's catalogue, Michelangelo Amerighi da
Caravaggio was classed among the Lombard painters, pro-
bably because Caravaggio, the birthplace of this painter, is
now in the province of Lombardy.   In his day, however,
all the district lying beyond the Adda formed part of the
Venetian Republic.   The question is of no consequence as
concerns Michelangelo Amerighi.   He only applied himself
to painting as a profession after he had left Caravaggio for
Rome, whither he went as a mason's apprentice.   He
therefore belongs to the so-called Roman school.   There
are several good and characteristic specimens of his art in
the Dresden gallery.   He is the principal representative
of that body of painters known as the ' Tenebrosi.'   The
Spanish painter Ribera also formed his style after him.

    The Dresden gallery has four good pictures by Ales-
sandro Magnasco, who was known at Milan, where he was
trained and where he laboured principally, as Lissandrino.
Two of these works (Nos. 649 and 650) have been in this
collection since 1741 ; the others (Nos. 651 and 652) were

only purchased in 1875, and were attributed by Dr. Hübner to Salvator Rosa, a distinction which has not unfrequently been conferred upon Magnasco in other European collections.[1]

THE TUSCANS.

The works of this school have also been subjected by Dr. Woermann to a thorough critical revision, and he has assigned to them more suitable places in the gallery than had been the case hitherto. Of the six pictures formerly ascribed to Sandro Botticelli, three [2] have now been recognised as works of his school. The "Madonna and Child" (No. 8) and the long low panel with scenes from the life of S. Zenobius [3] (No. 9) are acknowledged to be authentic, executed by the master himself, while the "Galatea" (No. 59A), which was also formerly assigned to Botticelli, has now been transferred by Dr. Woermann to the North Italian school [see p. 196, note 1]. This is, I think, a step in the right direction, and in time I hope that the identity of the painter will be indisputably established. The picture is not without interest, and I still adhere to my former opinion that it is the work of Jacopo de' Barbari.

The small "Annunciation" (No. 7) is assigned to the school of Fra Angelico, whereas it should, I think, be

[1] Dr. Eisenmann and Dr. Woermann both agree with me in attributing these landscapes to Lissandrino. They are clever but very mannered in treatment. It is much to be regretted that the great representatives of the early school of Milan, such as Foppa, Bramantino, Borgognone, Luini, Gaudenzio Ferrari, Boltraffio, Sodoma, Cesare da Sesto, Solario, Gianpietrino, and others, are not met with in a gallery of such importance as that in Dresden. It would, I think, be desirable if these deficiencies could, as far as possible, be supplied.

[2] No. 10, a "Madonna and Child with Angels"; No. 11, "St. John the Evangelist"; and No. 12, "St. John the Baptist."

[3] This composition, though full of life, is unpleasing, owing to the crude tone of red employed.

described as a feeble work by Benozzo Gozzoli. The principal pupils and imitators of Fra Angelico were his elder brother Benedetto, Zanobi Strozzi, Domenico di Michelino,[1] and Benozzo Gozzoli. It appears to me that the types of the faces in this picture, as also the manner of drawing and painting, recall Gozzoli more than any of the other pupils just mentioned. The question is, however, one of very minor importance.

The director of the gallery shares my opinion that the "Madonna and Child" (No. 19) is of the school of Filippino Lippi. With regard to the statement of the new catalogue, that Filippino was the pupil of Fra Diamante, his father's assistant, I must observe that such a view is not justified either by Filippino's own works or by any documentary evidence. Vasari clearly states that after the death of his father, Filippo Lippi, Filippino ' fù tenuto ed ammaestrato, essendo ancor giovinetto, da Sandro Botticelli ' ('he was kept and taught, being still very young, by Sandro Botticelli '). It is, therefore, purely arbitrary to suppose that he was in addition the pupil of Fra Diamante, by whom no authentic works have been preserved. At the death of his father in 1469, Filippino, who was born in 1457, was about twelve years old; it is far more probable that Filippo himself instructed his son in the rudiments of his art instead of entrusting him to his assistant, Fra Diamante.

The director agrees with me in regarding the very inferior picture, representing the "Holy Family" (No. 33), as the work of some feeble Sienese painter, possibly Pietro di Domenico. It was formerly assigned to Andrea del Castagno.

The fine "Tondo" (No. 20) of the "Holy Family," formerly attributed to Luca Signorelli, is now, with more discernment, restored to Pier di Cosimo.

[1] See Gaye, *Carteggio Storico*, ii. 4 and 7.

With regard to the panel picture representing the Madonna and Child with Saints (No. 21), I am not altogether of Dr. Woermann's opinion. He speaks of it as a 'work of the school of Raffaellino di Capponi.' I should substitute the 'school of Raffaellino del Garbo di Bartolommeo.' The two panels (Nos. 36 and 37), intended for the decoration of pilasters, are still ascribed to Luca Signorelli. I can only regard them as works of the school of that great master, though undoubtedly executed from drawings by him.

Two interesting pictures (Nos. 75 and 80), which are respectively by Franciabigio and Bacchiacca, are now more advantageously seen than was formerly the case. No. 75 is signed 'F. C. R.,' meaning 'Franciscus Cristofori (filius).' Cristoforo was the father of Francesco (Francia) Bigi.

Francesco Ubertini, known as Bacchiacca, was a pupil of the last-named painter, having first served his apprenticeship with Perugino. The two pictures just mentioned were painted in 1523 for a wealthy Florentine, named Benintendi. At that date Bacchiacca may have been about twenty-eight or thirty. I devoted some pages to this painter, who has received but scant notice hitherto, though he is by no means without interest, in the former volume of these studies, to which I refer those who may desire to know more of this master.[1]

We will now turn to Andrea del Sarto, a painter of undying fame. No. 76, the " Marriage of St. Catherine in the presence of St. Margaret," is an admirable composition, and though much injured by restoration, the hand of the master is still discernible in it. It was probably painted between 1512 and 1515. Vasari's Florentine commentators[2] —solely, it appears to me, on the authority of Dr. Aloysius Hirt—ascribe this picture to Domenico Puligo, a pupil and

[1] *Critical Studies in the Borghese and Doria Galleries*, pp. 101-13.

[2] viii. 289, note 3 (ed. Milanesi, v. 51).

imitator of Andrea del Sarto. Messrs. Crowe and Caval-
caselle pronounce it to be a genuine work of Andrea del
Sarto.[1] They describe it as 'very rich and sfumato in
colour,' and dating from the period when the master
imitated Fra Bartolommeo.

The second work by Andrea del Sarto in this collec-
tion is the "Sacrifice of Abraham" (No. 77). It was one
of the hundred pictures purchased from the gallery at
Modena. According to Vasari's commentators, it was once
in the collection of Alfonso Davalos, and passed from thence
into the Uffizi. It was still in the tribune of that gallery
in 1633; subsequently it was exchanged for a "Riposo" by
Correggio in the Modena gallery. Had it not been for
this transaction the Dresden gallery would probably have
been richer by a Correggio, though it would have forfeited
a work by Andrea del Sarto.

A very similar picture, also ascribed to Andrea del
Sarto, is in the Madrid gallery.[2] In the background of
that picture two of Abraham's servants are seen, answer-
ing to Vasari's description: 'Vi erano oltreciò, certi servi
ignudi che guardavano un asino che pasceva' ('there were
in addition several nude servants with an ass, which was
grazing').[3] There are, therefore, two pictures by the
master representing the same subject, that at Dresden
measuring seven feet in height by five feet in width, while
the example at Madrid is of much smaller dimensions.
The latter is, I think, the replica, on a smaller scale, which
Andrea del Sarto painted for Paolo da Terrarossa. 'Venne
voglia a Paolo da Terrarossa, veduta la bozza del sopra-
detto Abramo, d' avere qualche cosa di mano d' Andrea,
come amico universalmente di tutti i pittori; perchè richi-

[1] iii. 581.
[2] No. 819. It is ninety-eight
centimètres in height and sixty-nine
in width.
[3] viii. 289 (ed. Milanesi, v. 51).

estolo d' un ritratto di quello Abramo, Andrea volentieri lo
servì, e glielo fece tale, che nella sua piccolezza non fù
punto inferiore alla grandezza dell' originale. Il quadro
fù poi da lui mandato a Napoli.' ('Paolo da Terrarossa
having seen the sketch of the above-mentioned Abraham,
felt the wish to possess something by the hand of Andrea,
being the universal friend of all painters. He therefore
asked of him a reproduction of the said Abraham ; Andrea
willingly complied, and executed it in such a manner, that,
notwithstanding its small dimensions, it was in no way
inferior to the large original. The picture was then sent
by him to Naples.') The example in the Madrid gallery
has suffered from restoration as severely as that at Dres-
den.[1] There is another replica of this picture in the
gallery at Lyons, but I am not acquainted with it.

In addition to the Florentines of the golden epoch of
art, Carlo Dolci is also represented in the Dresden collection
by several very good pictures.

At this point our progress in the Dresden gallery is
suddenly arrested, and we are forced to pursue a difficult
and circuitous route in order to continue our onward course.
No one will be surprised to learn that the chasm which has
thus suddenly opened at our very feet divides us from
Drs. Bode and Bayersdorffer ; but it is with sincere regret
that I am bound to add that it also separates us from the
director of the Dresden gallery. Thus far I have noted
with satisfaction that his views coincide almost without
exception with my own, even as regards the Tuscan
masters ; but when we come to the Madonna bearing the
unlucky number 13, the case is different. In London,
where the picture was acquired by the late Dr. Hübner, it
was attributed to Lorenzo di Credi, but at Dresden it was
pronounced to be an early work of Leonardo da Vinci,

[1] See A. Hirt, *Kunstbemerkungen*, p. 80 (Berlin, 1830).

and as such we find it described in the former edition of the catalogue. A drawing, representing the Madonna, in the cabinet of engravings at Dresden, which had long passed for the work of Leonardo, was probably responsible for this bold attribution. The Madonna in the picture (No. 19) bears some resemblance to it, but is a mere caricature. Ten years ago I pronounced this picture to be a Flemish imitation of Lorenzo di Credi, for the drawing then appeared to me more probably by this painter than by his master Verrocchio. Dr. Woermann agrees with me in rejecting the name of Leonardo da Vinci as the author of this picture, which is a step in the right direction. But he then proceeds to ascribe it to Lorenzo di Credi—to an Italian artist, therefore, and not to a Fleming. I feel bound once more to return to this vexed question, though much against my will, for I know that I shall thereby still more irritate my opponents at Berlin. I fear that I shall also make enemies of that small but active body of young writers on art who have appeared in the interval, and have allowed themselves to be overruled by others in their conception both of Leonardo da Vinci and of his master Verrocchio, following unquestioningly in the footsteps of Drs. Bode and Bayersdorffer. But I consider it my duty to do my best to vindicate the reputation of two great Italian masters who, owing to the persistent efforts of these gentlemen, are in danger of being entirely misunderstood —at least in Germany. Of these two artists, one may, perhaps, be regarded as the most remarkable and versatile genius that modern Italy has produced. Yet never, I think, has the estimate of Verrocchio and Leonardo been so utterly false and perverted as in the present day. Had these erroneous views been merely propagated by one of the countless insignificant persons who have written on art the matter would be of no consequence. In this case, however, they emanate from one who has earned well-merited praise in another branch of art-criticism ; and it is, therefore, desirable to meet them at once with strenuous opposition, as they will, in all probability, cause the most dire confusion in the history of Italian painting.

A lengthy dissertation on Verrocchio, compiled by Dr. Bode [1] with praiseworthy industry, prompted me to make a more careful study of the Florentine sculptor than I had hitherto been able to do. I soon came to the conclusion that the heterogeneous productions, both paintings and drawings, which the Berlin critic so lavishly ascribes

[1] Dr. Bode's partiality for Verrocchio, which leads him to make continual discoveries of that master's influence, may perhaps be traced to the epitaph dedicated to Verrocchio by his friend and admirer, Ugolino Verino. It was as follows :

' Nec tibi, Lisippe, est Thuscus
    Verrocchius impar,
A quo, quidquid habent pictores,
    fonte biberunt.
Discipulos poene edocuit Verrocchius omnes,
Quorum nunc volitat Thyrrhene per oppida nomen.'

As all who have had experience of such things are aware, epitaphs, whether of former days or of recent date, are not usually conspicuous for veracity, and no art-historian of any learning would attach the slightest importance to an inscription commemorating the merits of a painter. The sculptor Civitali of Lucca, for example, was after his death likened to Praxiteles and Phidias (see Vasari, iii. 35 ; ed. Milanesi, ii. 180). Of Alesso Baldovinetti—an artist whom Dr. Bode holds of very small account—it was said : ' Cujus neque ingenio neque picturis quid-

quam potest esse illustrius ; ' and Cosimo Rosselli, another Florentine painter depreciated by Dr. Bode, is extolled in his epitaph ' for his brilliant manner of painting, in which, also, he instructed many of his contemporaries ' (Vasari, v. 32 ; ed. Milanesi, iii. 190). Even Vasari was spoken of in his day as *facile princeps* of all living artists (Vasari, xi. 28 ; ed. Milanesi, vi. 244). In Italy, and more especially in Florence, in the fifteenth and sixteenth centuries, it was the fashion to copy the Greeks in everything. At the time of Vasari, Pliny's writings were well known to all scholars in that country, and many anecdotes related by him of Grecian artists, and epitaphs were made to apply—by the humanists and also by historians of art—to the Italian painters. Thus the tale of the grapes of Zeuxis, which were so admirably painted that the birds came to peck at them, or that of the horses which were so true to nature that living animals neighed at the sight of them, have been related of Italian masters. In the present day such childish fables should be banished one and all from the history of art.

to his favourite artist, are for the most part the work of
other contemporary and inferior Florentine hands. No
competent critic of Italian art could seriously affirm that
the painter of the "Baptism of Christ" in the Florence
Academy also produced the three Archangels with Tobias
in the same gallery, the unpleasing Madonna (No. 104A)
in the Berlin Museum, and the "Tobias" in the English
National Gallery. In all these pictures the forms are
totally dissimilar, as are also the types and the scale of
colouring.

A closer study of Verrocchio's well-authenticated works
has therefore convinced me that the numerous paintings
and drawings which Dr. Bode sees fit to attribute to him
cannot possibly be by this master. On the other hand, I
have come to the conclusion that the silver point drawing
in the cabinet of engravings at Dresden is neither by
Leonardo da Vinci, as Messrs. Bode and Bayersdorffer
affirm, nor by Lorenzo di Credi, as I myself thought some
years ago, and as Dr. Woermann still considers, but that
it is undoubtedly by Verrocchio—that is, if the painting of
the "Baptism of Christ" and the head of an angel with
curly hair, a drawing in the Uffizi (Brogi, No. 1712), are
really by this master, which even Dr. Bode has never
disputed. On the strength, therefore, of a renewed study
of Verrocchio, I now confidently repeat that this picture of
the Madonna in Dresden (No. 13) is of Flemish origin,
executed from the silver point drawing by Verrocchio which
is now in the cabinet of engravings at Dresden. It is a
well-known fact that the drawings of the great masters in
Italy were utilised by many Italian artists, both painters
and sculptors, for their own work. Lorenzo Ghiberti, in
his commentary, observes : [1]—

'Ancora a molti pittori e scultori e statuari ho fatto

---

[1] See Vasari, ed. Le Monnier, i. xxxvi.

HEAD OF AN ANGEL. DRAWING BY VERROCCHIO.
(In the Uffizi, Florence.)

To face p. 266.

FEMALE FIGURE IN HALF-LENGTH.   DRAWING BY VERROCCHIO.

(In the Print Room, Dresden.)

To face p. 266.

grandissimi onori ne' loro lavori; fatti moltissimi provve-
dimenti di cera e di crèta, e a pittori disegnato moltissime
cose.' ('Likewise many painters, and sculptors, and
makers of statues have I brought to great honour in their
works; many sketches have I made in wax and in chalk,
and for painters have executed many drawings.')

Benvenuto Cellini also observes with respect to Antonio
del Pollaiuolo, Verrocchio's contemporary, who in his
day was accounted the best draughtsman in Florence :
'Questo orefice fù si gran disegnatore, che non tanto che
tutti gli orefici si servirono de' suoi bellissimi disegni, i
quali erano di tanta eccellenza che ancora molti scultori e
pittori, io dico de' migliori di quelle arti, si servirano de'
suoi disegni e con quelli si feciono onore.' ('This gold-
smith was so good a draughtsman that all goldsmiths made
use of his drawings, which being so admirable, many even of
the best sculptors and painters of our day employed them,
and thus gained honour for themselves.'[1])

We know from Vasari[2] that at the time of Benvenuto
Cellini, drawings by great artists were even sold : 'Onde si
vedono ancora gran numero di disegni (by Raffaellino del
Garbo) per tutta l' arte mandati fuori per vilissimo prezzo
da un suo figliuolo,' &c. ('A great number of drawings
by Raffaellino del Garbo are dispersed abroad among those
who practise art, having been sold dirt-cheap by one of his
sons.'[3])

---

[1] Verrocchio may be looked upon
as a case in point. He was an
excellent sculptor and draughtsman,
and sculptors, and probably also
painters, applied to him for draw-
ings. This accounts for the fact
that some pictures of his time bear
a certain resemblance to his man-
ner, and superficial connoisseurs of
Italian art have in consequence
been led to regard them as works of
his own hand.

[2] vii. 191-5 (ed. Milanesi, iv.
235-9).

[3] See on this subject—which is
not without importance for the
right understanding of many a
picture and statue—my Critical
Studies in the Borghese Gallery,
p. 141.

I may, however, add that Messrs. Bode and Bayers-
dorffer probably see and estimate the works of Leonardo
and Verrocchio with very much the same eyes as did the
Netherlanders who visited Italy in the lifetime of these
artists. This remarkable ethnological phenomenon, which
it is important not to overlook, may in a measure excuse
these German critics for having mistaken Flemish imita-
tions for Italian originals, and may furnish us with a clue
to understanding their opinions.[1]

It is in the nature of things that what occurs so
frequently in articulate language should also be met with
in the language of painting. Take the case of a foreigner
who has studied Italian grammatically in his own country.
He crosses the Alps, and finds himself by chance in the
company of several natives and also of one of his own
countrymen. The latter, we will suppose, has spent some
time in Italy, and has learnt to speak the language with
tolerable fluency. The new-comer will undoubtedly per-
ceive that the Italian, as spoken by his fellow-countryman,
is easier to understand than that of the natives themselves,
and it will appear to him more correct both as regards
accent, pronunciation, and grammar. He will accordingly
be inclined to declare that his compatriot speaks the best
Italian of the party. The same thing constantly occurs
among northern critics, where the language of painting is
concerned.[2] Messrs. Bayersdorffer and Bode have fallen

[1] In this respect I am quite of the opinion of the author of *Rembrandt als Erzieher*, a little volume which has found many readers.

[2] Baron Rumohr is said to have attributed to Leonardo a "Leda" at Cassel—now at Neuwied (?), and a "Madonna with flowing hair" in the Augsburg gallery, which was once much extolled as a Leonardo in the *Augsburger Allgemeine Zeitung*. Both these pictures are now acknow-ledged by every connoisseur to be the work of Flemings. Passavant believed the portrait of Joanna of Aragon in the Doria gallery to be by some Milanese pupil of Leonardo; and even Mr. Mündler held the repulsive picture in the Louvre—No. 1533, the head of St. John the Baptist—

into this mistake with respect to the pictures which they ascribe to Leonardo, and many equally learned writers before them have done the same. As the Flemings, technically speaking, handled their material more solidly and with greater precision than their contemporaries in Italy, such Flemish imitations appeared to these critics far more Leonardesque than originals by the great master, which have always been extremely rare.

Twenty years ago the great name of Leonardo was applied to the Madonna (No. 13) in the Dresden gallery. Ten years later we can scarcely be surprised to find Dr. Bode bringing to light, out of the depôt of the Berlin Museum, a large panel, which he proclaims *urbi et orbi* to be the work of the same great painter. Munich naturally did not wish to be outdone by Dresden and Berlin, and quite recently the learned custodian of the gallery, Dr. Bayersdorffer, also discovered a Leonardo. Thrice within the short space of twenty years has an injury thus been done to the memory of the great Florentine.

to be by Andrea Solario. This critic, however, was one of the first who recognised in the portrait of Joanna of Aragon just mentioned the manner of a Fleming in the garb of an Italian. In the former edition of 1880 of these studies, entitled *Italian Masters in German Galleries*, I drew attention to the following pictures at Munich as Flemish imitations, though they were described in the catalogue of that gallery as Italian works :—

1. "St. Cecilia," No. 546 of the old catalogue. This picture has now been removed from the gallery.

2. "A Madonna," No. 1042. In the present catalogue it is acknowledged to be a Flemish imitation.

3. A small work representing the "Repose during the Flight into Egypt," formerly attributed to Schedone. It is now placed in the school of Rembrandt (No. 334).

4. The so-called portrait of Garofalo by himself. The present director agrees with me in regarding it as the work of a Fleming. It is numbered 166.

It is satisfactory to note that even in Germany people are beginning to see through the disguise in which these Flemings have sought to hide their nationality. I cannot but hope, therefore, that in the course of another ten years the numerous pictures which I have pointed out in the galleries at Munich, Dresden, and Vienna as northern imitations will be recognised as such by the directors of these different collections.

The so-called "Leonardo" in the Munich gallery also represents the Madonna, and may be considered the counterpart on a larger scale of the picture in the Dresden collection. It is my firm conviction that both these pictures were painted by some very inferior Flemish artist from drawings by Verrocchio. These drawings may have been lent or sold to this Flemish painter either by Lorenzo di Credi—the pupil of Verrocchio and also his heir—or by some other Florentine artist.

After these long but needful preliminary remarks let us come to the point, and first let me endeavour to enumerate those characteristics of Verrocchio which we see in two of his authentic and undisputed works—the "Baptism of Christ"—a much injured picture in the Florence Academy, and the head of an angel with curly hair—a drawing in the Uffizi (see illustration, p. 266).

These characteristics are as follows :—

1. The forehead is high and slightly rounded.

2. The eye is very large; the eyelid boldly cut and with long lashes.

3. The eyebrows are but slightly indicated by a shadow.

4. The nostrils, as in Botticelli's pictures, are somewhat swollen; the opening, which with Botticelli is long, with Verrocchio is rounder, and not prolonged towards the root of the nostril.

5. The curves of the lips are full and undulating.

All these characteristics we meet with in the drawing in the Uffizi, which is always acknowledged to be by Verrocchio. They have enabled me to recognise the hand of the master in the following drawings :—

1. The beautiful female head with elaborately braided hair [1] in the Malcolm collection in London, No. 338 of the

[1] Vasari (v. 144; ed. Milanesi, iii. 364) observes of Verrocchio's drawings: 'Sono alcuni disegni di sua mano nel nostro Libro fatti

FEMALE HEAD.   DRAWING BY VERROCCHIO.
(In the Malcolm Collection, London.)

To face p. 270.

FIVE STUDIES FOR CHILDREN. DRAWING BY VERROCCHIO.

In the Louvre.)

To face p. 271.

catalogue, in which it is assigned to the North Italian school (†).

2. The silver point drawing in the cabinet of engravings at Dresden, which is closely related to the preceding example (†).

3. A silver point drawing in the British Museum, representing an angel—a study for the Forteguerri monument at Pistoia : register mark 1860-6-16-29.[1]

4. A sheet in the Louvre (Room X. No. 2021) containing various pen studies of nude *putti*, five on one side and four on the reverse (†). This sheet, which I had the good fortune to discover some years ago in the depôt of the Louvre, should be compared with the drawings by the author of the so-called sketch- and note-book of Verrocchio. Even an unpractised eye will then, I think, see the immense difference in capacity between these two draughtsmen.

If the drawings which I have enumerated are all, as I believe, by this great Florentine sculptor, which I think even Dr. Bode will not dispute, it follows that the pictures extolled by him as the work of Verrocchio cannot possibly be by the same hand, as none of them exhibit the characteristics which I have cited as distinctive of that master.

' That may be,' some of my inveterate opponents may

con molta pazienza e grandissimo giudizio ; infra i quali sono alcune teste di femmina con bell' arie ed acconciature di capelli, quali, per la sua bellezza, Lionardo da Vinci sempre imitò.' (' There are some drawings by his hand in our book, executed with much patience and great judgment, among which are some female heads, attractive in appearance and in the arrangement of the hair, which were always imitated by Leonardo by reason of their beauty.')

[1] The other pen drawings marked 1875-6-12-15 and 1875-6-12-16, which, incredible as it may appear, have been hitherto attributed to Verrocchio, all formed part of the sketch-book of some feeble sculptor whose drawings are scattered in different collections—at Berlin and Lille, in the collection of the Duc d'Aumale, in the Louvre, and elsewhere. One of these drawings is dated 1489. Verrocchio, it is well known, died in 1488.

reply, ' but this by no means proves that Leonardo did not execute the Madonnas in the Dresden and Munich collections, during his early Florentine period, from the drawing by his master Verrocchio you have just mentioned.'

To this I may reply, that, in the first place, the type of these two Madonnas bears no resemblance to that of the Virgin in the small "Annunciation" in the Louvre (No. 1265) attributed to Lorenzo di Credi, and still less to that of the "Vierge aux rochers" in the same gallery; both these pictures being placed by Dr. Bode in Leonardo's early Florentine period.

Secondly, I would observe that there is nothing fresh or youthful in either of these pictures at Munich and Dresden; both show a feeble, indeed, but a mature and practised hand. No especially keen artistic perception is required to see this. In order, however, that students may judge for themselves of the merits of the two pictures, I have appended illustrations of both.

I may, of course, be mistaken in my opinion ; yet it appears to me that no impartial observer, with any feeling for art, could fail to remark in the Dresden picture the defective modelling of the Child's body, with the disfiguring rings of fat; the unnatural drawing of the chest, the unsightly feet and misshapen right hand, which looks more like a claw. The modelling of St. John's arm, too, is execrable, and his expression of countenance silly. As to the curtains of the bed and the ridiculous little pillow, they look as though they were made of wood. No Florentine painter could have produced such a picture, and least of all Leonardo, who was an artist of most refined taste. The work is undoubtedly Flemish. It appears to me to be by the same feeble hand as a drawing in the Uffizi (No. 428 ; Braun, No. 429), which, though ascribed to Leonardo da Vinci, is a Flemish copy after Verrocchio.

MADONNA AND CHILD. ATTRIBUTED TO LORENZO DI CREDI.
(In the Dresden Gallery.)

To face p. 272.

MADONNA AND CHILD.　ATTRIBUTED TO LEONARDO.

(In the Munich Gallery.)

To face p. 272.

I am well acquainted with the Dresden picture, having several times examined it critically, but its counterpart in Munich I only know from the photograph—an excellent reproduction taken by Hanfstaengel. The picture was formerly at Günzburg, where it was ascribed to Albert Dürer. It was, therefore, regarded as the work of a Northern master, and this attribution, though it cannot be said to hit the bull's-eye, falls at least, I think, within the target. The picture owes its present ascription to Leonardo, to the exertions of Dr. Bayersdorffer, who took steps to make his important discovery known in all the leading German periodicals. And thus it came to pass that even Professor Lübke, who is well known and justly celebrated throughout Germany as an art-historian, was unfortunately induced to decide in favour of Dr. Bayersdorffer's attribution. It certainly requires courage to be the only one to raise a dissentient voice amid such a chorus of approval, but, as the Italian proverb says, 'Ogni viltà convien che qui sia morta.'

To connect such a caricature with the great name of Leonardo is treason not only to Italian art but to good taste, and I can scarcely think that any modern painter of repute in the present day will be disposed to agree with Dr. Bayersdorffer. An Italian critic of much insight, who happened to be passing through Munich, went at my request to look at the picture, and has given me his impression of it, which I may repeat in his own words : ' I had expected that this picture would prove to be one of those numerous paintings of the Milanese school which are all more or less Leonardesque in feeling, or at least an old copy of one of them. But this Madonna at Munich is much further removed from Leonardo, and all idea of its being an Italian work is dispelled at the first glance. Moreover, it is unpleasing in the extreme. The inspector of the

gallery is said to be a man of considerable learning, which
certainly cannot be said of our directors and inspectors in
Italy, yet I feel convinced that not one of them would ever
have thought of ascribing to Leonardo a work containing
types so common as those of the Madonna and Child in
this picture.'

This view coincides entirely with the opinion which I had
formed from merely studying the photograph of the picture.

My opponents will perhaps retort that the critical stand-
point of a superficial Italian is very different to that of a
German specialist on matters of art. I may, therefore,
quote the opinion of one of their own countrymen, a
diligent and impartial student of art.

'I think,' he observed, ' that this Munich " Leonardo "
even beats the one at Berlin. I have as yet not seen the
picture itself—which is now exhibited in the Munich gallery
as an example of the master's early Florentine period—
but the autotype reproduction is quite sufficient. The
square forehead of the Madonna, which is altogether
Flemish or Low-German in type, the upturned eyes of
the Child, the hard folds, the unpleasing lifeless hand of
the Madonna, the misshapen left foot of the Child, the
fidgety treatment of the flowers, and finally the land-
scape, which is of a character only adopted by Leonardo
after he had migrated to Lombardy—all this, in my
humble opinion, goes to prove that this picture is an
imitation of Leonardo da Vinci rather than the work of
the master himself.'

I can most fully endorse the opinion of this promising
young German critic, and I should further like to point
out a few more defects in this picture, which will enable
even a beginner in art-criticism to understand why this
feeble production cannot possibly be the work of a great
artist like Leonardo da Vinci.

First, I must state that I consider the Munich picture to be an earlier and much more feeble example of the same subject as at Dresden. In the latter picture, instead of the miniature-like vase of flowers, the little St. John was introduced. All the faults of modelling in the Body of the Child, which we noticed in the Dresden picture, occur also in that at Munich. In the latter picture the left arm of the Child is, moreover, so completely out of drawing, that it appears to have no connection with the shoulder, but to be hanging in mid-air. The number of unpleasing and meaningless folds on the breast of the Madonna and on her left arm are not in character with the system of drapery as seen in the clustered folds on the lower part of her mantle, for while the first named are wholly Flemish, showing, moreover, on the Madonna's left side certain of those hook-shaped folds which at once prove the Flemish origin of the picture, the latter are undoubtedly copied from some study of drapery by Leonardo or Lorenzo di Credi. In the name of all lovers of Italian art, let me once more protest against such a perversion of the truth, and express a hope that sooner or later this production may also find its way to Schleissheim.

As the Dresden picture, No. 13, necessitated my discussing this thorny question more exhaustively than heretofore, I may also take the opportunity of pointing out several imitations of Italian originals which I have met with in collections of pictures out of Italy, and which many years of study have enabled me to discover. In the first volume of these ' Studies ' I touched upon the Flemish imitations in the Italian galleries. As far back as 1880, after the publication of my first book—' Italian Masters in German Galleries '—some German critics, I am told— and among them even several who were not unfavourably disposed towards me—taxed me with having made Northern painters responsible for all inferior Italian pictures. I scarcely expected such an accusation, particularly now in my old age, when I am more than ever conscious of having shaken off such chauvinistic prejudices. I think my knowledge of European nations is sufficient to forbid my imputing to one only good qualities and to another evil, a practice which, however, is very common in these days. A German, whose eye has been trained principally by studying the works of his own countrymen or of Flemish painters, will naturally find it more difficult than a native of France or Italy to discriminate between an Italian original and a Northern imitation. I have, however, had occasion to observe that a German, who is something more than a ' learned specialist,' and who is gifted with artistic perception and with powers of observation, may attain to a surprising degree of proficiency in a relatively short space of time.[1]

The following are so-called Italian pictures which I believe to be the productions of Flemish or German artists :—

At Vienna.

In Prince Lichtenstein's Gallery.

1. The copy of Raphael's so-called " Madonna di Francesco I.," there ascribed to Polidoro da Caravaggio.

In the Collection of the Academy of Fine Arts.

2. " Christ with the Canaanitish Woman " (No. 55), there assigned to the early Florentine school.

---

[1] I should recommend students to procure photographs of the two following drawings, with studies of hands: One is at Oxford under the name of Raphael (Braun, 19), and belongs, I consider, to the school of Holbein. The form of the nails in this drawing should be compared with the form of the thumb-nail in Holbein's portraits. The other study is at Chatsworth, and is attributed to Parmegianino (Braun, 158). In this also the form of the nails is extremely characteristic.

3. "Christ with the Woman of Samaria " (No. 60),
with the same attribution as the preceding.

4. The "Enthroned Madonna" (No. 1084), ascribed
to the school of Padua. The Madonna is taken from
Mantegna's celebrated "Madonna della Vittoria "—now
in the Louvre (No. 1374)—the unpleasing angels were
added by some Northern painter.

5. The "Martyrdom of St. Sebastian" (No. 1128),
assigned to the North Italian school of the fifteenth
century.

6. No. 464, the "Infant Saviour with the little St.
John."

In the Public Gallery.

7. The portrait of a young man with a brown beard in
three positions (No. 244), ascribed to Titian. The form of
the nails should be especially noted. This portrait was
ascribed by Storffer to Martin de Vos, by Mechel to Johann
of Calcar. Both critics, therefore, rightly regarded it as
the work of some Northern painter. Messrs. Crowe and
Cavalcaselle, the historians of Italian art, have, however,
assigned it to Lotto.

8. The portrait of a man of aristocratic appearance,
his left hand resting upon his sword-hilt (No. 268). This
picture is attributed to Titian, while Messrs. Crowe and
Cavalcaselle give it to Girolamo da Treviso.

9. "Christ bearing the Cross," assigned to the school
of Leonardo. In my opinion, it is a Flemish imitation of
Luini.

10. The "Rescue of Andromeda " (No. 48), a Flemish
copy.

In Count Harrach's Collection.

11. There are several Flemish imitations in this gallery,
among them a "Christ bearing the Cross." The subject

seems to have been one for which the Flemings had a special predilection, and we meet with works of this description in the Borghese gallery at Rome, at Dresden, and at Lützschena.

AT MUNICH.

In the Gallery.

12. A male portrait (Cabinet XVII. No. 996), which, incredible as it may appear, is assigned to the early Florentine school, though it is unmistakably a German production.

13. No. 1032, the "Pietà," wrongly ascribed to Marco Basaiti.

14. No. 1084, a company of nine persons singing, attributed to Sebastiano Florigerio.

15. No. 1088, "St. Jerome," ascribed to a Brescian artist.

16. No. 1041, a "Madonna," an imitation of Leonardo da Vinci.

17. No. 1042, a "Madonna." What was said of the preceding applies also to this picture.

AT DRESDEN.

In the Gallery.

18. No. 102, "Christ bearing the Cross," attributed to Sebastiano del Piombo.[1]

19. No. 197, "Christ and the Woman taken in Adultery."[2]

20. No. 195, the Madonna and Child with four saints.

[1] The form of the thumb-nail on the right hand is characteristic in this picture.

[2] This copy, after Lotto, affords us a good example of the Flemish method of treatment. Everything in this picture is caricatured. The form of the nails should be observed as distinctive of this naturalistic painter of the Netherlands.

A copy by some feeble Fleming of Lotto's original in the Bridgewater gallery.

21. No. 199, the " Calling of St. Matthew," ascribed to Giovan Antonio da Pordenone.

22. The exaggerated figure of the Madonna ' di Caitone,' a German production of the last century.

23. The " Magdalen," attributed to Correggio.

AT FRANKFORT.

In the Staedel Institute.

24. " St. William," attributed to Dosso Dossi; the original is at Hampton Court.

AT OLDENBURG.

. 25. The " Daughter of Herodias," attributed to Solario. A Flemish imitation of that master.[1]

AT PARIS.

In the Louvre.

26. Male portrait, ascribed to the Venetian school. No. 520 of Vicomte Both de Tauzia's catalogue.[2]

IN ENGLAND.

In the National Gallery.

27. No. 1052, male portrait, assigned to the Milanese school.

In the Christ Church Collection at Oxford.

28. Two children embracing one another.

29. A copy of Raphael's Madonna in the Bridgewater gallery. A similar Flemish copy is in the Naples Museum.

[1] This is evident, even in the photograph of the picture.

[2] Ascribed to Giulio Campi by M. Mesnard (*Chronique des Arts*, 1889).

AT DARMSTADT.

In the Collection of the Grand Duke.

30. The recumbent Venus, ascribed to Titian. A
German imitation of the last century of Giorgione's Venus
in the Dresden gallery.

I could name many more of these Flemish and German
imitations, but those I have enumerated will, I think,
suffice.

The Dresden gallery contains an admirable early work
by Bernardino Pintoricchio. It is the charming portrait of
a boy (No. 41), and must have been produced about 1480.
The picture is interesting, too, from another point of view,
for both the technic and the quality of the tempera point,
I think, to the school whence Pintoricchio proceeded, viz.
that of his fellow-countryman Fiorenzo di Lorenzo.

An inferior picture of the Madonna (No. 22) is not, I
consider, by Lorenzo di Credi, but is more probably by some
feeble contemporary of that master, who worked with Botti-
celli. Messrs. Crowe and Cavalcaselle [1] and the director of
the gallery are of the same opinion.

Two genuine works by Lorenzo di Credi were, however,
purchased not long since : No. 14, which represents the
Madonna adoring the Infant Saviour, who turns his head
to look at a goldfinch ; and No. 15, the Madonna with the
Child in the act of blessing, between SS. Sebastian and
John the Evangelist. Both pictures have been much
injured by restoration.

The small picture representing St. Crispin (No. 38) is
only a work of the school of Perugia, which Dr. Woermann
admits. Messrs. Crowe and Cavalcaselle would identify
the painter of this unimportant fragment, and ascribe it to

[1] iii. 413.

an equally insignificant artist, Melanzio of Montefalco, near Foligno.[1] No connoisseur in these days would, I think, agree with Baron Rumohr in ascribing the " Adoration of the Magi " (No. 42) to Marco Palmezzano of Forlì. This wretched production is copied from some picture of the school of Perugia. I should recommend the director of this collection to have it removed to its ·proper place—the depôt of the gallery.

DRAWINGS BY ITALIAN MASTERS
IN THE PRINT-ROOM.

The collection of drawings at Dresden, though not so rich in originals by the great Italian masters of the fifteenth and sixteenth centuries as that in Munich, yet contains a certain number which appear to me deserving of study. When I last visited the Saxon capital I found the director engaged in rearranging this valuable collection more systematically, rectifying the attributions where it seemed to him to be desirable. From what Dr. Woermann gave me to understand, I may conclude that most of the changes which I suggested ten years ago in the attribution of the Italian drawings have now been adopted. I am not aware, however, what the present arrangement in the Print-Room may be ; I shall therefore begin my examination of the drawings with the Umbrian school and conclude with the Venetian.

My opponents will, no doubt, note with satisfaction various mistakes in the attribution of the drawings which I unfortunately committed ten years ago. Having in the

[1] iii. 254.

interval made a close and diligent study of the subject, I am now able to correct these mistakes. I may here once more repeat that the study—and consequently the right understanding—of drawings and sketches by the old masters is by no means so easy as some young and hot-headed German critics appear to think. It demands years of constant practice in order to acquire even a tolerably intimate knowledge of the forms peculiar to the great masters, and, what appears to me a yet more difficult matter, to grasp the mode of conception and representation characteristic of each. Let there be no illusion on the subject. Even with the most brilliant endowments, an enthusiastic and diligent student of art will take years to attain to an approximate degree of certainty in his judgment, but without natural artistic perception the most strenuous and laborious efforts will be of no avail.

According to the catalogue of Braun's photographs, there are no less than nine drawings by Raphael in the Dresden collection. We will consider them in order :—

1. The first which arrests our attention is a large sheet of circular form (Braun, 74). This poetically conceived pen drawing was evidently designed for the border of a bronze or silver salver. It represents Neptune in a chariot drawn by sea-horses; in his train are naiads riding on dolphins, amorini borne by sea-monsters, Silenus mounted on a tortoise, and sea-horses led by centaurs; the whole, in short, is like a scene from Homer. The drawing was apparently sketched in lightly with red chalk, and was then gone over and finished with the pen. According to Passavant, it is the same drawing which Vasari stated had been made by Raphael for his patron, Agostino Chigi, a wealthy Sienese merchant settled at Rome. The design was then to be carried out in metal by Cesarino Rosetti of Perugia. Ten years ago this drawing appeared to me to be by

Raphael. My subsequent studies have, however, convinced me that the forms in this interesting example are not those of the master, but coincide with those in drawings by his gifted imitator, Perino del Vaga (†). The horses are of the same build as those in Perino's fine drawing in the Louvre,[1] "Moses passing through the Red Sea," which is also wrongly attributed to Raphael. The example in Dresden shows a yet closer connection with another admirable washed drawing by Perino in the Albertina at Vienna (Braun, 21), which again represents Neptune and his train. The movement of the sea deity and the types of the horses are identical in both. A similar composition by Perino (†) is in the University galleries at Oxford.[2] Passavant attributed this drawing to Raphael.

2. Another pen drawing in the Dresden collection represents the standing figure of Eve. She holds the apple in her left hand (Braun, 75). Neither the form of the hand nor that of the ear nor the character of the line-work point to Raphael himself. The lower part of the body is too imperfect in modelling for so great a master. I look upon it as a copy by some painter of his school (†).

3. The nude figure of a flying genius holding a bow in his left hand, executed in red chalk (Braun, 76). The modelling of the mouth with the swollen upper lip, the over-prominent knee-joints, the treatment of the hair, the fine pen-strokes, which do not accord with Raphael's usual method of drawing, all point to Giulio Romano, the pupil of Raphael, rather than to the master himself (†).

4. Three nude flying *putti* drawn with the pen (Braun, 77). Everything in this feeble drawing is defective and meaningless, and I therefore look upon it as a forgery (†).

5. A small pen drawing for a frieze (Braun, 78). If I

---

[1] Salle aux Boîtes (Braun, No. 275).

[2] No. 83 of Sir J. C. Robinson's catalogue.

am not mistaken, this drawing more probably belongs to the school of Fontainebleau than to that of Raphael (†). The forms of the boy point to Primaticcio, or perhaps even to his imitator, Niccolò dell' Abbate.

6. A copy of a part of Leonardo's celebrated cartoon, the "Battle of the Standard." This pen sketch is far too coarse and exaggerated for Raphael. The treatment of the hair and of the manes of the horses should be observed, as also the defective modelling of the arms, and the drawing should then be compared with an exquisite little sketch of the same subject by Raphael in the Taylor Institution at Oxford (†) (Braun, 15).

7. The charcoal study of a head (Braun, 80). A feeble drawing, very modern in character.

8. The same applies to the drawing of a woman and a child (Braun, 81).

9. The washed drawing of the Martyrdom of St. Cecilia (Braun, 82) is evidently one of those examples by Perino del Vaga which, as we have already seen in the first volume of these ' Studies,' [1] are continually attributed to Raphael (†). The Dresden collection of drawings, therefore, cannot boast of a single genuine example by the great master himself.

10. Luca Signorelli of Cortona is represented by an authentic, though much rubbed, charcoal drawing (Braun, 44). It represents four nude male figures in various attitudes, and is probably a study for some part of Signorelli's "Last Judgment" in the Cathedral at Orvieto.

11. A pen drawing, representing two Apostles (Braun, 70), is attributed to Perugino, but is probably a copy by one of his school.

12. A pen and wash drawing with a crowd of nude figures (Braun, 39). This unattractive example is wrongly

[1] *Critical Studies in the Borghese and Doria Galleries*, pp. 139-50.

ascribed to Antonio del Pollaiuolo. It is unquestionably by Girolamo Genga (†), the pupil and imitator of Signorelli. This eclectic painter, who, though working in a *baroque* style, is not without talent, is confounded with the most divers masters, both in drawings and paintings, as I pointed out in the first volume of these 'Studies.'[1] I should recommend those who desire to gain some knowledge of this master to procure Braun's photographs of those drawings by Genga which I there mentioned.

13. The Dresden collection contains a pen drawing by Baldassare Peruzzi, "Hercules holding his Club" (Braun, 37). It belongs to his middle period. In his early period he was much influenced by Sodoma. This is seen in two good pen drawings in the Louvre,[2] both representing a triumphal procession. In his later period Peruzzi imitated Raphael, and to this epoch of his career I should attribute the cartoon of the "Adoration of the Magi" in the English National Gallery (No. 167), and the drawing for the same subject in the library of the Palace at Sigmaringen.

14. Among the drawings by Florentine masters we find an admirable example by Fra Angelico, representing two angels (Braun, 26).

15. There are also a few excellent drawings by Filippino Lippi. One of them—in black chalk heightened with white—represents two men ; the younger is seated, while the elder with a long beard stands before him holding an open book (Braun, 32). Another drawing—St. John the Baptist and a young man seated beside him—is also by this master (†) and not by Cosimo Rosselli, to whom this example is attributed in Braun's catalogue (40 and 41).

---

[1] *Critical Studies*, vol. i. pp. 93–5.
[2] No. 487, the "Triumph of Vespasian," and No. 1967, Room X.   The former is ascribed in the catalogue to the ' Venetian or Lombard school,' the latter to Sodoma.

Filippino is easily recognised by his characteristic forms of ear, hand, and foot; nevertheless, he is confounded not only in drawings, but also in paintings, with his pupil Raffaellino del Garbo, with his father Fra Filippo, with Perugino, Andrea del Castagno, and even with Masaccio.[1]

16. Another Florentine master, Verrocchio, is represented in the somewhat rubbed silver point drawing which we have already discussed at length (pp. 266, 271). This drawing is wrongly attributed to Leonardo (Braun, 49). Three other examples are also ascribed to that master in Braun's catalogue, but they have no claim to his name, and only those disposed to follow the reckless example of Leonardo's latest German biographer would dream of ascribing them to him.

17. Among the Lombard masters we find Gaudenzio Ferrari, represented in Dresden by an admirable pen drawing with two nude *putti*, which in Braun's catalogue is attributed to Correggio (No. 84) (†).[2]

18. By Correggio himself there is one example—the sketch for his picture of the Madonna with St. George—in this gallery (Braun, 85). The handling resembles that of contemporary Venetian masters, pictorial effect and a right distribution of light and shade being evidently the principal aim of the artist.

19. The red chalk drawing of two nude *putti* is far

---

[1] It appears to me that Filippino is confounded with Fra Filippo in two drawings in the Louvre (Braun, 230 and 232); with Perugino in one in the British Museum (Braun, 148); with Andrea del Castagno in a picture in the Florence Academy; with Masaccio in the British Museum (Braun, 31), and in the Uffizi in two male portraits in fresco (Nos. 286 and 1167); the head of the old man, No. 1167, has been photographed by Brogi under the name of Masaccio, that of the young man —Filippino's portrait of himself—he has reproduced under its right name.

[2] Pen drawings by Gaudenzio are very rare. They are mostly executed in wash on blue paper, and heightened with white. A considerable number are in the royal library at Turin.

too coarse for this master himself, and is probably only one of the many copies which have come down to us of the school of the Caracci.

20. A good red chalk drawing by the Milanese artist Cesare da Sesto is in Portfolio I. of ' the Lombards ' (No. 2). It represents the Madonna and Child seated between St. Elisabeth with the little St. John, and an angel. For some notice of other drawings by this master I refer my readers to the first volume of these ' Studies.' [1]

21. Another Milanese artist of far less merit— Aurelio, the son of Bernardino Luini—we also meet with in this same portfolio (No. 18). This example—the " Scourging of Christ "—is executed, like all the master's drawings, with the pen, and heightened with white. The handling is similar to that of Aurelio's drawing in the Archbishop's palace at Milan, the sketch for his large picture in the Brera, the " Martyrdom of St. Andrew."

22. Among Venetian masters I will first mention that rare artist Jacopo de' Barbari. He is represented by a most characteristic example—the " Rape of a Siren by a Triton." This pen drawing was formerly in the collection of Mariette, the French connoisseur, and passed for the work of Lorenzo di Credi. The large round form of skull, the half-open mouth, and the clumsy rounded shape of the thumb all bespeak the hand of Jacopo de' Barbari.

23. A large washed drawing, representing the Madonna and Child enthroned between SS. Faustinus and Jovita, the patron saints of the city of Brescia; on the steps of the throne are two angels playing on musical instruments, and in the background is a hilly landscape. On the upper part of the sheet is inscribed ' Johan Bellino,' and it was formerly attributed to that master.[2] It is, how-

[1] *Op. cit.* pp. 165-8.
[2] Photographed by Braun under the name of Giovanni Bellini (No. 51).

ever, an undoubtedly genuine and characteristic example
by Bellini's contemporary, Vittore Carpaccio. It is the
sketch for a large panel picture by the master, which some
thirty years ago was in the Averoldi collection at Brescia.
It was subsequently sold to the English National Gallery,
but is said to have perished on the voyage to England.
The picture was signed and dated 1519; it was, therefore,
one of the last works of this simple-minded and delightful
painter. For the benefit of students I will here enumerate
five other drawings by Carpaccio, which are all in the
Uffizi: (1) "Hebrew Judges condemning a Christian to
Death" (Philpot, 919); (2) the "Presentation of the Ma-
donna in the Temple" (No. 1292 of Signor Ferri's cata-
logue; Brogi, No. 1857); (3) "St. George overcoming the
Dragon in the open Square of a City," the sketch for one
of Carpaccio's pictures at Venice (No. 1287 of Signor Ferri's
catalogue; Brogi, No. 1856); (4) the "Circumcision" (Phil-
pot, No. 918); (5) the "Madonna and Child between
SS. Roch and John the Baptist" (Philpot, No. 917).[1]

Another drawing in Dresden, representing the "En-
tombment," is, for no reason at all, attributed to Giovanni
Bellini.

24. A pen drawing in which we see a fortified town on
an island in a river. Several ships are in the river, and
on the bank are two halberdiers. In Braun's catalogue
(No. 63) this drawing is attributed to Titian, and it is cited
by Messrs. Crowe and Cavalcaselle in their life of that
painter. Ten years ago another drawing in Dresden was
also ascribed to this master. It represents a horseman, to
whom a man on foot appears to be explaining an inscrip-
tion on a stone. In my opinion, these two drawings are by
Domenico Campagnola.

This artist, who is by no means without interest, was

[1] These two drawings have also been photographed by Brogi.

endowed with a rich imagination. His name is frequently mentioned by the ' Anonimo,' and his fantastic landscapes, delicately executed with the pen, were evidently sought after by Venetian art-patrons in the early part of the sixteenth century. Subsequently, however, he was so completely overshadowed by his great contemporary and colleague, Titian, that he has not met with the appreciation which I consider he deserves, but has, on the contrary, down to the present day been entirely neglected. His engravings of 1517 and 1518, which are signed with his name, are, however, well known to collectors. In the second decade of the sixteenth century Domenico was employed to execute frescoes in the Scuola del Santo at Padua. In these, as also in his drawings and engravings, he shows himself an ardent follower and imitator of Giorgione, or rather of Titian in his Giorgionesque period. This is seen not only in the modelling of the human body, more especially of the female form, but also in his choice of subject and in his manner of treating it. Campagnola is certainly less refined than Titian, and still less so than Giorgione. Drawings by him are more frequently attributed to Titian than to Giorgione. All, however, as we shall see, bear unmistakable traces of the hand of Campagnola.

I will now enumerate certain characteristic examples by him which are either signed with his name or which are universally admitted to be his work. By studying them we shall then be enabled to recognise the hand of this forgotten artist in many other drawings which are usually ascribed to those greater masters whom he imitated.

1. The large design for the "Massacre of the Innocents," which is well known to collectors. In 1517 it was engraved in wood by Luc'antonio di Giunta of Florence, and bears the name of Domenico Campagnola in addition to the date. In this example the type of the female faces,

with the straight nose and the sharp touches of light on the hair, should be particularly noted.

2. Another woodcut, of which we give a reproduction, is signed 'Dominicus.' It represents a hilly landscape, in the centre of which we see a lion furiously attacking a bear. St. Jerome, whose meditations have been disturbed by the commotion, has hurried to the spot, and anxiously watches the issue of the combat in which his faithful lion is engaged. In the background two men with an ass, alarmed by the terrific noise, are seen making good their escape. In this example the peculiar form of the bank of clouds on the right should be observed, as also the precipitous rocks of the Dolomite mountains in the landscape, the abnormal size of St. Jerome's hands, and the arrangement of the lines.

The following pen drawings are, I consider, rightly ascribed to Campagnola :—

3 and 4. In the Uffizi.[1] One represents the seated figure of a bearded old man, to whom a boy, standing before him, appears to be making some offering. Beside the latter, on the right, are two female figures. (Photographed by Philpot, No. 1045.) In the other we see Christ seated on a stone bench in a landscape, with SS. Peter and Paul beside him on the left; before him is a kneeling woman in supplication, behind whom are two boy angels (Philpot, No. 1341). In these drawings the straight form of nose, the sharp touches of light on the hair, and the characteristic crumpled folds of the drapery should be studied.

5 and 6. At Chatsworth. The first represents a fantastic landscape, with castellated buildings and temples on a rocky promontory overhanging a winding river, across which several bridges are thrown. On the right, in the foreground, is a woman who has been pointing out the way

[1] These drawings have been photographed by Brogi.

ST. JEROME. WOODCUT BY DOMENICO CAMPAGNOLA.

To face p. 290.

to a rider, who gallops off in the direction she has indicated ; on a bridge in the centre are two men on horseback and several foot-passengers, and on the left two donkey-drivers and other figures. In this example (Braun, No. 186) we notice Campagnola's keen observation of nature, as also the characteristic treatment of the clouds and the peculiar arrangement of the lines. The other drawing in the collection is also a landscape with castellated buildings and a massive stone bridge in the middle distance. In the foreground, on the right, is the nude figure of Andromeda ; before her is the sea-monster, about to attack her, while Perseus is seen flying through the air to her rescue (Braun, 183). Here, again, we find the peculiar form of the clouds, while both Andromeda's hand and the shape of her nose are equally distinctive of Campagnola. In these six drawings, which either bear the master's signature or have always been attributed to him, I have noticed that the following characteristics constantly recur :—

(a) The small and crumpled folds of the drapery, such as we find in the works of Giorgione or of Titian in his Giorgionesque period.

(b) The sharp touches of light on the hair.

(c) The straight form of the nose in the female faces.

(d) The abnormally large hands.

(e) The characteristic bank of clouds.

(f) The petty treatment of the foliage, as compared with the treatment of the same subject in Titian's drawings.

(g) The laboured regularity of the pen strokes, which contrast unfavourably with the breadth and freedom of Titian's flowing lines.

Having mentioned some of the most apparent characteristics which will enable even an unpractised eye to recognise Campagnola's works, I will now point out some drawings which I am firmly persuaded are by this master,

though they are ascribed to Giorgione, to Titian, and even
to Raphael.

In the Albertina at Vienna, a pen drawing [1] (Braun,
197), representing a mountainous landscape with buildings
in the middle distance, is attributed to the latter master,
though it is undoubtedly by Campagnola; and the small
woodcut of "Hercules in combat with the Lion," falsely
inscribed—'RAPH . VR . IOS . NIC . VICEN'—must certainly
also have been executed from a design by Campagnola (†).

The drawings in the Uffizi under the name of Giorgione
are almost without exception by Campagnola. I have
already dealt with several of them on p. 225, as also with
three drawings by this master at Chatsworth, which are
there ascribed to Giorgione.

Mr. John Malcolm's well-known collection contains,
I think, no less than thirteen drawings by Campagnola,
nine of which are assigned to Titian in the catalogue.[2]
Among them is the celebrated pen drawing representing a
rural concert, which, to add to the confusion, has been
photographed by Braun under the name of Giorgione
(Braun, 'Beaux-Arts,' 191). The remaining four drawings
are rightly ascribed to Campagnola (Nos. 388, 389, 390,
and 391).

His drawings, as we have already observed, are for the
most part attributed to Titian. In addition to the nine
examples just mentioned in the Malcolm collection, there
are six by him at Chatsworth[3] and three in the Louvre[4]
which are all wrongly given to Titian.

In the choice collection of the well-known painter,

---

[1] This drawing is mentioned by
Passavant (see *Raphaël d'Urbin*, ii.
445, No. 239).

[2] They bear the following numbers:
369, 870, 371, 373, 374, 381, 883, 884,
385 (†).

[3] Two of these have been photo-
graphed by Braun (185, 199).

[4] Braun, 428 (the "Rape of
Europa"), 432 (the "Judgment of
Paris"), and 437.

A RURAL CONCERT.   DRAWING BY DOMENICO CAMPAGNOLA.

(In the Malcolm Collection, London.)

To face p. 292.

THE JEALOUS HUSBAND STABBING HIS WIFE. DRAWING BY TITIAN.

(In the Malcolm Collection, London.)

To face p. 243.

STUDIES FOR A ST. JEROME. DRAWING BY TITIAN.
(In the British Museum.)

To face p. 293.

M. Bonnat, there are two pen drawings by Campagnola, again under the name of Titian : one, an admirable example, represents a satyr climbing a tree.   In the British Museum a drawing by Campagnola has also been dignified with the name of Titian,[1] and the same is the case with several examples in the Albertina at Vienna, such as those photographed by Braun under the numbers 283, 284, and 285.

I could mention many other instances in which Titian and Campagnola have been confounded, but I think those I have cited are sufficient to instruct the student how to distinguish these two artists from one another.   In conclusion, I should like to point out a few genuine drawings by Titian, for no study trains the eye so effectually as that of comparative examination.   I am unable, however, to name many, as Titian's drawings are extremely rare both in public and private collections.   Mr. John Malcolm is the fortunate possessor of five, if I am not mistaken ; a sixth is in the collection at Lille (Braun, 41) ; a seventh—a sketch for the picture in the Church of the ' Salute ' at Venice—is in the Louvre ; an eighth is in the British Museum ; a red chalk drawing by him, but under the name of Padovanino, is in the Christ Church collection at Oxford ; two are in the Morelli collection ;[2] one is in the Venice Academy ; and another is at Chatsworth.   The last named represents St. Jerome in a rocky landscape ; he is kneeling near a cavern, whence a lion issues, and holding a large book.   There are also a few fine examples by Titian in the Albertina at Vienna and in the Staedel Institute at Frankfort.

In addition to these drawings some woodcuts have

---

[1] (Vol. 34, register mark F. f., I., No. 65), Braun, 138.

[2] See *Collezione di 40 disegni scelti dalla Raccolta del Senatore* *Giovanni Morelli, descritti ed illustrati dal Dott. Gustavo Frizzoni* (Milano, Hoepli, 1886).

been ascribed to Titian, which he either executed himself or for which he must at all events have furnished the designs; for instance, that representing Samson and Delilah and another of larger size, St. Jerome kneeling before a crucifix in a wild landscape, near him two lions and a lioness—a splendid composition, which would not be unworthy of Rubens. Art-historians cannot agree as to the year of Campagnola's birth or that of his death. The date usually assigned for the former is 1484. We may here bring this notice of Campagnola, which has, perhaps, assumed undue proportions, to a close.

It is very possible that in the course of this second survey of the drawings in Dresden I may again have committed some mistakes, for good intentions are not the sole requisites for such an undertaking. I am, however, persuaded that the greater part of my attributions will in the end establish their claim to be accepted. Literary work has always been distasteful to me, but I shall feel amply rewarded for all my trouble should these ' Critical Studies' induce even a small number of students to devote themselves to the laborious but most interesting task of studying the original drawings by the great masters.

GENERAL INDEX.

X

INDEX OF PLACES.

NOTE.—*The numbers printed in italics indicate that the works referred to are not accepted as genuine by the Author.*

PRINTED BY
SPOTTISWOODE AND CO., NEW-STREET SQUARE
LONDON

CPSIA information can be obtained at www.ICGtesting.com
Printed in the USA
BVOW05s0914110715

408147BV00008B/32/P